Here are fresh and practical insights
in spiritual discussions that are authe
must-have guide to becoming stronger salt and brighter light in
the twenty-first century!

LEE STROBEL
Bestselling author of *The Case for Christ* and professor of Christian Thought
at Houston Baptist University

"Go and make disciples." That was one of the commands Jesus
gave to his followers, but it often ranks low among American
Christians' priorities. That's why churches, small groups, and
those who consider themselves to be disciples of Jesus should
read this book. *The 9 Arts of Spiritual Conversations* is an essential
resource for accomplishing the mission Christ gave his church.

RICH STEARNS
President of World Vision US and author of *The Hole in Our Gospel* and
Unfinished

The nine arts are a culmination of years of real-life stories. If you
want tried-and-true concepts that will become reality for you and
your friends, I highly recommend this unique resource.

HUGH HALTER
Author of *Flesh*, *Brimstone*, and *The Tangible Kingdom*

John and Mary present a compelling case for how to maximize
moments for Kingdom good. This book will profoundly alter the
way you engage with humanity. It's a must-read for anyone who
is serious about having spiritual conversations!

STEVE CARTER
Teaching pastor at Willow Creek Community Church

When you can't put a book down, you know that you are
on to something important. As I read *The 9 Arts of Spiritual
Conversations*, I found myself simultaneously instructed,

challenged, inspired, and equipped. I was given hope that I could actually engage people in a way that could lovingly bring them to Jesus over time. The ministry of Young Life has popularized the phrase that we need to "earn the right to be heard." This book puts flesh on that phrase like nothing else I have ever read.

GREG OGDEN

Writer, speaker, teacher on discipleship, and author of *Discipleship Essentials*

Fear of rejection and a lack of understanding on how to communicate the gospel has shut the mouths of many sincere Christians for too long. *The 9 Arts of Spiritual Conversations* is a shot of encouragement for all of us who want to *live* and *proclaim* a gospel that is truly good news!

CAESAR KALINOWSKI

Author of *Transformed* and *Small Is Big, Slow Is Fast*

For introverts like me, the first four arts (Noticing, Praying, Listening, and Asking Questions) are especially helpful. Gifted extroverts can help us with the other five! I am impressed with the vitality and deep faith of the authors: They really want to help us reach out for Christ, and they do so winsomely.

FREDERICK DALE BRUNER

Author of commentaries on the Gospel of Matthew (2004) and the Gospel of John (2012)

In *The 9 Arts of Spiritual Conversations*, John and Mary make the art of connecting with the people whom Jesus misses most doable, human, and fun. Put these arts to work in your church today and watch evangelism move from being a gift shared by only a few to a practice shared by everyone.

JIM HENDERSON

Author of *Jim and Casper Go to Church*, executive producer at Jim Henderson Presents

**The 9 Arts of
Spiritual Conversations**

Walking
alongside
people
who believe
differently

The 9
Arts of
Spiritual
Conversations

Mary Schaller & John Crilly

TYNDALE
MOMENTUM®

The nonfiction imprint of
Tyndale House Publishers, Inc.

Visit Tyndale online at www.tyndale.com.

Visit Tyndale Momentum online at www.tyndalemomentum.com.

Visit Q Place online at www.qplace.com.

TYNDALE, Tyndale Momentum, and Tyndale's quill logo are registered trademarks of Tyndale House Publishers, Inc. The Tyndale Momentum logo is a trademark of Tyndale House Publishers, Inc. Tyndale Momentum is the nonfiction imprint of Tyndale House Publishers, Inc., Carol Stream, Illinois.

The 9 Arts of Spiritual Conversations: Walking alongside People Who Believe Differently

Edited by Karin Stock Buursma

Designed by Daniel Farrell

For information about special discounts for bulk purchases, please contact Tyndale House Publishers at csresponse@tyndale.com, or call 1-800-323-9400.

Library of Congress Cataloging-in-Publication Data

Names: Schaller, Mary.
Title: The 9 arts of spiritual conversations : walking alongside people who believe differently / Mary Schaller and John Crilly.
Other titles: Nine arts of spiritual conversations
Description: Carol Stream, IL : Tyndale House Publishers, Inc., 2016. | Includes bibliographical references.
Identifiers: LCCN 2015038074 | ISBN 9781496405760 (sc)
Subjects: LCSH: Interpersonal relations—Religious aspects—Christianity. | Oral communication—Religious aspects—Christianity. | Christianity and other religions. | Witness bearing (Christianity) | Apologetics.
Classification: LCC BV4597.52 .C75 2016 | DDC 248/.5—dc23 LC record available at http://lccn.loc.gov /2015038074

Printed in the United States of America

24   23   22   21
8   7   6   5   4   3

Table of Contents

Preface

NOW THAT YOU'VE PICKED UP THIS BOOK, you may have a burning question about the cover: Why the dinosaurs? Are we saying spiritual conversations are extinct?

When I (Crilly) think of dinosaurs, I immediately am taken back to a childhood memory of my grandma's home. My Grandmother Crilly was a child of the Depression. She grew up a fatherless immigrant and married very young, only to divorce her abusive first husband and marry my grandfather, a quiet and gentle man. My grandma was a neat freak, probably with an obsessive-compulsive disorder that manifested itself in cleanliness. She put paper towels between every plate in the cabinet. She was constantly concerned about bugs getting into her home. She had clear plastic covering her nice sofa and chairs.

Into this squeaky-clean environment entered my brother and I. We did not look forward to visiting her home because we had to be clean and quiet there—two very difficult tasks for young boys. In addition, Grandma did not keep many toys on hand, though she was thoughtful enough to store a few simple children's toys in a walnut-laminate cabinet in the living room. As I grabbed both handles and opened wide the cabinet doors, I could smell the waxy, plastic odor of the Mold-A-Rama models, remnants of a field trip to the Museum of Natural History. There they were: *Tyrannosaurus rex* and *Triceratops*. From the museum's odd, bubble-topped molding machine, they had made their way to my grandma's toy cabinet and were about to be engaged in epic prehistoric battles of my imagination: T-rex vs. Triceratops. A fight to the death.

For many of us, that's how we view spiritual conversations as well. Somehow, we assume that any attempt to love and understand each other is bound to end in a battle: herbivores versus carnivores. When it comes to topics such as faith, religion, or God, we're afraid it's impossible to have a conversation with someone who believes differently without ending up in a standoff that would damage the relationship. We're convinced that followers of Jesus and people who believe differently will end up on opposite sides of any discussion, finding little common ground. And if we have the courage to broach the topic at all, we feel confined to a formula or series of steps. Then the flood of obstacles, fears, and expectations constrains us from winsomely living in the love of Christ and sharing that love with others.

Mary and I are here to say that it doesn't have to be this way. Meaningful, noncombative spiritual conversations are not extinct—they're possible for all of us.

When I was a boy, the dinosaurs invited me to a place of playfulness, free from the rigid expectations and rules of my grandma's sterile home. Mary and I hope this book will help you find joy, freedom, and pleasure in talking about God with people who believe differently. We also hope this book will provide simple tools for amateurs and experts alike to engage naturally in the Great Commission. So we, like Jesus, can be winsome and unashamed when we speak of the Kingdom.

Mary Schaller
John Crilly

CHAPTER 1

The Heart and Habits of Jesus

Whoever claims to live in [God] must live as Jesus did.
1 JOHN 2:6

Our most serious failure today is the inability to provide
effective practical guidance as to how to live the life of Jesus.
DALLAS WILLARD

MY (MARY'S) SISTER TERRY had a window seat in the second-to-last row of a full plane. A young man in his early twenties occupied the coach seat next to her. He was nicely dressed and had gotten out a Bible to read when he sat down. Curious, she asked if he was attending a Bible or divinity school. No, he said, he worked in a sawmill, but he was very involved in his church and loved the Bible. He said he read it a lot.

"Do you believe in Jesus?" he asked boldly in return. Terry said yes, but felt a little uncomfortable disclosing such personal information within the first minute of conversation with a stranger. He immediately followed up with an even more intrusive question: "When you pray, do you pray 'with tears' and 'great anguish'?"

Shocked by the question, but trying to assume this discussion was headed in a normal direction, she said she did pray, but typically not with that kind of passion. "If you are not praying *right* like that, God doesn't hear," the man exclaimed, raising his voice and spitting out the words with a mixture of excitement and judgment. If she didn't "pray right," he said, she wasn't saved and would go to hell when she died.

The young man started leafing through his Bible, referencing passages that reinforced his claims. The plane was just taking off, and he was shouting all of this above the engine noise.

What have I unleashed? Terry thought, feeling trapped in the far back of the plane. For the next twenty minutes, she couldn't get a word in edgewise as her seatmate zealously justified his position on prayer.

Finally, when Terry could no longer stand the lecture, she held up her hand and said, "STOP! Don't tell me what to believe, and don't judge me! He's my God, too. I believe only God can judge people." To her astonishment, the man immediately stopped his discourse, closed his book, bent over the tray table, and started to weep.

After about an hour, he finally sat up. Terry didn't want to look at him; she was afraid he might start yelling again or even pull out a weapon. She thought it best not to make eye contact and pretended to ignore him for the rest of the trip, silently praying for him and for God's protection. It seemed like the flight would last forever.

When they were finally exiting the plane, the young man helped her get her bag down and said he was sorry that she didn't see things the same way he did. It didn't feel like an authentic apology to Terry, but rather a halfhearted effort to make peace. She was just happy to be free of him.

When Terry called me later that day, she said, "The first thing that came to mind when I got off that plane was, 'I can't wait to tell my sister what happened.' You're in the spiritual conversation business, Mary, but I can tell you that I will think twice before I start another conversation with someone holding a Bible! Before that incident, I would think, 'Oh, they are Christians. So am I. It will be great to get to know them.' Not anymore!"

With exasperation, Terry asked me, "When you talk to someone about God, shouldn't it be give-and-take? It was completely one-sided, and his approach was totally wrong. He made me feel like I didn't want to know the same God that he knows. Why couldn't he portray God as loving rather than making it sound like he is condemning or hate filled? The whole time he was talking I was asking myself, 'How can I end this conversation?'"

Beyond the misguided theology about prayer, this poor young man somehow thought that his aggressive approach of intimidation and Scripture quotations would persuade my sister to believe as he did. I am not sure who should be pitied more in this situation—my sister or him. Both were a little spiritually disoriented by the experience. Both walked away wounded from the encounter. Both would classify the interaction as anything but good news.

Sadly, we all know this is not an isolated incident. We've all heard or read stories like this from unsuspecting "victims" of Christ followers who wanted to share the Good News but lacked the sensitivity or timing to effectively represent Jesus.

Midlife Crisis

I must confess that I have occasionally been one of those well-intentioned Christians whose attempts to share the good news about Jesus ended with experiences that were simply *bad* news—though not nearly as extreme as the situation my sister encountered! Because Jesus had made such a huge difference in my life, I wanted to share about him with others. But I lacked the spiritual maturity, as well as the social skills, to talk about God in a way that was grace giving, winsome, and attractive with people who believed differently than I did. When I reached the age of fifty, this became part of an unusual midlife crisis.

This crisis didn't make any sense on a worldly level. I had been a successful entrepreneur, having started three high-tech companies, two of which had done well. I was still married to the same guy, Paul, with twenty-eight years of marriage behind us and the future looking good for continued marital bliss. We had three nearly grown children who had somehow survived our parenting. I had also recently decided to go into full-time ministry and had already served for three years in a large evangelical church in California before entering seminary to work toward a master's of divinity.

So what was the big crisis? It had to do with a short passage in the Bible that made me feel that I was missing something really important. The verses in question were Matthew 28:18-20, summarized briefly as "Go make disciples." In other words, Jesus told his followers, "You followed me for three years; now find others who are spiritually open and ready to commit to exploring who I am and following me. Pass on what I taught you so that they, too, can pass it on." Jesus said that he would be with all of us as we did this important work and that all authority in heaven and on earth was at his disposal to help us. I knew these verses well, as do most Christians. But did I really understand and obey them? Like many followers of Jesus, I knew in my heart that I didn't.

Even having been involved in many Christian ministries over the years, and having nurtured a lot of believers along in their faith, I had never made *one single new disciple of Jesus.* Not one! The prospects of doing so in the future seemed pretty grim given my track record, even though I was in seminary at the time and was now "in the business" of ministry as a paid professional. But in reality, I didn't know how.

Adequate knowledge of God and the Bible wasn't my biggest problem, though I was clearly no biblical scholar. My understanding of Jesus and how he lovingly related with those who believed differently seemed to be my leading challenge. I knew if I didn't figure out how to relate well to people with different views about God and to walk alongside those who were being drawn toward Jesus, I'd go to my grave as a failure at the Great Commission. This was too important to disregard.

Over the years I had been taught two main ways to make new followers of Jesus. The first recommendation from church leaders was to invite people I knew to church so that the expert who was giving the sermon that day could tell them about Jesus and his life giving promise of redemption. If they, drawn by the Spirit of God, found this attractive and compelling, they could keep coming to church and learning what it means to become a follower of Jesus. It was assumed that if they learned about Jesus, they would want to follow him too.

My church had great preaching and worship. This first approach should have been a slam dunk, but so far it hadn't worked well for me. Occasionally someone would come with me to church, but usually just once and that would be the end of the conversation. The one-hour lecture and sing-along wasn't compelling enough to them. Plus, people in northern California, where I lived at the time, were resistant to giving up their precious Sunday mornings, and many of them weren't actively seeking God.

The second recommendation I'd been given was that I *tell* everyone about Jesus ("present the gospel") during a one-time conversation and hope that they received the Good News with open arms, ideally saying a prayer to seal the deal. Then I could invite them to church and Sunday school classes so that someone else could keep teaching them more about Jesus.

Whether the initial gospel presentation came at church or from me, all the discipleship paths I knew basically relied on church programs to help people grow in their understanding of what it means to be a Christian. Love and relationships didn't seem to be predominant factors in either of these approaches, yet I noticed that Jesus was relational with his followers. In fact, so much of what his disciples learned was "caught" rather than "taught."

A Better *How*

In our increasingly secular Western culture, Christ followers have been stifled by a lack of direction on *how* to live out and share their faith in ways that are both biblical and magnetic. Yet Jesus showed us how. He modeled a more relational, conversational way of living and sharing the good news of the gospel.

John Crilly (from here on, we'll simply call him by his short-hand nickname, Crilly) and I have written this book because we believe that many Christians desire to share the good news about Jesus with family, friends, neighbors, and coworkers but in a way that is natural rather than intrusive. We have seen, both from our own personal experiences and from the experiences of Christians who have begun to engage with people the way that Jesus did, how conversations about God can unfold naturally and powerfully.

At the time we wrote this book, Crilly and I were both part of Q Place, an organization that empowers ordinary Christians to engage in meaningful conversations about God with people who believe differently. The *Q* stands for *questions*, and a *Q Place* is a small group of two to twelve people in which the majority are not Christians. These people get together on a regular basis to discuss questions about life, God, and the Bible. The mission of Q Place is to mobilize Christians to facilitate group discussions with spiritual seekers so that those seekers can find God as he is revealed in the Bible.

Before joining the staff at Q Place, both Crilly and I led several small groups in which the majority of the participants were not Christians. As facilitators rather than teachers, we created safe havens where spiritually curious people could wrestle with their big questions about God, consider what the Bible says about those questions, and figure out what they believed. These groups relied heavily on an inductive learning approach, built on the premise that people learn best when they discover truth for themselves through questions, discussion, and study, rather than through lectures by experts presenting information.

After twenty three years in the business world, Crilly led our field operations at Q Place from 2011 to 2015. He brought leadership and project management expertise to the organization, as well as his experience as a writer and a certified professional life coach. Crilly's life had been transformed by Jesus Christ shortly after he completed engineering school at the University of Illinois. With a new heart and a passion for helping others discover God, Crilly directed his enthusiasm and energy into seeker small groups and sports ministry. He helped equip others in the seeker-small-group movement by training adults, church leaders, and university students.

As for me, I worked in the high-tech industry for most of my adult life before ending up in leadership at a large church. I also went back to school and earned a seminary degree, and by 2006 I was ready to go into full-time ministry. At the same time, I had been getting an unofficial seminary degree in my own living room. In 2002, in the midst of my midlife crisis, the thought had occurred to me that, if Jesus had invited a handful of ordinary people to explore God together during his earthly ministry, it might be worth trying to do the same thing in my own community of Portola Valley, California. What the heck! Given that all of my other evangelistic ventures had seemed to bomb most of the time, I figured I had nothing to lose.

Applying my entrepreneurial skills to this faith challenge, I invited two other Christian friends to start a small group with me that was primarily a place for people to figure out what they believed about God. We called it the "Tough Questions Group." I was amazed at the depth of relationships, stories, honesty, doubts, and faith that quickly emerged. This was the answer to my midlife crisis! Suddenly, many people were meeting Jesus for the first time and choosing to follow him through their involvement in this group. What a privilege for me to be there when they made that decision.

This transformational experience started to creep naturally into my relationships with other friends and family members; more and more I found myself talking about God without a debate or argument. For example, my dad and I had decided long beforehand that we couldn't talk about God because it always ended badly. We had increasingly polar views about social issues, politics, and religion, and of course we both thought we were right. But I learned some important new skills in my Tough Questions Group that I hadn't had before. As I co-facilitated our group over time, I improved at genuinely *praying* for people who believed differently, *listening* to them tell stories about their faith journeys, and *asking* them questions to help me understand how they had arrived at their current beliefs.

As I put these skills into practice, God gradually gave me a heartfelt curiosity about my dad's faith journey. Rather than judging him and what he believed, I truly wanted to understand those beliefs. When he sensed that my curiosity was genuine, he started opening up both about what he really believed regarding God and all of the questions he had about the Bible. It turned out that no one had ever given him a safe place to air his own doubts and questions. Yet when he was seventy-nine years old, this became our favorite topic to discuss, rather than one to be avoided at all costs. That was the year he decided one day at my kitchen table to follow Jesus wholeheartedly and begin studying the Bible with me. What had changed?

Asking versus Telling

When I examined the core difference between my approach with my dad and the Tough Questions Group and my approach in earlier attempts to share my faith, I realized that I had made a subtle but significant shift from a *telling* approach to an *asking* approach.

In a telling approach, I do most of the talking, and I give you information that I believe is important and true. You are the passive listener receiving this information and deciding whether to believe it. You'll evaluate this information internally, based on what you already believe to be true, your openness to new information that contradicts what you believe, and my personal credibility with you. It's hierarchical: I, the teller, have most of the power over your and you, the listener, have very little if any voice.

The telling approach is efficient. Because not much response is expected, the teller could be talking to one person or a thousand. Many people like the telling approach because it gives them a sense of control. Telling also tends to be transactional: I tell you something, and you decide whether to listen, believe it, reject it, or obey it. Putting two "tellers" with different views in the room causes conflict; they both want to talk, and each of them thinks he or she is right. Few of these conversations end well or continue productively. Two people with different beliefs who both want to *tell* the other what to believe is at best a recipe for getting stuck and at worst a relational crisis.

In an asking approach, on the other hand, I am curious about you, and my primary goal is to understand you, not just to give information. Our developing relationship is more valuable to me than any single moment of conversation. My respect for you and desire to know you takes precedence over my verbal content.

The asking approach can be messy. The initiator of the conversation is not in control of how it goes because he or she assumes that the other person also has something significant to share. There is give and take. It's a dialogue, not a monologue. Two essential ingredients are listening and asking good, open-ended questions that are not easily answered with one or two words. These practices require the other person to think in order to respond.

We see the asking approach in the first recorded conversation between God and Adam and Eve in the Garden of Eden. Adam and Eve had disobeyed God's command not to eat the fruit from the tree of the knowledge of good and evil. God was walking through the Garden and wanted to talk with them. Since God is all-knowing, he obviously knew what had happened. And yet instead of *telling* Adam and Eve what they did, he *asked* a sequence of four questions: (1) Where are you? (2) Who told you that you were naked? (3) Have you eaten from the tree that I commanded you not to eat from? (4) What is this you have done? (See Genesis 3:8-13.)

This has always puzzled me. If I had been God, I would have blasted Adam and Eve with the facts: "You could eat from any tree in the entire garden and yet you chose to eat from the one tree I said was off-limits! You shouldn't have listened to anyone who was contradicting me, and besides that, snakes are not supposed to talk." (Good thing I'm not God!)

Why did God ask questions? I think he wanted Adam and Eve to consider what they had done. To own their actions. To notice that they were now feeling ashamed in their nakedness. To see that they had chosen to disobey him. Perhaps he also wanted to approach them in a respectful way, to start a dialogue and continue the relationship. Whatever the reasons, I am overwhelmed at this loving response from God in spite of Adam and Eve's disobedience. This response is repeated throughout the Old Testament, as God continued to ask questions of his people.

Walk the Way of Jesus

Reading the New Testament, we see that Jesus also majored in asking much more than in telling. He asked questions, responded with questions, and filled his teaching with questions and parables that required people to puzzle through what he was saying. You can easily imagine people, long after Jesus' teaching was over, continuing to discuss what he had said as they tried to get to the heart of his message.

Mark 8 provides one example of Jesus' tendency to ask questions. In just one chapter, Jesus asks sixteen questions, including the all-important one: "Who do you say I am?" (Mark 8:29). We see the same scene in Matthew 16:15-16. When Jesus asks his disciples to voice their belief in their own words, Peter responds: "You are the Messiah, the Son of the living God." We can imagine the thrill it must have been for Peter to hear Jesus' affirmation: "Blessed are you, Simon son of Jonah, for this was not revealed to you by flesh and blood, but by my Father in heaven" (Matthew 16:17). Because Peter had reached this conclusion on his own, his realization was much richer than if Jesus had directly told the disciples, "I am the Messiah."

Let's look beyond the questions to the bigger picture of what Jesus did to advance the Kingdom of God around him. Jesus made disciples by selecting a few people into whom he poured his life— just twelve ordinary men. The plan was that they would "be with him" for the majority of his earthly ministry (Mark 3:14). Jesus wanted to give his followers as clear a picture of God as he could. He wanted them to walk alongside him to ensure the lasting nature of his mission. I think Jesus knew that disciples could not be impersonally mass-produced but would be the product of intimate and personal investment. Could this be true of disciples today as well?

Evangelism or Discipleship?

Most Christians and non-Christians can agree on one thing: They don't like the "e" word—evangelism. Although *evangelism* comes from the Greek word *euangelion*, which means "good news," the term has been hijacked by an approach that has not always delivered good news to its intended recipients, and it now elicits negative emotions from many.

It seems that the church at large has separated evangelism from discipleship so that there are two main buckets: everything *before* someone has a conversion experience with Jesus, which we call "evangelism," and everything *after* that conversion experience, which we call "discipleship."

Author Alan Hirsch has long been a prophetic voice to the church in the twenty-first century. If you haven't read any of his books on evangelism and discipleship, I'd encourage you to explore his writings, starting with his best-known work, *The Forgotten Ways*. Hirsch talks a lot about "reframing evangelism" within the context of discipleship in his recently released digital download, *Disciplism*.

Hirsch explains that treating evangelism and discipleship as part of the same continuum makes space for long-term, loving, authentic relationships with people in our lives. It gives credibility to our message and meaning to our relationships. It forces us to think of evangelism as a process, not as a transaction where someone prays a prayer and then graduates to the next class called "discipleship."

Reimagining evangelism through the lens of discipleship requires that we let go of seeing salvation as something we can deliver on demand, or when a person says a certain formulaic prayer. Rather, we need to reconceive discipleship as a process that includes pre-conversion discipleship and post-conversion discipleship. A person's salvation really is God's business, isn't it? Our part in it is to simply devote meaningful time and commitment to making disciples of whoever wants to share the journey with us—as we go. We don't need to rush to share the standard formulas in an unnatural, non-relational, forceful way. Surely, if we love our Lord Jesus and love the people we are investing in, we will get to share the Good News of His saving impact on our lives in a less forced manner. And surely we believe that it is the Holy Spirit who awakens interest in those that He is calling into God's kingdom?[1]

Maybe another "e" word is a better place to start with the people whom God is drawing to himself: *engagement*. What if simple times of engagement and respectful dialogue are what's needed to build relationships? What if they can serve as a bridge that is able to bear the weight of truth as people choose to explore Jesus? Perhaps we are becoming too preoccupied with what we label pre-evangelism, evangelism, and discipleship in the church today. If discipleship is helping those around us engage with God by engaging with them, that all starts the minute we choose to love them with his love—not just after their moment of salvation. Let's have conversations about God flow naturally from our interest in others and see whom God leads toward more intentional discipling and ongoing discussions about Jesus. We've made it harder than it needs to be.

Making New Disciples: Love Like Jesus

Author Francis Chan helps us understand what counts as good news: "God's definition of what matters is pretty straightforward. He measures our lives by how we love."[2] Our mandate from Jesus in Matthew 22:36-39 is clear: Love God, love people. Could it be that simple? We may have complicated evangelism by separating this Great Commandment from the Great Commission. Loving God and loving others is the foundation of the Great Commission.

To make disciples of people outside of our church doors, we start by loving them, building authentic friendships based on ordinary life circumstances and proximity (our neighborhoods, local coffee shops, workplaces, fitness classes, basketball courts, golf courses, or preschool play groups). These are the early stages of discipleship. The people we have identified may not all become followers of Jesus, but when we actively love them, we are in a better position to discern whom God might be drawing to himself.

One of our best snapshots of Jesus' love and compassion is found in Matthew 9:36: "When he saw the crowds, he had compassion on them because they were confused and helpless, like sheep without a shepherd" (NLT). If we are honest with ourselves, do *we* have compassion on the people we see every day? It starts with that deep, unsettled, heartfelt sympathy for people whose lives are full of problems and who are living without hope, meaning, or a clear direction for their future.

Jesus is called "a friend of sinners." Through his life we see that making new disciples starts with love and compassion for those we want to point toward him. Greg Ogden, a well-known author on the topics of discipleship and leadership, reminds us that "the Bible teaches us not only the message of our faith but also the *method* by which that faith is to be passed on to future generations. *We are called to do God's work in God's way.* The manner in which the Lord works is incarnational: life rubs up against life. We pass on Christlikeness through intimate modeling."[3]

The apostle John reminds us, "Whoever claims to live in [God] must live as Jesus did" (1 John 2:6). Are we ready to walk the way of Jesus? What does that look like in day-to-day, 24/7 life?

In the remainder of this book, Crilly and I will present nine relational practices of Jesus that we see in the Gospels. These practices provide tangible skills (the "how") for those who want to walk in the way of Jesus—to develop relationships and use an asking approach to pursue vibrant, vital conversations about God. Walking in the way of Jesus is a tremendous privilege and an exciting adventure that we hope you will take seriously. It will enable you to make disciples in a way that is natural and life giving. It will change your life and the lives of people around you.

In a recent book, missional leader Hugh Halter declares,

> If the kingdom of God is good news, then the King of this kingdom is also good news. Here's some encouraging info that should give you more confidence to have a conversation. Almost everyone loves Jesus. . . . He set people free and gave them license to live again . . . , and He was constantly blessing, healing, protecting and saving people around Him. All of this was done way before He did his greatest act of going to the cross for our sins. Who wouldn't love a man like this? Who wouldn't love it if God was like this?[4]

How about you? Are you trying to walk in the steps of Jesus to set people free with his good news? Would you like to genuinely model the practices of Jesus, who blesses, heals, protects, and saves people? Putting it in the broadest terms, do you want to be loving and compassionate like Jesus in the way that you interact with those around you? If you desire to improve in how you relate to people who believe differently (and let's face it, we all believe slightly differently from one another), this book can equip you to bless others by talking about God in a way that is always good news.

Discover

1. What is your definition of discipleship? When do you think discipleship starts?

2. Have you ever been involved in making a new disciple of Christ? If so, what did you find to be an effective method?

3. How did you become a follower of Jesus? If you are not a Christ follower, what would be the most attractive way to explore the possibility?

Practice

1. Think about people you see on a regular basis at work, in your neighborhood, or wherever you spend time each week. Ask God to show you the people with whom he would like you to have a meaningful conversation about him, and write down a few names. We'll come back to this list in some future chapters.

2. Try using an asking approach rather than a telling approach in a conversation this week where there are differences of opinion. How did it work out?

CHAPTER 2

Rediscovering Nine Relational Practices of Jesus

This is a large work I've called you into, but don't be overwhelmed by it. It's best to start small. Give a cool cup of water to someone who is thirsty, for instance. The smallest act of giving or receiving makes you a true apprentice. You won't lose out on a thing.

MATTHEW 10:42 (MSG)

We don't change markets, or populations, we change people. One person at a time, at a human level. And often, that change comes from small acts that move us, not from grand pronouncements.

SETH GODIN

WE LOVE THE BIG STUFF. The star athletes and celebrities. The crowds. The grandiose events. The spectacular 2012 Olympic opening ceremony in London was viewed on TV by an estimated 900 million people. According to Nielsen ratings, 2014's Super Bowl XLVIII started with 108 million viewers and peaked during the halftime show at 115.3 million! Fans love the game-winning, last-second shot to win the championship. People are drawn to the glamorous red carpet and opulent celebrity weddings.

We often carry this perspective into how to spread our faith, valuing big outreach events featuring celebrity preachers and a polished production. We admire the evangelists who can "close the deal" with the all-important sinner's prayer . . . on an airplane at 30,000 feet with a whole row of atheists.

The Christian culture has embraced the mind-set that evangelism should be done by the experts, the gifted, the professionals and the pastors; the theologians, apologists, and Masters of Divinity; the Bible-answer-men and -women. The rest of us can cheer them on, set up chairs, and throw a few bucks in the offering.

I (Crilly) have a friend who calls this the "Barry Bonds" mentality. Despite the controversial steroid scandal that clouded his career, Bonds was an outstanding baseball player. He played twenty-two seasons (1986–2007), received seven National League MVP awards and fourteen All-Star selections, and is considered to be one of the greatest baseball players of all time. An exceptional hitter, Bonds finished his career with the most home runs in baseball history. Bottom line: Bonds was elite. If you needed a home run, you would call in Barry Bonds.

In the church, the Barry Bonds mentality translates to our admiration for all-stars and professionals who spread the good news about Jesus—not with a little base hit, but with a flashy grand slam. The ordinary stuff seems boring. The little stuff doesn't seem to matter as much to us, so we're content to sit on the bench—or maybe even decide we're not needed on the team at all and head for the bleachers.

But what if this is a perspective we need to challenge and reconsider? What if the ordinary stuff *does* count?

Have you ever seen children playing tee ball? Tee ball introduces kids to baseball by helping them develop simple skills and have fun. If you watch the game, you will see little Jordan step up to home plate, where a stationary ball sits atop a plastic tee. Little Jordan takes a whack at the ball but misses it and instead hits the black plastic stem of the tee. The ball falls to the ground and rolls a few feet toward the infield. At once, all the parents start cheering for Jordan, who heads off running with all his might—down the third-base line, peering out the earhole of the crooked helmet on his head. His coach and his dad jump up to cheer him on and redirect him to first base. All the while, the crowd of parents is going wild because Jordan gave it his best try. In tee ball, everyone plays. Everyone cheers for attempts. Everyone gets a trophy. They don't even keep score!

If we applied this tee ball mentality to evangelism, what would happen?

First, I want to remind each one of you that, as a follower of Jesus, you have been picked for the team! Jesus himself said, "You did not choose me, but I chose you and appointed you so that you might go and bear fruit—fruit that will last" (John 15:16). And, in Ephesians 1, Paul further expanded this truth that we were chosen to be part of God's amazing plan from the beginning:

> Long before [God] laid down the earth's foundations, he had [you] in mind, had settled on [you] as the focus of his love, to be made whole and holy by his love. Long, long ago he decided to adopt [you] into his family through Jesus Christ. . . . He set it all out before us in Christ, a long-range plan in which everything would be brought together and summed up in him, everything in deepest heaven, everything on planet earth.
> EPHESIANS 1:4-5, 9-10, MSG

The God of the universe has hand-selected you to be on his team. Let that soak in a little. You are his first string, his A-team, his top choice. You are not created to sit on the bleachers and watch someone else play in the game. You are not his B-team or his last choice. God has specially picked you to be adopted into his family and to play a critical role in his redemptive plan to reconcile the world to himself. You are picked to be a Great-Commission Christian.

If we are chosen for the team, then how can each of us get in the game of making disciples?

Cups of Cold Water

What if some simple steps helped us all get in the game? What if the little stuff counts? The little things seemed to matter to Jesus. He heartily applauded the widow who gave the two tiny coins she had to offer. He blessed and multiplied the little loaves and fish from a boy's lunch until they fed thousands of people. He said, "If anyone gives even a cup of cold water to one of these little ones who is my disciple, truly I tell you, that person will certainly not lose their reward" (Matthew 10:42).

In Jesus' view, an activity as small as giving someone a cup of cold water is so important that a reward is associated with it. In today's evangelistic economy, little things don't seem to count for much. But in reality, it's the modern-day "cups of cold water"—like paying attention to people, listening to them, and praying for them—that bring refreshment and give others a taste of Jesus' love.

In tee ball, attempts matter. Regardless of the outcome, your simple attempt shows courage and grows you as a baseball player. The same can be true of making new disciples. Simple attempts matter because every action requires risk, faith, and courage, and repeated practice will help you grow as a disciple of Jesus. God will handle the outcome. He is most interested in our willingness to obey and follow in the ways of Jesus.

A New Perspective

In order to share the good news about Jesus intentionally today, we may have to start with a new perspective: focusing on the little things, the cups of cold water. In his book *You Lost Me*, David Kinnaman, president of Barna Group, writes:

> The Christian community needs a new mind—a new
> way of thinking, a new way of relating, a new vision of
> our role in the world—to pass on the faith to this and

future generations. As it turns out, this "new" mind is not so new. . . . I am convinced that historic and traditional practices . . . are what this generation really needs.'

We can discover a clue to this "new-old" way of relating by taking a look at Matthew 22:36-40, often called the Great Commandment: "Jesus replied, 'Love the Lord your God with all your heart and with all your soul and with all your mind.' This is the first and greatest commandment. And the second is like it: 'Love your neighbor as yourself.'"

Here Jesus presents the life-guiding principle given by God through Moses in the Torah. Jesus encourages a return to the basics—and loving God and loving others covers all the bases! What if this is the way for all of us to get involved in our Kingdom mission? After all, making disciples is a natural outcome of loving God and loving others. As you actively love people who don't yet know Jesus, you are building trusting relationships with them and earning the right to engage in spiritual conversations.

If our role in making disciples is to love people, then small, simple, everyday activities really do count! All of the little actions that build relationships count, and those are what we are responsible for. That's what God asks us to handle; he takes care of the rest. I don't know about you, but I find this extremely liberating. I am free to build loving relationships without the pressure of following the right formula. I don't have to be the one to convict, convince, or convert anyone. Thankfully, it's God's job to change hearts and minds and produce fruit that lasts. I am free of the pressure to "save" someone because it is God alone who can transform a human heart.

Simple Building Blocks

So then, what is our job? Author and pastor Peter Scazzero says, "Telling people to love better and more is not enough. They need practical skills incorporated into their spiritual formation."[2] These practical skills are a lot like simple machines. Remember them from grade school? There are six: the lever, the wheel and axle, the pulley, the inclined plane, the wedge, and the screw. The Greeks identified them, but all throughout history, people have used these fundamental tools to accomplish what would be impossible without them. Archimedes said of the lever: "Give me a place to stand on, and I can move the Earth."

Renaissance thinkers took these basic elements and combined them to create more sophisticated machines such as the printing press and the bicycle. The rediscovery of these building blocks of mechanics also paved the way for inventions from the steam engine to the cotton gin, and for cultural shifts like the Industrial Revolution—all from six machines so simple that people used them even before the machines had names!

If six simple machines played a critical role in the development of the machinery that drove the Industrial Revolution, then what are the building blocks we need to rediscover for a different kind of revolution—a revolution of the heart? And where will we find them?

Is it any surprise that we would find the answer in Jesus? If you think about *how* Jesus interacted with people around him and about the practices that made up the activity of his early church, you can see patterns that are very different from the habits of our Western lifestyle. Jesus' method of disciple-making was thoroughly relational, involving simple foundational practices.

For example, consider how Jesus initiated a conversation with the Samaritan woman at the well, recorded in John 4. He intentionally went out of his way to engage with her. He took time to notice her. He asked her a simple question: "Would you give me a drink of water?" Jesus could have made water flow from a rock or provided a way to draw his own water from the well. He did not need to interact with this woman, but he did. He engaged her naturally and winsomely—not in a way that was weird or canned.

Why? Relationships start with questions and actions that build bridges and encourage trust. With simple relational skills, Jesus demonstrated love and compassion. Jesus' question initiated a deep conversation with rippling spiritual consequences.

In other encounters, we see Jesus intentionally notice people like Zacchaeus (Luke 19) and the crippled man at the pool of Bethesda (John 5). We read of Jesus' regular practice of prayer (Luke 5:16, among others) and the apostles' devotion to prayer (Acts 2:42). We observe Jesus listening and asking questions, intent on engaging in meaningful conversations about God with people such as his disciples at Caesarea Philippi (Matthew 16:13-16) and a blind beggar in Jericho (Luke 18). Then we read of the early church walking as Jesus did, on mission with God, practicing the same behaviors as Jesus. Think about Philip asking questions and facilitating an interaction with the Ethiopian (Acts 8) or Peter noticing a beggar and reacting with compassion and healing (Acts 3).

What if we began to apply these patterns and practices of Jesus?

The interaction with the Samaritan woman started with Jesus' ability to engage her in a meaningful conversation. The same is true for you and me. Philosopher Martin Buber wrote, "When two people relate to each other authentically and humanly, God is the electricity that surges between them."[3] Even if people don't know God personally, they recognize the power of a significant conversation within a relationship that allows them to be authentic. Our challenge, though, is that a discussion about spiritual matters so easily becomes negatively charged. Even simple interactions and ordinary conversations can be difficult for us.

Why? Well, generally, we are poor conversationalists. Some of us talk way too much and listen very little. Often we offer our unsolicited opinions. Our attention spans are short, and we formulate our responses while others are speaking. We'll often make hasty generalizations and jump to conclusions. Some of us talk over people and talk for them. We tend to cast quick judgments.

Most of us are generally not curious; we are more inclined to talk about ourselves than ask about others. Some of us avoid entering into conversations at all.

If we are not good at ordinary conversations, how can we talk well about spiritual matters? We must be honest with ourselves. Even if we can handle everyday conversations, most of us still are not good at "God talk" with our family, friends, neighbors, classmates, or coworkers. Loving people and participating in the Great Commission will inevitably mean talking with people in ways that we hope will nudge them toward Jesus. So, to be Great-Commission Christians, we all need to improve in our conversational ability, to engage the spiritually curious, and to begin a journey of discovery with them about God and the Bible.

Pastor Francis Chan reminds us that we all need to grow in this area.

> Wherever you are, you need to figure out how to get into the lives of the unbelievers. To me, the biggest problem with evangelism . . . is that it's gotten too impersonal. People in the church don't know how to look an unbeliever in the eye and actually love him or her and carry on a conversation with them. . . . It's a lot harder to go out, be in the world, and build relationships with people who don't believe like you and think like you. Most people don't make the effort to do that. . . . I think overall, the church is going to get weaker and weaker in this area, and it's not because they don't love Jesus. It's not because they don't have a heart for the Lord. They just don't know how to engage with people who don't believe like they do.[4]

We could take the pessimistic route and make gloomy predictions about what this behavior portends for the future of the church. But as Christians with a desire to see the world renewed and redeemed, we could instead see an opportunity. After all, people crave *engagement*. They want someone who will acknowledge and respect their thoughts and feelings. For Christians living in this technologically interconnected but relationally disconnected culture, engaging in simple conversational practices will communicate the unconditional love of Christ to people all around us and could reverse the downward spiral of our churches.

Maybe we don't need more apologetic arguments, but simple conversational "arts." When it comes to spiritual conversations, we are talking about a craft that you can cultivate and practice over time—and that's more art than science anyway. As Vincent Van Gogh said, "The more I think it over, the more I feel that there is nothing more truly artistic than to love people."[5]

Moving from a lifestyle of few, if any, spiritual conversations with people who believe differently to a life of ongoing spiritual conversations is a big leap for a lot of people. If making new disciples is going to become a normal part of our lives, it will have to be something we enjoy doing and can envision doing tomorrow, next month, and five years from now. That's why we need to provide a pathway to spiritual conversations through simple, memorable activities that can be done by ordinary people as part of their normal routine. No special training or unusual courage required. It's the little stuff that counts, like cups of cold water.

So That

Over and over in Jesus' life, we see simple behaviors that reflect a life on mission with God. But that lifestyle isn't the end in itself—Jesus' behaviors and practices are always a means to a much greater good. Paul gives us insight into why we should adopt these loving practices of Jesus:

Be wise in the way you act toward outsiders; make the most of every opportunity. Let your conversation be always full of grace, seasoned with salt, *so that* you may know how to answer everyone.

COLOSSIANS 4:5-6, EMPHASIS ADDED

When I am with those who are weak, I share their oppression *so that* I might bring them to Christ. Yes, I try to find common ground with everyone *so that* I might bring them to Christ.

I CORINTHIANS 9:22, EMPHASIS ADDED

These two key words are critical: *so that*. You have been picked for God's team "*so that* you might go and bear fruit—fruit that will last" (John 15:16, emphasis added).

What if simple practices—such as noticing people, praying for them even before your first conversation, listening to demonstrate love and value to them, and asking them engaging questions to discover how God may be at work in their lives—could provide an easy pathway so that you could engage people in your life in ongoing spiritual conversations and help them discover Jesus?

To get good at anything takes practice. Take driving a car, for example. Truck drivers started in Driver's Ed. School bus drivers started in Driver's Ed. Indy 500 drivers started in Driver's Ed. We all sat in a classroom learning the road signs and what they meant. We sat at the simulator, watching the same videos with the beach ball bouncing across the road, the dog running out into the street, and the car backing into our path. We all took the multiple-choice tests. But the simulator videos and the "Rules of the Road" booklet didn't make us drivers.

We didn't become drivers until we actually got behind the wheel and practiced. And the reality is, people all drive differently, and each of us learns specific skills that fit into our context. A person who lives in the city gets really good at parallel parking. A truck driver gets really good at driving for long hours and backing up a forty-foot tractor-trailer into a narrow loading dock. A school bus driver gets really good at safely driving a load of children to school.

Most of us drive every day just to get us where we want to go. Most of us never aspire to drive like a professional NASCAR driver, but almost all of us aspire to drive. And almost all of us—from all walks of life, educational backgrounds, and demographics—can learn how to drive. It doesn't take an immense amount of coordination or a high level of education. We're not all going to be NASCAR drivers, but we all get to drive and enjoy the freedom it brings.

Just like anyone can learn how to drive, everyone can learn simple practices to make disciples. That's our purpose! But we do need some equipping, we need an on-ramp of learning, and we need to get out there and practice.

What are the behaviors that will help us to make new disciples?

The 9 Arts of Spiritual Conversations

Looking at the behaviors and practices of Jesus, we have identified nine practices that we call The 9 Arts of Spiritual Conversations. These nine simple practices provide a pathway for you to engage people in your life in ongoing spiritual conversations. They are building blocks of an incarnational lifestyle—a way of life that brings Jesus into the lives of people because he is in you and you are with them. They are simple, doable behaviors for an ordinary Christian that get you on the journey of making disciples. They are skills that help you move from a lifestyle of few (if any) spiritual conversations to ongoing spiritual conversations. Just like learning how to drive, anyone can learn and practice these Arts. It doesn't take a lot of upfront training; you can practice as you go. In fact, it's likely that you are already doing some of them.

It's easy to feel intimidated, inadequate, and ill-equipped to get on mission with God and make disciples. But the book of Acts tells us that Jesus' disciples were just like us. Look at what Acts 4:13 says about them: "When [the Sanhedrin] saw the courage of Peter and John and realized that they were unschooled, ordinary men, they were astonished and they took note that these men had been with Jesus."

These were ordinary men and women who became world changers because they went through Jesus' training school. He took them with him and, along the way, they gained real experience in these nine simple Arts that lead to disciple-making.

Like learning how to ride a bike or drive a car, getting good at spiritual conversations with those who believe differently from you takes practice. Learning how to relate to people, especially those unlike you, calls for a change in your perspective. You need to experience it—not just learn about it, hear about it, or talk about it. These nine practices will help you begin. We have broken them down into three categories:

Arts for Getting Ready for spiritual conversations:
  Noticing
  Praying
  Listening

Arts for Getting Started with spiritual conversations:
  Asking Questions
  Loving
  Welcoming

Arts for Keeping It Going:
  Facilitating
  Serving Together
  Sharing

With practice, these 9 Arts become building blocks of a trustworthy relationship with almost anyone, no matter what they believe about God. And anyone can do them. Whether you are introverted or extroverted, gifted in evangelism or not, you can put these 9 Arts into practice. We can be ordinary people in our ordinary days doing little things but having extraordinary impact—because we have "been with Jesus."

Notice that the Art of Sharing—as in sharing your faith with others—is the last of the 9 Arts on the list. Christians have historically considered this to be the exclusive practice of evangelism and have often bypassed normal conversational decorum to leap to the action of *telling* the gospel. However, the other eight Arts not only count; they lay a significant relational foundation and create a safe environment for sharing the good news about Jesus. By following the Holy Spirit's lead in noticing, praying, listening, asking questions, welcoming, loving, facilitating, and serving together, we can be respectful of the relational process and will earn the trust to share our story and God's story.

Ordinary folks like you and me can purposefully practice these simple Arts, which are small, incremental steps to building relationships with people who believe differently. These relationships could eventually lead to ongoing spiritual conversations resulting in a life-changing decision to follow Jesus.

One important caveat: These 9 Arts are intended to make it easier to engage with people who believe differently, not add eight additional steps that you have to climb in order to have a gospel conversation. Please do not view these as an order or formula to be rigidly followed. View the Arts more as nine tools in your tool belt that are at your disposal to use when needed. Maybe in the past you have operated with one gospel tool—the hammer. This book hopes to provide you with a variety of relational tools to help you get on mission with God in his Kingdom expansion.

Practicing the 9 Arts

In chapter 1, Mary Schaller shared some of her stories. Now it's my turn.

I (Crilly) met Ed after he had turned eighty. I had recently moved into a townhome, and Ed was my neighbor. Ed lived independently and was full of life, still dancing, dating, and driving. When I noticed him sitting on his back patio, I would intentionally go out to sit with him and chat. Over time, we established a warm friendship, despite the fifty-plus-year age difference. I grew to love Ed. We enjoyed walks in the park, parties, holidays, and birthdays together.

Ed's life story captivated me. Often in our conversations I would find myself asking him about his youth, his war experience, his marriage, his adventures, and his career. Ed shared that he was a teenage Ping-Pong champ, a successful lawyer, a ballroom-dance instructor, and an adventurer who once rode horseback across Cuba. I found out that Ed was a courageous war veteran who had defended his country in the Pacific theater during World War II. His life was rich and deep and abundant with experiences—and the only way I discovered his story was by being interested enough to ask questions. Sixteen years later, when Ed was ninety-six years old, I had built the trust to ask him other meaningful questions, resulting in a spiritual conversation that impacted Ed's relationship with God for eternity.

For some reason I'll never understand, God wants ordinary men and women in their ordinary days to make an extraordinary impact with an extraordinary message. What's the message? *God is madly in love with all people!* With an awesome message like that, how can we all get in the game? Where do we practice?

Getting in the Game = Making Disciples

We have all heard Jesus' command to *go and make disciples*. But *go* where? I didn't know, so I tried all kinds of different opportunities.

I went into the big city to serve the urban homeless at a soup kitchen. I connected with suburban under-resourced folks at a care center. I tutored kids in a struggling part of the city an hour's drive from my home.

All of these experiences were formative and powerful, yet none were sustainable activities I could integrate into my daily life. I didn't want to do "hit and run" disciple-making only a few days or weeks of the year. I wanted to follow my Master's command right where he had placed me. I wanted an opportunity to foster relationships, engage with people, and create a longer-term connection I could build on.

It seemed to me that God's plan for his Kingdom to come meant I had to *go*. As I prayed that God would reveal to me where I should go, I began to desire a greater understanding of different people in our pluralistic, melting pot of a society. I felt like the world was getting smaller and God wanted my heart for the world to get bigger. I specifically prayed for a chance to engage with people of different races, colors, and religions. That prayer seemed unreasonable. How would I, a white suburban guy, have that prayer fulfilled without traveling somewhere far away? But I prayed anyway.

During that time, my wife, Danielle, and I volunteered for a local service project through our church to help clean up a low-income apartment complex in a nearby town. As we were picking up trash and sweeping the sidewalks, the children from the complex came out to see why we were there. Many of the people living in the apartments were refugees from Africa. Almost immediately, I was drawn to two adorable little girls—sisters from the same family who were Muslim Bantu refugees from Somalia. We got to know them a little, played games together, and met their sisters, brothers, and mother. After that day's experience and relational connection, Danielle and I decided we would return to visit the family—and we did. We came to see them every month or so and began a friendship with the whole family, especially the oldest son.

Around the same time, Danielle joined a new women's group in the area and met a woman who worked for World Relief, a refugee placement agency. In conversation with her, Danielle found out that she also coordinated tutoring for Bantu refugees on Saturday mornings at a church five blocks from our home. Danielle mentioned that we had recently met a Bantu family from Somalia, and we discovered that the two little sisters and their siblings actually attended this tutoring! We felt like pieces were coming together and we were in the midst of God's activity.

Curious about this opportunity, Danielle and I showed up one Saturday morning and were quickly put into action. I was assigned to the older boys and Danielle to the younger girls. In talking with the kids, we found out that several of the refugee families lived in an apartment complex only two blocks away from our house! We knew that only God could pull off a global intersection like this. That was in 2005, and Danielle and I have been involved with these refugee families ever since. The close physical proximity has allowed us to deepen relationships with a family of twelve and many of the older boys over time. As an added bonus, we found rich friendships with the teacher and the couple who founded this ministry.

Because these children live nearby, we have been able to sustain the relationship over the long haul, connecting on a consistent basis outside of the regular tutoring time. We have learned together—math, science, reading, and writing. We have had fun adventures together, like taking the kids to their first baseball game. We have experienced deep sorrow together, like the death of one of the younger boys after a struggle with leukemia.

Now, as the children have transformed into young adults, we are able to have meaningful spiritual conversations with them— to seek to understand their culture and religious perspectives, to ask questions about their beliefs, to answer their questions about our faith, and to challenge them to seek truth for themselves, not blindly embrace the faith of their fathers.

Cultivating the friendship naturally, over time, we have earned the mutual trust to speak openly to each other about God, our faith, and our questions. In friendship, we can engage in spiritual conversations without hostility as we try to love and understand each other better. As the older boys have now turned into young men, we have been able to do many more social activities with them, including inviting them to attend special Christmas services with us. The past three years, they heard (and some even sang!) some of the great incarnational carols and listened to the story of Christ's birth with us. This sparked wonderful conversations.

Our friend Hugh Halter has said, "When I start a relationship with a seeker, I plan on a five-year commitment." Well. I knew when we began this journey that it would be a long-term investment. Discipleship works that way. The relational capital invested has begun to take root in the hearts of my young friends as they are slowly discovering *Isa al Masih* (Arabic for *Jesus the Messiah*). It has been wonderful to watch God's Spirit reveal truth to these young men. In response to one year's Christmas service, one of them wrote a poem about what he experienced entitled "Love and Praise the Lord." Here are a few lines he shared:

> *All the poetry ever written*
> *Every verse and every line*
> *All the love songs in the world*
> *Every melody and rhyme,*
> *If they were combined,*
> *They would still be unable to express,*
> *What I want to define*
> *When I try to describe my love for you.*[6]

It all started with praying for God's direction, noticing the children around us, and asking questions as we sought to get to know them. And because of that, I am experiencing the joy of discipling young men *to* Jesus and seeing God's power and truth revealed to them. It is a long walk in the same direction—but it is worth every step. What about you? Where will you *go* to live out the Great Commission? Where will you practice these 9 Arts of Spiritual Conversations?

Recently, I drove past a familiar corner in the town of Wheaton, Illinois. Yes, Wheaton—the home of Wheaton College, with its beautiful Billy Graham Center, which chronicles the wonderful history of the Billy Graham ministry and of evangelism in America. In fact, Trivial Pursuit claims that Wheaton has "more churches per capita than any other town in America."

I knew this corner because it was the site of a once-thriving church. The church had come on hard times and had foreclosed, leaving the property inactive for the previous year. As I drove by, I noticed new activity in the parking lot. I was surprised to discover that a new church had not moved into this foreclosed property, but a mosque—the first mosque in Wheaton.

It hit me again that the world—all colors, religions, ethnicities—is already right in my neighborhood. It also revealed to me in a graphic way how important it is for me to *go* into my own community.

When you look around, you may be surprised at just how close *all the nations* already are. You may also be surprised by how spiritually hungry and confused people are right where you live. Most of us don't have to *go* too far. You can go to the office or cubicle next to you. You can go to your neighbor or roommate. You can go to the park or to the pub. You can go and walk alongside your own son or daughter. Disciples are waiting to be made all around us.

I'm reminded of what Jesus said to the man from the region of the Gerasenes. The man, whom Jesus delivered from demon-possession, begged to go with Jesus away from his home. But "Jesus sent him away, saying, 'Return home and tell how much God has done for you.' So the man went away and told all over town how much Jesus had done for him" (Luke 8:38-39).

We can all make disciples of Jesus, but we will have to put one foot in front of the other and go. Many of us will find that we don't have to go very far. As you pray and discern where God is leading you to go, your next questions may be *How? How will I do this? How will I make a move again?*

With a fresh perspective and simple everyday practices, any Christian can engage in the Great Commission. To do it, we need memorable skills that can be done by ordinary people as part of our normal routine, and that will be positively received as good news by everyone.

Mary and I will spend the rest of this book providing you with simple, practical ways to develop those skills. We'll incorporate many more of our stories along the way. We hope you'll also see how God has used these simple practices to help us relate with people around us, and how God is really the one doing the powerful work all the time. He is in the business of making disciples, and he wants to work through you, too.

Discover

1. Describe a time when you had a spiritual conversation with someone who believed differently. Did it go well? Why or why not?

2. What do you think is scarce in today's culture that people are thirsty for?

Practice

1. Take a minute to perform your own quick Spiritual Conversation Assessment below. Rate your level of effectiveness with each

of the 9 Arts on a scale of 1–5 (5 = totally satisfied, 1 – not satisfied at all). There's no passing grade here! The aim is to help you get an idea of where your strengths lie and where you might need to focus some attention.

____ **Noticing** those around me and paying close attention to what God might be doing in their lives.

____ **Praying** for those I meet in my day-to-day life and asking God to show me what he wants me to do to bless them.

____ **Listening** with genuine care, interest, and empathy as I interact with others without editorializing or offering my own unsolicited opinions.

____ **Asking questions** that arise from genuine curiosity, drawing others out with great questions and seeking to understand more than to be understood.

____ **Loving** others authentically because I personally know God's love and see them with his eyes.

____ **Welcoming** people by valuing their presence so they feel that they belong.

____ **Facilitating** good discussions in a group setting so that every person feels honored and respected, even when they believe differently than I do.

____ **Serving together**, gathering people to serve and know God and each other better through service.

____ **Sharing** my own story, learning others' stories, and expressing God's story of forgiveness through Jesus in a way that is respectful and meaningful.

2. Discuss your assessment with someone. In which practices would you like to improve? (Examples: Notice people more, ask better open-ended questions, listen more empathetically.)

PART I

Getting Ready

THE 9 ARTS OF SPIRITUAL CONVERSATIONS are divided into groups of three. The first three Arts do not require you to say or know much at all. We call this grouping *Getting Ready* for spiritual conversations. Whether you are a quiet introvert or a garrulous extrovert, gifted in evangelism or not, you can put these Arts into practice. They include the Arts of Noticing, Praying, and Listening. If you do not know how to begin engaging in spiritual conversations with people in your life who may believe differently, these practices will launch your journey.

CHAPTER 3

The Art of Noticing

When he saw the crowds, he had compassion on them, because they were harassed and helpless, like sheep without a shepherd. Then he said to his disciples, "The harvest is plentiful but the workers are few. Ask the Lord of the harvest, therefore, to send out workers into his harvest field."

MATTHEW 9:36-38

If we are to love our neighbors, before doing anything else we must see our neighbors. With our imagination as well as our eyes, that is to say like artists, we must see not just their faces but the life behind and within their faces. Here it is love that is the frame we see them in.

FREDERICK BUECHNER

FOR A NUMBER OF YEARS in my commute to work, I (Crilly) entered the highway at the same toll ramp almost every day. I would wait in the line of cars, along with all the other impatient commuters, wanting to get through the tollbooth as quickly as possible and be on my way. Paying the toll was irritating enough, but sitting in line made it doubly frustrating. As I waited to pay, I would see an anonymous hand reach out of the booth and go back in, then repeat this mechanical motion over and over for each vehicle. Toll attendants have a thankless job. Most drivers do not even acknowledge their existence. My guess is that most people see them as part of the machinery—a means to an end. But for some reason, probably prompted by God, I decided to pay attention to this particular toll attendant. The first time

I noticed her, I slow-rolled up to the booth and greeted her with a pleasant smile and cheerful, "Hello!" handing her my toll money and making eye contact. As I pulled away, I shouted, "Have a great day!"

She was there every day. So in future interactions, I noticed her nameplate and greeted her by name. We engaged in pleasant small talk each time I pulled up to her booth. Over time, our conversation added a personal dimension. I eventually learned the names of her children, details of her family life, and her weekend plans. In fact, we even exchanged Christmas gifts! This relationship was built in a matter of a few seconds over time—how long each day depended on the honking of the cars behind me. Noticing her did not add much time or activity to my day, but it did add the rewarding feeling of being on an adventure with God. It was the simple, intentional turning of my attention that made the difference.

It All Starts with Noticing

A precursor of knowing someone is noticing them. As Doug Pollock writes in his book *God Space*, "noticing is a prerequisite to caring about others and serving them in tangible ways that smuggle the gospel into their hearts."[1] Relational interaction has the same starting point for all of us—simply in noticing another person. Noticing is not only a first step in becoming aware of another person but also in paying attention to God's activity in your world. Pastor John Ortberg writes of noticing as the spiritual discipline of seeing God at work all around you. Exercising this discipline challenges us to broaden our focus, slow down our pace of life, and witness God's grace in ordinary people, things, and events. In the study on grace in the Pursuing Spiritual Transformation series, Ortberg shares what it means to live in grace and how it relates to noticing:

If we want to live in grace, we must develop eyes that see. We must learn what might be called the discipline of *noticing*. To notice something—to truly pay attention—is a powerful thing. . . . The practice of noticing is a skill. It involves learning to pay attention to gifts that we otherwise take for granted. . . . They are gracious gifts. And what's even more amazing is that their Giver is lovingly present with you even as you are experiencing them.[2]

Jesus was a noticer. "When he saw the crowds, he had compassion on them, because they were harassed and helpless, like sheep without a shepherd. Then he said to his disciples, 'The harvest is plentiful but the workers are few. Ask the Lord of the harvest, therefore, to send out workers into his harvest field'" (Matthew 9:36-38). Jesus was moved with compassion for the crowds when he *saw* them. He *noticed* the crowds first and consequently expressed his desire for workers who could shepherd them. The disciples might have missed the tremendous needs of the crowd if Jesus had not pointed out their harassed and helpless condition.

Jesus Is Our Model of Noticing

Jesus was masterful at noticing people. In Luke 19, we read that Jesus was walking through the big city of Jericho. Crowds of people lined the street to catch a glimpse of him. Yet amid the activity, Jesus was attentive enough to notice one guy up in a tree, and because of that, the man's life was transformed.

Jesus entered Jericho and was passing through. A man was there by the name of Zacchaeus; he was a chief tax collector and was wealthy. He wanted to see who Jesus was, but because he was short he could not see over the crowd. So he ran ahead and climbed a sycamore-fig tree to see him, since Jesus was coming that way.

When Jesus reached the spot, he looked up and said to him, "Zacchaeus, come down immediately. I must stay at your house today." So he came down at once and welcomed him gladly.

All the people saw this and began to mutter, "He has gone to be the guest of a sinner."

But Zacchaeus stood up and said to the Lord, "Look, Lord! Here and now I give half of my possessions to the poor, and if I have cheated anybody out of anything, I will pay back four times the amount."

Jesus said to him, "Today salvation has come to this house, because this man, too, is a son of Abraham. For the Son of Man came to seek and to save the lost."

LUKE 19:1-10

It's amazing in this account that Jesus even noticed Zacchaeus. While Zacchaeus had a desire to see Jesus, it was Jesus who took the first step to personally initiate contact with him. It makes me wonder if I would have noticed Zacchaeus in the crowd. I might have seen him in the tree and wondered what he was doing there, but would I really have seen him as a person who needed Jesus? Would you have?

Jesus came to seek and save the lost. The action verb *to seek* means "to go in search of, to try to find or discover by searching or questioning." This was a pattern and practice of Jesus. He noticed people personally and collectively, and it moved him to compassion and action. Consider what happened later in the same chapter: "As [Jesus] approached Jerusalem and saw the city, he wept over it" (Luke 19:41).

Or in an earlier chapter:

Jesus went with his disciples to the village of Nain, and a large crowd followed him. A funeral procession was coming out as he approached the village gate. The young man who had died was a widow's only son, and a large crowd from the village was with her. When the Lord saw her, his heart overflowed with compassion.

LUKE 7:11-13, NLT

Do we want to live like Jesus, to notice people *and* have compassion toward them? Noticing people can move us to compassion and action as it humanizes the nameless faces around us. People become real to us, with real lives and real problems in need of a real Savior. As Frederick Buechner said, "If we are to love our neighbors, before doing anything else we must see our neighbors." While Jesus is our model for this important practice, ordinary people can do this too. You probably already do it, but now you can practice it more intentionally. Remember—as in tee ball, success is in the intention and the attempt, not in the results.

Noticing is such a simple activity that we can miss how powerful it can be. How many of us, for example, long to see people we care for reconciled to God? Noticing can be a critical step toward that result. John Paul Lederach, professor of international peacebuilding at the University of Notre Dame and widely known for his pioneering work in conflict transformation, identifies "noticing mutual humanity" as the first of three "Reconciliation Arts." Lederach explains:

When we approach the challenge of reconciliation, we tend to ask for the steps, the model, the process, the toolkit, and the techniques. . . . When we approach the life of Jesus, however, questions of method or technique may not be the best starting point. His ministry did not rise from recipes or in the words of the environment around him or from the law. Jesus' ministry had roots in grace expressed primarily through the *quality of presence*: the way he chose to be present, in relationship and in the company of others, even those who wished him harm. . . . The key to this presence was his capacity to notice the humanity of others. . . . [For Jesus], compassion starts with a quality of attentiveness that requires the simple act of noticing the other as a person. So simple is the idea that we far too often take it for granted. In truth, I believe this simple act forms a spiritual discipline.[3]

We don't notice just for the sake of noticing. Seeing another person through God's eyes has a purpose: It's the first step in the ministry of reconciliation. In 2 Corinthians 5:16, Paul calls us to see people through the eyes of Christ: "So from now on we regard no one from a worldly point of view." In our busy, self-absorbed culture, noticing is the equivalent of a cup of water—a small, rebellious act against the idolatry of self.

When Jesus noticed people, it was good news for them! When we notice people, it should be good news for them, too. Because people matter to God, they should matter to us. Giving people the gift of our time and attention demonstrates their value to us as a treasure of God. The evil one accuses, devalues, blames, shames, and slanders people so that they think they are not worthy to be truly seen by others or God. When we notice people, we assign worth to them as image bearers of the Most High God. Our noticing says, "You are worthy of attention from me and from God." This simple practice begins to break down the accusations of the enemy and to call out the image of God in each person. But because we all are also "image breakers," as Andy Crouch puts it, we need to be reconciled to God through Jesus. As Christ's followers, we are assigned to be representatives of Christ's life-giving message of reconciliation, partnering with him to bring people to

God. Noticing another person opens the door to relationship and to this life-changing message.

The apostle Paul writes about the ministry of reconciliation:

> All this is from God, who reconciled us to himself through Christ and gave us the ministry of reconciliation: that God was reconciling the world to himself in Christ, not counting people's sins against them. And he has committed to us the message of reconciliation. We are therefore Christ's ambassadors, as though God were making his appeal through us. We implore you on Christ's behalf: Be reconciled to God. God made him who had no sin to be sin for us, so that in him we might become the righteousness of God.
>
> 2 CORINTHIANS 5:18-21

In his book *My Name Is Asher Lev*, Chaim Potok's main character is an awakening artist, beginning to see the world with a different perspective. The author captures a simple moment at a family dinner from the emerging artist's point of view:

> That was the night I began to realize that something was happening to my eyes. I looked at my father and saw lines and planes I had never seen before. I could feel with my eyes. I could feel my eyes moving across the lines around his eyes and into and over the deep furrows on his forehead. He was thirty-five years old, and there were lines on his face and forehead. I could feel the lines with my eyes and feel, too, the long straight flat bridge of his nose and the clear darkness of his eyes and the strong thick curves of the red eyebrows and the thick red hair of his beard graying a little—I saw the stray gray strands in the

tangle of hair below his lips. I could feel lines and points
and planes. I could feel texture and color. . . . I felt myself
flooded with the shapes and textures of the world around
me. I closed my eyes. But I could still see that way inside
my head. I was seeing with another pair of eyes that had
suddenly come awake.[4]

What if we changed the way we looked at people? What if we
paid attention to people with a new set of eyes that "suddenly came
awake"? Might we see the helpless and hopeless condition of people
with whom we come into contact every day?

While noticing may be the first step in bringing someone the
good news about Jesus and the Kingdom of God, the single most
significant benefit is that it transforms you and me. We begin to
see others, ourselves, and even God differently. People we never
noticed before (not because they weren't there, but because we
never paid attention to them) quite suddenly matter to us in
ways we can't explain. We find that the more we pay attention
to others, the less we are absorbed with our own agenda and
life. Jerry Root and Stan Guthrie, authors of *The Sacrament of
Evangelism*, explain: "Evangelism doesn't 'do anything' to God—
it does something to *us*. It opens our eyes to His work and grace."
It provides us with "the opportunity to experience participating
with this omnipotent, omnipresent God as He woos others to
Himself."[5]

Common Barriers

Noticing is the spiritual discipline of intentionally paying attention
to someone who is in your view at the moment, wherever you are.
But our everyday lives are filled with obstacles that keep us from
noticing others and that need to be overcome. Four potential barriers
can prevent us from practicing the Art of Noticing—the busyness

of our lives, focusing on ourselves, living in a Christian bubble, and having an unloving attitude.

1. PACE OF LIFE

Everybody is busy these days, and being rushed usually keeps our focus sharply on ourselves, our agendas, and our needs. This makes it almost impossible to focus on anyone else, even if they're right in front of us. With so much coming at us, we need to develop a greater capacity for noticing. When we are preoccupied with ourselves and our own busy lives, we have a low capacity for noticing others. We cannot easily see the image of God in another person. Our eyes are affected; we have spiritual myopia. Noticing people opens our eyes and awakens us to God's continuous activity in our world. Our vision begins to align with God's vision.

Author Melody Allred said it this way:

> My new perspective of understanding and loving God like never before gave me a new set of eyes through which to view people. With these new God goggles, I didn't just see people. I saw lost people. People with a name. People with a story. Good people. Good parents. Good neighbors. Yet they are lost people, and I barely even knew their names.[6]

Noticing is not another thing to put on your already full to-do list. It's a way of living that causes regular intersection with God's activity in the routines of your ordinary life. Look for what God is up to in people of all kinds, wherever you normally go. This practice transforms you into a spiritual archaeologist, discovering God's activity in people all around you and becoming more and more fascinated by what you find.

One way to overcome the barrier of busyness is to break up your schedule with thirty-second noticing sessions. Go where you normally go and do what you normally do, but plan on spending at least thirty seconds paying attention to someone who is there with you. You may find yourself slowing down a little because you enjoy the experience.

2. SELF-FOCUS

To notice someone, you have to take your eyes off yourself and be willing to be interrupted. What if we welcomed the possibility that an interruption might be a divine appointment? Too often we respond to interruptions as impediments to our own agendas.

One way to overcome this barrier of self-focus is to intentionally direct your full attention toward whoever is in your peripheral view. Consider the possibility that God is inviting you to engage in what he is doing at the moment.

Several years ago when my (Mary's) son was a sophomore in college, I received a frantic call from him one day explaining that he had just been kicked out of class because I hadn't paid his tuition. My first reaction was, *What? Impossible! Of course I paid his tuition!* But the school was right. With my busy work and travel schedule, I had forgotten. The only way to rectify it quickly was to wire funds to the school.

Distraught and feeling like I was the worst mother in the world, I rushed to my local bank and asked for a wire transfer. As I waited for a banker to help me, I was having the biggest pity party. *How could I have done something so stupid!* I thought. *I want my son to get his college education, not be forced to drop out.*

Then it occurred to me that God might have allowed this to happen for a purpose. What could it be? He whispered, "Pay attention. I am doing something here." I became increasingly curious, temporarily taking focus off of my own problem. As I sat in the banker's cubicle while she took the information for the wire transfer, I noticed that her name card said "Rebekah," spelled like the wife of Jacob in the Bible.

When she finished the wire transaction, I said to her, "Your name is spelled exactly like the Rebekah in the Bible. Is there any biblical connection to your name?" She turned red in the face and said that her mother, a strong Christian, had given her that name. However, she was estranged from her mom because she had made some bad decisions in recent years, including using drugs and having a child out of wedlock. Rebekah didn't think God wanted anything to do with her now.

I heard quite a bit of her story in the next few minutes, and by the time I left we had exchanged contact information and set a time to meet again at a local coffee shop. A relationship and a conversation about God had begun! As I drove back home, I smiled at how God had a purpose in all of this, which I might have missed had I not taken focus off myself and noticed someone's name.

3. CHRISTIAN BUBBLE

My (Crilly's) pastor friend shared a conversation he had with one of his elders. They were discussing the idea of having spiritual conversations with people who did not know Jesus when the elder confessed, "I don't know any non-Christians!" I often hear this from pastors, elders, and church attenders alike. Those of us who are involved in churches tend to spend much of our free time absorbed in "fellowship" or church work with other Christians and rarely interact closely with people who don't move in our Christian circles.

To overcome this barrier, you can make a point of recognizing others who are already part of your everyday life—at the store, at work, at school, at the gym, in your neighborhood. Every day, wherever you go, you're surrounded by hundreds of people who are desperate for someone to pay attention to them.

4. ATTITUDE

We tend to be judgmental of, rather than open to, those around us whom we don't know. Often, we don't view people the way God views them. In Luke 15, Jesus paints a clear picture of God's heart for each of us. In three separate stories he describes something that is greatly missed—the lost sheep, the lost coin, and the lost son—and someone who desperately wants to find their possession again. What if our attitude toward those who are "missing" reflected this picture of the heart of God?

Our attitude can cloud our view from seeing people the way God does. Greek Orthodox bishop and author Kallistos Ware states:

> This idea of openness to God, openness to other persons, could be summed up under the word *love*. We become truly personal by loving God and by loving other humans. By love, I don't mean merely an emotional feeling, but a fundamental attitude. In its deepest sense, love is the life, the energy, of God Himself in us. We are not truly personal as long as we are turned in on ourselves.[7]

One way to overcome this barrier is to turn outward and go on a treasure hunt, looking for the image of God in each person. Follow Jesus' example and treat each person you notice with love and respect, recognizing his or her intrinsic value as an image-bearer. As Bill Hybels often says, "We have never locked eyes with someone who did not matter to God." Pray that God would re-form your habit, replace a judgmental attitude with a generous spirit, and cultivate an attitude of love and openness in you. Meditate on Scripture passages like Luke 15 that remind you of God's compassion for the lost.

Ken Sande, founder of Peacemaker Ministries, says that instead of judging critically, we can choose to judge charitably. "Making a charitable judgment means that out of love for God, you strive to believe the best about others until you have facts to prove otherwise."[8] We can choose to believe the best about people first. Hunt for the positive attributes in those around you.

Three Simple Noticing Practices

While we may need to deal with these barriers periodically, simply being aware of them will help us set them aside. Once we do that, we can follow three simple ways to practice noticing in our everyday lives: *paying attention, secret prayer,* and *genuine listening.*

The first of these simple practices is *paying attention.* It costs you something—whether time, attention, or money—to stay focused on someone else, even for a few minutes. This simple, nonspeaking practice refers to more than a quick glance at another human being. Rather, paying attention means concentrating on someone long enough to wonder about him or her. This "spiritual peripheral vision" is not hunting for a victim; it's simply paying attention to people you ordinarily come into contact with and opening your heart to where God may be at work. Think about questions such as *What is her story? Where is he from? Does she seem happy, sad, angry, lonely?* Make a mental note about what you observe. This practice helps you begin to see another person with God's eyes of love and compassion. Nobody knows you're doing this except God, who is always delighted when we take our focus off ourselves and our own agendas for a moment to pay attention to someone else. This takes no bravery—just intentionality.

The second way to practice noticing is *secret prayer*—or what we might call noticing's first action. In the next chapter, we'll talk in more detail about why and how we pray for others, but here our focus is on what we could call "praying behind people's backs." When you're praying secretly, nobody but God knows you're praying. It's a covert operation. It's discreet. You don't stare, but you just send up a silent prayer while you are in the vicinity of someone you have noticed. You don't close your eyes or move your lips. Just pray for people as you see them. Pray that they would sense the presence of God in some undeniable way. Pray for their day. Pray for their peace. Pray for their relationships. It doesn't have to be a long prayer, either; just a quick one will do.

You could also call secret prayer "unauthorized prayer" because you are not asking people for permission to pray for them. Though they know nothing about your prayer, it counts with God.

Jesus, of course, is our model for this practice because he seemed to have a thing for praying in secret: "When you pray, go into your room, close the door and pray to your Father, who is unseen. Then your Father, who sees what is done in secret, will reward you" (Matthew 6:6). Once you are secretly praying for someone, God begins to change your heart toward that person. Secret prayer prepares you to cooperate with God as he seeks out the lost sheep in our world. It invites you into this search.

The most challenging part of secret prayer is our willingness to surrender the outcome to God. By releasing control of the results, we submit to God's will and align our hearts with his plans for the people around us. This secret prayer practice affects the way we look at ourselves, others, and God.

The third simple Noticing practice is *genuine listening*, which is part of the broader topic of listening that we'll look at in chapter 5. Paying attention to someone may prompt you to start a dialogue; this may be your chance to *engage.* Genuine listening requires that you look the person in the eye, conveying your interest and attention; hold the look; lean in a little; and say, "How are you?" Then keep quiet. I'm serious . . . it's that simple. Simone Weil said, "The love of our neighbor in all its fullness simply means being able to say to him, 'What are you going through?'"[9] Be genuinely interested in hearing the other person's story—the truth of what is going on right now. Don't correct, preach, talk over, or editorialize. Don't offer your own opinions. Just listen to theirs.

If you genuinely listen to people this way, they will almost always tell you how they really are. They may even tell you things that shock you. People become extraordinarily open when they sense that you're really paying attention. Use a couple of phrases liberally as you are genuinely listening, such as "Wow!" or "That's really interesting." This helps you deal with your own response in the moment without having to hijack the conversation.

Genuine listening opens the possibility of entering into an authentic conversation in which we allow God to control the outcome. When you've already noticed someone by paying attention and secretly praying for them, listening is a natural next step.

A Simple Way to Start

The Art of Noticing is a starting point for building more genuine, caring relationships with people who are separated from God. It involves doable, everyday practices that get you "in the game" during your normal life routines. To develop any habit, you follow a certain behavior pattern regularly until it becomes almost involuntary. For example, a parent teaches a child the habit of looking both ways before crossing the street. With regular practice, before long, the child develops the habit. The same is true of noticing. What if you practice paying attention to people throughout your day? Small attempts count. The more you practice, the better you get.

By practicing the Art of Noticing, you will begin to recognize that people are longing for your attention (which is like a cup of cold water to them), you will become aware of what God is up to right where you are as you secretly pray for people behind their backs, and you will find yourself authentically engaged in conversation as you learn to really listen to others. This practice is unintimidating and life-giving; in fact, the Art of Noticing is a stealth gift you can give to anyone. By taking the time to intentionally pay attention to others, you take your eyes off yourself and create an opportunity to get to know them and recognize them as treasured creations of God. It doesn't require memorizing or presenting anything. It doesn't call for any courage on your part. The important thing is that you start *doing* it.

Noticing changes your view of God. (He gets bigger!) It changes your view of others. (They begin to matter to you in ways you can't explain.) And it changes *you!*

Discover

1. How do you recognize when God is up to something in the lives of people around you? How can noticing raise your awareness of God's activity?

2. What small changes in your day would help you to develop a habit of paying more attention to people?

Practice

1. Commit to spending thirty seconds each day paying attention to people in your ordinary routine and being unusually curious about them. Whom can you notice in thirty seconds at school pickup? At the grocery store? In the elevator on your way to work? On the highway in traffic? What do you notice happening inside of you as you pay attention to others?

2. After a few days of paying attention, now commit to spending sixty seconds per day paying attention to *and* secretly praying for people behind their backs based on what you noticed. Share your experience with a friend and celebrate that you made the attempt!

CHAPTER 4

The Art of Praying

My prayer is not for them alone. I pray also for those who will
believe in me through their message, that all of them may be one,
Father, just as you are in me and I am in you. May they also be
in us so that the world may believe that you have sent me.

JOHN 17:20-21

If we truly love people, we will desire for them far more than it
is within our power to give them, and this will lead us to prayer.

RICHARD FOSTER

WHEN I (CRILLY) GO TO CONFERENCES, I am often moved by the content or the speaker. Unfortunately, the fire of inspiration quickly cools as I reenter my daily rhythms. But something changed in me after hearing a presentation in 2011 by pastor, church planter, and speaker Lon Allison. The topic was evangelistic prayer.

Lon explained that the spheres of influence in our lives are generally divided into four categories: friends, family, work, and neighborhood. He explained the value of focusing prayer on these four simple categories to see a harvest in each one. When I arrived home that evening, I resolved that, each night as I put my head on the pillow, I would pray to see God's harvest in these four areas. I invited my wife to join me too.

On my neighborhood block, there are eighteen homes, with

thirty-one adults and twenty-four children: a total of fifty-five people. (*My neighborhood.*) Before I left my marketplace job, I had a team of twelve that I interacted with daily and a workforce of about 250 that I knew by name. (*My work.*) I have a whole slew of aunts, uncles, and cousins. (*My family.*) I also have friends from grade school, high school, and college. I have a bunch of acquaintances—the guys at the gym, the owner and staff at my favorite café, and the clerks at the cleaners. I have connections through tutoring and mentoring as many as forty African refugee children and young adults. (*My friends.*) All in all, that is a pretty large network of connections that I interact with on a regular basis, full of many people who are not particularly interested in following Jesus. Now, I realize that I am an extrovert who finds it relatively easy to build relationships. But I believe we all have many more relational connections with people than we think we do—people who are spiritually curious (John 6:2; 1 Corinthians 1:22), spiritually poor (Matthew 16:26; Luke 12:20-21), spiritually blind (1 Corinthians 2:14; 2 Corinthians 4:3-4), spiritually bound (Ephesians 2:1-2; 2 Timothy 2:25-26), spiritually helpless (John 6:44), and spiritually hopeless (Ephesians 2:12).

As Danielle and I have prayed each day, I have come to realize more than ever the privilege of being invited by God to be an ambassador of his love to these folks, guiding them out of the darkness into his wonderful light. Almost every night, as we drift off to sleep, we pray for the people in our lives whom we long to introduce to Jesus. We pray for spiritual awakening among an entire refugee community, for longtime friends to bow to Jesus, for baptisms to occur in the sprinklers of our neighborhood. We pray that God would use us and mobilize other followers of Jesus to bring the Good News to these people we know and love.

I would be thrilled to see dramatic results in the lives of all the people we pray for. But I have been surprised to discover that, although we have seen God's activity in the lives of many of these folks, the results have not been the primary benefit for me. The biggest personal impact of this practice is that it has changed *me*— my heart toward people, my trust in God, and my love for those who do not have God's help and hope.

The Struggle

A lot has been written on prayer by people much smarter, more theologically astute, better read, and generally wiser than I am. This chapter is intentionally targeting folks like me who have struggled with evangelistic prayer. I honestly don't have any business writing on the topic other than as a fellow sojourner who desires to pray for people in my life to come to know Jesus and see God's power flow through me for the advancement of his Kingdom.

I often suffer from practical prayerlessness. I want to pray without ceasing, but I don't. I want to ask God for my heart to be attentive and open to his promptings, but I don't. I want to pray persistently for the people in my life who do not yet know Jesus, but I don't. In my years of following Christ, I admit that over the long haul I have not had a consistent prayer life for people separated from God.

At some unconscious level, I used to think that their conversion was up to me and my clever presentation of the gospel, my compelling apologetic, my solid argument. I thought it was my job to convict, confront, and convince people of their theological errors. I thought that if I won the argument, then surely they would convert—but I did not find that to be the reality. In fact, if I won an argument or debate with a friend, it often wedged greater distance between us. Of course, I felt good that I won and proclaimed the truth to my friend, but he left the interchange feeling bullied, judged, and diminished. Somehow, I can't believe that is what Jesus had in mind when he invited us to announce the Kingdom of God. The Kingdom is loving, enchanting, beautiful, exciting, attractive, inviting, gracious. Yet my approach did not seem to convey those attributes. As I have operated from my own strength, I have seen the powerlessness of my words in the absence of God's influence. Paul reminds me in Romans that "the gospel [not my profound words added] . . . is the power of God that brings salvation to everyone who believes" (Romans 1:16).

I am faced with the humbling reality that I cannot save anyone. I cannot convict or convince anyone. This is not my role, as Jesus reveals; it is the Spirit's role:

> When [the Holy Spirit] comes, he will convict the world
> of its sin, and of God's righteousness, and of the coming
> judgment. . . . When the Spirit of truth comes, he will
> guide you into all truth.
> JOHN 16:8, 13, NLT

My job is to pray to the One who can convict, convince, and save, as Jesus teaches in John 6:

> No one can come to me unless the Father who sent me
> draws them to me, and I will raise them up at the last day.
> As it is written in the Scriptures, "They will all be taught
> by God." Everyone who listens to the Father and learns
> from him comes to me.
> JOHN 6:44-45

I have also discovered that I must depend on God in prayer because my own strength is insufficient to combat our spiritual adversary. Yes, a spiritual adversary. We easily forget that we have an opponent in this spiritual battle for the hearts, minds, and souls of our friends and neighbors. C. S. Lewis provides a sobering perspective when he writes, "There is no neutral ground in the universe: every square inch, every split second, is claimed by God and counterclaimed by Satan."[1]

Similarly, Paul reminds us of this reality in Ephesians 6:12: "For we are not fighting against flesh-and-blood enemies, but against evil rulers and authorities of the unseen world, against mighty powers in this dark world, and against evil spirits in the heavenly places" (NLT).

God is the source of all the power we need, and he alone can defeat the enemy and rescue a human heart. We cannot fight our adversary with our own strength. We need the weapon of prayer.

Prayer is powerful because the God to whom we pray is all-powerful. He lovingly draws people to Christ—even the most unlikely men and women. As Lon Allison says, "It is the prayers of God's people that break down the strongholds that the enemy holds over the people in our lives who do not know God."[2] When we become aware of prayer's transformative power, we are motivated to pray to the only one who can change a person's condition: God.

Invited to Participate

With the burden of results lifted, God invites me to participate with him in his redemptive activity in the world first through prayer. To believe that my prayers could have an impact requires me to believe that my prayers are heard—that they are valued. Revelation 5:8 captures the significance of our prayers: "The four living creatures and the twenty-four elders fell down before the Lamb. Each one had a harp and they were holding golden bowls full of incense, which are the prayers of God's people."

All our prayers reach God; each one is treasured by him. Each one of my prayers and yours is held before God's throne in a gold bowl. He does not ignore them, forget them, or misplace them. They are precious and constantly before him. He hears you intercede for your friend, brother, coworker, and roommate.

Focusing on the four spheres of influence and interceding for the people in my life has helped me pray regularly for God's power of transformation and blessing on the lives of friends, colleagues, relatives, and neighbors. It is empowering to know that prayer has gone before any encounter I have with a friend or any conversation I have with a neighbor. Wheaton College professor Rick Richardson, author of *Evangelism Outside the Box*, states the principle quite simply: "Before we can talk to people about God, we need to talk to God about people."[3]

Most of us think introducing people to Jesus is primarily about our talking—verbally sharing our story or God's story. We have friends or neighbors who are disinterested in God, skeptical of Christianity, or apathetic toward spiritual things, and we want to tell them about God and his impact in our lives. But what if that is not where it starts? What if God has already initiated pursuit of your friends and simply invites you to join him? Richardson notes,

> Collaborating with God and what He is doing in another life is the evangelism strategy. Because He is the witness. He is the one bringing people forward. He is the one interacting with people's pain. So asking God good questions about people is, I think, the first task in evangelism.[4]

To understand what God is doing in others' lives and what our role might be, we can ask him. Here are three key questions we can start with:

God, where are you already at work?

God, what does this person need right now?

God, how can I invite this person to experience Jesus in a fresh way?

Ask God, "Where?"

The adventure of God's Kingdom is discovering where God is at work and joining him on his mission to reconcile people to himself. Since he is already at work all around us, we can ask him to show us where he wants us to participate in his activity of love and grace. Praying behind people's backs (i.e., secret prayer, mentioned in chapter 3) can be the first step of engagement in what God is up to so that you can recognize where God is at work and join him. In his book *Experiencing God*, Henry Blackaby explains,

> When Jesus passed through a crowd, he always looked for where the Father was at work. . . . [God's] desire is to get us from where we are to where he is working. When God reveals to you where he is working, that becomes his invitation to join him in his activity. When God reveals his work to you, that is the time to respond to him.[5]

The secret-prayer approach provides an opportunity for all Christians—whether talkative or quiet, outgoing or shy, silly or serious—to experience God more and to participate in his work.

God may already be moving in the people around you, even if they don't realize it. And even if you don't see the evidence of his activity, he may already be using their pain, joy, fear, or confusion to woo them to himself. When you're praying and watching for where God is working, you will be more ready to recognize it and join in.

Picture the early church, constantly in prayer for people to know Jesus—their friends, neighbors, coworkers, and even their persecutors. The book of Acts says, "They devoted themselves to the apostles' teaching and to fellowship, to the breaking of bread and to *prayer*. . . . And the Lord added to their number daily those who were being saved" (Acts 2:42, 47; emphasis added). God heard their prayers and moved, transforming lives every day! In Acts 4:31, we see that after the believers prayed, the Holy Spirit demonstrated his saving power and galvanized this new community to share the Good News: "After they prayed, the place where they were meeting was shaken. And they were all filled with the Holy Spirit and spoke the word of God boldly."

I can imagine the early church praying for Saul, their most zealous persecutor, to find Jesus. Think how crazy this is! It's the equivalent of today's persecuted Christians in the Middle East praying for the leaders of ISIS to come to know Jesus or of believers in Nigeria praying for the leaders of Boko Haram. From a human perspective, it is ludicrous. But then in Acts 9, we witness God taking action in Saul's life. Around that time, I imagine Ananias praying that God would show him *where* God was at work and *where* Ananias could join him. Next thing you know, God tapped Ananias on the shoulder and gave him the startling instruction to go and meet Saul! Ananias did not know how God had been at work in Saul's life, but he trusted God's prompting. As a result, Ananias had the opportunity to participate in the healing and transformation of the one whom God would use to offer salvation to the Gentiles, and to welcome him into the new community! What could we miss if we don't ask God, "Where?" What could we miss if we don't obey when he prompts us?

Throughout Scripture, God involves people in his activity. Blackaby reminds us that Jesus always looked to God to see what he was up to.

> The first thing Jesus recognized is that his Father was always at his work. God did not create the world and then just leave it to run all by itself. He is not just sitting in some heavenly place passively observing all the activity on earth. God is orchestrating history. He is present in the middle of all history. God is the One who is at work redeeming a lost world. His desire is to involve his people and his servants. . . . Because of his love he wants us to have the privilege of working with him as his ambassadors.[6]

As we follow Jesus' example and the example of the early church, we can watch for God's invitation to join him in the spiritual drama unfolding in the lives of others, to collaborate with him in bringing people to himself. When we ask him *where* he is already working, we get to reach out to others *with* God, not just *for* God.

Ask God, "What?"

A second question you can ask God as you seek to pray for others is, *What does this person need right now?* Not only does God know exactly what he's up to in each person, he knows each person's heart and exactly what he or she needs at this very moment. Psalm 139 communicates this truth:

> You have searched me, LORD,
>   and you know me.
> You know when I sit and when I rise;
>   you perceive my thoughts from afar.
> You discern my going out and my lying down;
>   you are familiar with all my ways.
> Before a word is on my tongue
>   you, LORD, know it completely.
> You hem me in behind and before,
>   and you lay your hand upon me.
>
> PSALM 139:1-5

Sometimes we think that having a significant spiritual discussion with someone who doesn't know God requires a well-rehearsed script or canned delivery. However, chances are that our practiced reasoning or argument is more likely to stunt a conversation rather than lead to a compelling discussion. In particular, a person who is grieving the recent loss of a relationship, loved one, or job isn't going to respond well to a script or any approach that doesn't meet them where they are. The right words at the wrong time are still the wrong words.

Many years ago I (Mary) knew a wonderful Christian couple with three daughters. After years of waiting, they finally got the son that they had so wanted to complete their family. Caleb was an adorable baby boy who was loved by his mom, dad, and big sisters, all of whom doted on him constantly. But when Caleb was about nine months old, he suddenly died in his crib during a routine nap. It was later determined that an unusual virus had caused his heart to stop beating suddenly. As you can imagine, his family and the entire community were devastated by this horrible news.

At the memorial-service reception, which was held in this family's backyard, I ran into a mutual friend, Diane, who had been a teacher of one of the daughters. I knew she had different beliefs about God than I did because we had discussed faith matters periodically in the past, but we had not kept up our relationship in recent years. I could tell that Diane was struggling to understand how God would allow such a terrible thing to happen to this couple who had regularly professed faith in Jesus and were active in caring for their community.

In retrospect, I might have had an opportunity to set up a time to meet and discuss some of her thoughts about God in the upcoming weeks when our emotions were not so raw. But instead, galloping straight ahead like a racehorse out of the starting gate, and without inviting God to guide the process, I asked an inappropriate question right there at the reception: Where did she stand with God at the moment? It was totally insensitive! Her response was essentially, "None of your business!" which I wholeheartedly deserved. I had failed miserably to ask God where he was working and what Diane needed *before* opening my mouth to have a spiritual conversation.

The good news is that while God certainly uses our words, he is not limited to them. He knows exactly what each person needs and also uses our service, prayers, kindness, generosity, and blessings to meet those needs in a way that will open the pathway to that person's heart. Rick Richardson experienced this change in perspective at a secular arts festival some years ago. He explains:

> I've long said that Christians are a very rationally dependent culture, and we think that our words are what gets the thing done. I did the same thing at that festival, praying, "God, give me the killer argument to get through to these experientially oriented, self-at-the-center people." And I felt like God said to me, "Why don't you just let me show up? It is not words, it is my power that moves people."[7]

When Rick began praying for the people in attendance, he saw a fresh openness toward God that his preplanned words never would have accomplished. We have experienced this same response. With loving engagement preceded by prayer, we have witnessed hard hearts softened and opportunities opened.

Ask God, "How?"

We tend to invite people to experience God in ways that can feel clichéd. We invite them to a church service. We tell them he can meet all their needs. We say God is always with us and gives us joy, and ask whether they want that too. But it's too easy for people to dismiss our attempts as uninspired and not universal: "That's nice *for you*," they might say. For people who haven't grown up in the church and haven't experienced the truth—and even for those who have—it can all sound kind of phony or trite.

Let's be honest: Many people's stereotypes about Christians, church, and God aren't very positive. Many have been burned by the church. Many have been hurt by Christians. Many have based their understanding of God on his most extreme bullhorns: people who yell about his judgment on the evening news, street corner, or college campus.

So when we use stale approaches, terms, and concepts to introduce a person to Christ, they bring to mind these unfortunate examples. For people with a negative religious background or none at all, we need to get creative to communicate the real, wondrously life-changing truths about Jesus. Many of these people are skeptical about our words and need to experience God's love and grace in action.

In addition, we're all wired by God differently, and therefore we will experience and respond to him in a variety of ways. Our Creator, who knows each person's baggage and wiring, can show us how to introduce his Son to those who need to meet him. This is the God who used a burning bush and a talking donkey to get people's attention. He knows how to win people's hearts. Doesn't it make sense to ask God, *How can I invite this person to experience Jesus in a fresh way?* For example, what are their hobbies and interests? How can you connect with them around their areas of passion? Will art, music, or poetry open them to God's creativity and beauty? Can a service project reveal God's love in action? If you open up about your struggles and talk honestly about God's help in your life, will they get a glimpse of God in a new way? If you serve them, will they experience Christ's self-sacrificial love personally and uniquely? How can you help them discover God's activity and Jesus' presence in their lives today?

When you ask God these few simple questions about people—"Where?" "What?" and "How?"—you get to participate in his work as he draws them to himself. This type of intentional prayer for people who are exploring faith opens up the door for natural interactions that point to God.

As you pray for people in the various spheres of your life, it may also help to keep three goals in view—to make your prayers

(1) personal, (2) purposeful, and (3) a priority, inviting God to minister directly to others in a profound way.

Making Prayer Personal

Nineteenth-century evangelist George Müller was a godly man known for his tenacious practice of personal prayer. It was his belief that prayer could influence people toward true faith in Christ, and his life evidenced this conviction. He prayed faithfully, he prayed daily, and he prayed by name for people without Jesus.

In the book *George Müller: Man of Faith and Miracles*, Basil Miller recounts George Müller's experience of praying for five not-yet-Christians in his life:

> In November 1844, I began to pray for the conversion of five individuals. I prayed every day without a single intermission, whether sick or in health, on the land or on the sea, and whatever the pressure of my engagements might be. Eighteen months elapsed before the first of the five was converted. I thanked God and prayed on for the others. Five years elapsed, and then the second was converted. I thanked God for the second, and prayed on for the other three. Day by day I continued to pray for them, and six years passed before the third was converted. I thanked God for the three and went on praying for the other two.[8]

In an interview near the end of his life, Müller was asked how much time he had spent in prayer for the last two unsaved people on his five-person list. He earnestly responded, "I have been praying every day for fifty-two years for two men, sons of a friend of my youth. They are not converted yet, but they will be! How can it be otherwise?" Shortly after Müller's death in 1898, the two young men for whom he had prayed over half a century turned to God. It is hard to overemphasize the power of praying intentionally for specific individuals.

In Luke 22:31-32, Jesus tells Simon Peter that he has prayed personally for him: "Simon, Simon, Satan has asked to sift all of you as wheat. But I have prayed for you, Simon, that your faith may not fail. And when you have turned back, strengthen your brothers." Think of how the words of this prayer must have brought comfort to Peter later on, pulling him up from his guilt in the aftermath of his betrayal of Christ: *Jesus prayed that my faith would not fail.* Imagine Peter, trusting in those words, choosing not to wallow in regret but to turn back to God. How meaningful, purposeful, and powerful that specific prayer must have been in Peter's life!

When we pray specifically and personally, our hearts are engaged in a way that doesn't happen when we only pray generally for people separated from God. When we pray about the specific circumstances pertinent to the person we care about, we can see God's work step by step. Individuals also begin to matter to us in a deeper way, and the details of their lives become more important. In praying for them by name, with concern for their unique circumstances, we go beyond generic prayers to genuine, compassionate, heartfelt intercession.

Making Prayer Purposeful

A Jewish legend tells about an eccentric prophet named Honi from the first century BC, at a time when Israel was experiencing a severe drought. Even though God had been silent for hundreds of years, Honi believed that God was still listening to the prayers of his people. So to demonstrate how serious he was about prayer, Honi stood outside of Jerusalem, took his staff, and drew a circle around himself in the dry ground. Then he dropped to his knees, praised God, and prayed from the deepest part of his soul, committing to remain in that circle until God showed Israel mercy and provided rain.

Rain began to sprinkle, amazing the crowd of onlookers. But Honi was not satisfied with a drizzle. From inside the circle, Honi prayed again for rain to fill cisterns, pits, and caverns. Miraculously, the gentle drops turned into a torrential downpour, triggering flash flooding. Again, Honi interceded from his circle with more specificity: "Not for such rain have I prayed, but for rain of your favor, blessing, and graciousness." At once, a constant, peaceful rain began to fall, quenching the parched land and bringing joy to the people. The circle became a sacred symbol to the Jewish people, and the legend of Honi the circle maker testifies to the power of prayer.[9]

Honi was clear about the purpose of his prayer. As an exercise in purposeful, personal prayer, take a few minutes to think about your relational spheres. Draw four circles, labeled with the four categories I mentioned at the beginning of this chapter: *friends*, *family*, *work*, and *neighbors*. In each circle, write down the names of specific people whom you know and love and who are likely not to have a relationship with Jesus. Can you pause right now to intercede for the people in your circles, asking God to draw them to himself?

When we pray by name and with purpose for spiritually astray family members, friends, neighbors, coworkers, and classmates, our interactions with them become more deliberate and meaningful. We are more invested in their lives. We begin to wonder about their family and friends, their dreams and desires, and their movement toward or away from spiritual matters. Our specific focus before God opens us up to being more compassionate for the sake of Christ and these people. Our love for them grows.

Praying is a secret act of love to others, as we intercede on their behalf and partner with God for their good. Evangelistic prayer warms our hearts to the subject of our prayer, while declaring that only God can change a human heart. French theologian John Calvin explained it well:

Our prayer must not be self centered. It must arise not only because we feel our own need as a burden which we must lay upon God, but also because we are so bound up in love for our fellow men that we feel their need as acutely as our own. To make intercession for men is the most powerful and practical way in which we can express our love for them.[10]

In John 17, Jesus modeled praying purposefully. He first prayed for his immediate circle of followers, who were within earshot, for their future protection and unity. Then he widened the circle of prayer to include everyone who would eventually turn to God through him for salvation:

My prayer is not for [the disciples] alone. I pray also for those who will believe in me through their message, that all of them may be one, Father, just as you are in me and I am in you. May they also be in us so that the world may believe that you have sent me.

JOHN 17:20-21

He prayed with purpose for unity and faith among his followers, both for their own sake and for the sake of a watching world that would see God through the transformation of those who followed him. As Jesus faced the Cross, the deepest, most passionate prayer of his heart was wrapped up in those who would one day believe in him. When we intercede for people who have not yet come to trust in Jesus, we are not only opening our hearts in a new way to those people; we are also drawing close to the deepest desire of God's heart—and to God himself.

As we seek to pray more and more purposefully for those we know who are disinterested in matters of faith, we can look to Scripture for specific guidance for our prayers:

Pray for openness to know the truth (2 Corinthians 4:4-6;
　　1 Timothy 2:3-5).
　　Ask God to shine his light in people's hearts so they will
　　come to recognize the truth.

Pray for receptivity to God's grace (Romans 3:23-24; Titus 3:4-7).
　　Salvation is a free gift, but we must receive it to experience
　　it. You likely know people who are full of pride or who
　　feel unforgivable. Pray that they will come to recognize
　　God's greatness and goodness, his unconditional love, and
　　his forgiveness that takes care of our sins and failures.

Pray for heartfelt conviction of sin (John 16:8-11; 1 Thessalonians
　　1:4-5).
　　The Holy Spirit convicts people of their imperfection in
　　relationship to God. You can pray specifically that the
　　not-yet-Christians whom you know will pay attention to
　　the work of God's Spirit as he points out where sin exists
　　in their minds, words, and actions.

Pray for genuine steps of repentance (2 Corinthians 7:10).
　　Pray that the spiritual explorers you know will humbly
　　turn toward God—and away from the destructive clutches
　　of sin—as God faithfully draws them to himself. Pray that
　　they will feel the life-giving conviction brought by the
　　Spirit, rather than the crushing self-loathing that comes
　　from guilt and shame incited by the enemy.

Pray for deep spiritual roots in Christ (John 15:5; Colossians
　　2:6-7).
　　When a person you care about is on the edge of becoming
　　a follower of Christ, pray that the decision will be

reinforced by complete surrender and stable faith. Pray specifically for his or her love of God to be nurtured by engaging in his Word, through prayer, and through relationships with other Jesus followers.

Pray for God's love to be clearly experienced (1 John 4:7-10, 19-21).
Pray that people you know will feel the need to give and receive sincere love, and that they would clearly experience the love of God in a way that will help them trust in Jesus.

Making Prayer a Priority

When it comes to loving people toward Jesus, prayer is not optional. It is the primary way we will shift from relying on our strength to relying on God's power in our spiritual engagements, and it's the means by which our efforts actually become spiritually effective. In *Prayer: Finding the Heart's True Home*, Richard Foster writes about the practice of intercessory prayer and how it flows first from a spirit of genuine humility and compassion: "If we truly love people, we will desire for them far more than it is within our power to give them, and this will lead us to prayer."[11] When we realize that on our own we cannot provide people with what they really need, prayer will surface as our only viable alternative.

Setting aside regular times in our schedules and being diligent to keep "prayer appointments" with God are beneficial commitments. We can each choose to make prayer a priority and to use this powerful spiritual weapon that God provides. Yet prayer is not a priority arising from stark obligation; it is a priority based in love. Our best intentions to go to God on behalf of people who are separated from him will only take us so far. Only love can move us to carve out dedicated time to pray in a targeted way.

To take this further, our motivation—*why* we pray—may

very well be as important as *what* we pray. How effective will our requests be if they come from a place of pride, obligation, or contempt? When praying for spiritual movement in people's lives, we must remember that the subject of our prayers is a real person, not a project. As our hearts align with God's heart and we start praying in accordance with what matters most to him, our God-honoring prayers will move both the people we pray for and us—believers who can help.

Praying for Workers

When Jesus came face-to-face with the masses of people who were experiencing life without hope, his heart broke for them. The apostle Matthew records his reaction: "When [Jesus] saw the crowds, he had compassion on them, because they were harassed and helpless, like sheep without a shepherd" (Matthew 9:36). Jesus' concern for the people was not just a passing response to a pitiful situation. Love compelled Jesus in everything he did. Deeply moved, Jesus looked at all the people who were still separated from the Father, and he commanded his followers to invest their hearts—not just their time and talents—and *pray* for more Kingdom workers: "The harvest is plentiful but the workers are few. Ask the Lord of the harvest, therefore, to send out workers into his harvest field" (9:37-38). This was probably not the first thing on the minds of the disciples, but in the face of such great need, *praying* for workers was what Jesus said to do.

According to Jesus, when we pray, people are stirred to get God's good news out. Then the "few workers" are joined by many more—most likely just ordinary people, all bringing in the harvest. Our own hearts will also be kindled with a new love for those who don't know God. Imagine: While you're praying for more workers, you just might be the answer to someone's request for a worker to be available!

The Tipping Point

Everything has a first cause. It's a law of nature. For a movement to begin, it has to start somewhere. Think of Rosa Parks. Nelson Mandela. Jackie Robinson.

Two ordinary men are mentioned rather offhandedly at the end of Paul's letters. They are virtually unknown among Christians, and yet their surrender to Jesus was a pivotal tipping point resulting in a tectonic shift for their cultures:

> Greet my dear friend Epenetus. He was the first person from the province of Asia to become a follower of Christ.
> ROMANS 16:5, NLT

> You know that Stephanas and his household were the first of the harvest of believers in Greece, and they are spending their lives in service to God's people.
> I CORINTHIANS 16:15, NLT

Epenetus was the first spark of a Jesus movement in Asia Minor. Stephanas was the first domino of a Jesus revolution in Greece. They do not have celebrity status in the Bible, but they are each the starting point of the powerful work that God did in their cultures. The good news of Jesus would later sweep through both of these geographical areas, transforming their societies and the lives of millions.

Imagine Epenetus on the early church's prayer list. Picture the followers of the Way circled in prayer, interceding for Stephanus. Envision the joy surging through the early disciples when God's Spirit moved and Epenetus and Stephanus chose to follow Jesus.

What if God's Spirit swept through my block and yours? Who is the Stephanas who could lead the way for every household on my block to experience the love of Jesus? Who is the Epenetus who will launch the transformation of those families and extended families?

Maybe it's time for all of us to ask the Lord of the Harvest to raise up the workers and to bring a harvest in our domains. Will you pray with me for the first domino to tip in your spheres of influence? For the Epenetus at your office? For the Stephanas at your school or in your neighborhood? For an awakening to begin that sparks a movement?

That's what I am praying for.

Discover

1. Why do you think we commonly forget to pray for someone before we start talking with them about God?

2. Describe a time when you were moved to pray for an unbelieving family member, friend, or stranger. What caused you to start praying? How has prayer changed the way you relate to that person?

Practice

1. Pull out the list of names you put together at the end of chapter 1—people you feel God might be calling you to engage with in meaningful conversations. Set a challenging but attainable goal to pray at a consistent time for these people who do not yet have a relationship with Jesus. Share your list with at least one other person who can encourage you, pray alongside you, and hold you accountable.

2. Over the next week, commit at least five minutes each day to ask God three questions about someone on your list: Where are you already at work in this person's life? What does he or she need right now? How can I invite this person to experience Jesus in a fresh way?

CHAPTER 5

The Art of Listening

My dear brothers and sisters, take note of this: Everyone should be quick to listen, slow to speak, and slow to become angry.

JAMES 1:19

Listening is such a simple act. It requires us to be present, and that takes practice, but we don't have to do anything else. We don't have to advise, or coach, or sound wise. We just have to be willing to sit there and listen.

MARGARET J. WHEATLEY

YEARS AGO, my buddy Dave and I (Crilly) invited several spiritual explorers to discuss their tough questions about God and the Bible. This was the first time we had tried anything like this, and we had no idea what we were doing or how we would respond to their questions. We just knew these people were looking for a place to have this important spiritual discussion, and we were willing to show up and try.

We gathered in the home of one of the participants on a weekly basis. We had not been meeting for long when one evening, a group participant named Eileen (not her real name) raised the "hell" question. She asked, "Do people *really* go to hell if they don't follow Jesus? That seems awfully harsh for a loving God." Everything was a blur from that point on. Without asking any further questions or listening for what God might be whispering to

79

us, Dave and I launched into a tag-team explanation of hell—and, while we were at it, we covered sin and eternal damnation, too.

We used lots and lots of words and lots and lots of passion. Unfortunately, we were unaware of our relational impact and did not pick up on the group's nonverbal cues as they became quiet and withdrawn, eyes focused down at the carpet. At the beginning of our monologue, some people offered differing opinions and counterarguments. But we had gained a head of steam and were determined not to let their opinions interfere with our speaking the truth! By the end of our hellfire-and-brimstone lecture, the room was filled with tearful and angry people. The group departed from the apartment that night, and Eileen never returned.

A few months later, we were talking to another group participant, Eileen's friend Cathy. Cathy informed us of the backstory: Eileen's mother had been diagnosed with cancer. In desperation, she made a pilgrimage to the healing shrine in Lourdes, France. Unfortunately, on the return flight home, she died. Can you imagine how gut-wrenching that must have been for Eileen? Then, a short time before our group began meeting, Eileen's father, her sister, and a family friend were leaving an airport in their private plane when something went wrong and the plane crashed, killing all three occupants. Horrific! Eileen was greatly grieved about their deaths and the possibility that they might be in hell.

With this insight, Dave and I immediately felt both profound sadness for Eileen and anguish because we realized that her question about hell had other layers below the surface. I deeply regretted that we had not stopped, sent a prayer up to God, listened empathetically, and asked a few more questions to try to understand Eileen's perspective—all instead of giving a homily on hell. I learned the wisdom of Proverbs 18:13: "To answer before listening—that is folly and shame."

Our error was that we did not listen and then ask clarifying questions to understand the nature of Eileen's question—that is, what were the questions *behind* her question? Why did she want to understand where people go when they die? What did she believe about hell and about Jesus?

I could have responded differently. Maybe I could have validated the importance of her question and suggested we talk about it privately. Maybe I could have honored her courage to ask such a big question and assured the group that we would tackle that topic in the future, after we had some time to build more trust.

Instead, we answered before listening. I didn't bother to seek to understand Eileen. I had an agenda to convince her of the truth, and I didn't check with God to see if that aligned with his plan for her that night. As Bono of U2 sings, "It's hard to listen while you preach."[1] Many spiritual topics, like the topic of hell, are emotionally charged for a spiritual explorer and worthy of gentle handling, not a data-dump lecture. This was a hard lesson to learn.

Have you ever answered before listening? If you have, I am sure you are familiar with the feeling of regret I experienced. Have you ever been in a conversation when others did not listen to you? Honestly, it can be quite irritating. You speak and they interrupt. You present your perspective and they load up for their rebutting ambush. You talk and they finish your sentence. You share a challenge you are experiencing and they try to diagnose and fix you. It's so frustrating, yet we all do it at times.

But Jesus gave us a different way of behaving. He taught us how to truly listen. He was deeply attentive to the expert in the law who tried to justify himself by asking, "Who is my neighbor?" (Luke 10:29). He understood the most important needs of the paralyzed man (Matthew 9:1-7), pronouncing him forgiven of his sins before healing him. He dialed in to the Samaritan woman's questions and rejoinders and saw her heart during the discussion in John 4:7-26.

Imagine the scene in Mark 5:21-34 as if it were a Hollywood movie. Jesus arrives in town and is swarmed by a crowd. Jairus, an important community leader, rushes up to Jesus and begs him to come heal his young daughter, who is dying. As Jesus sets out, the people press in on all sides.

In the midst of this urgent moment, a subplot emerges: a hemorrhaging woman in the crowd. This Jewish woman has endured over a decade of social isolation because of her illness. She has spent everything she has on painful, ineffective treatments, and now she puts all her faith in Jesus by simply touching his cloak. She reaches out. Suddenly Jesus stops and asks, "Who touched me?"

Luke's Gospel reports that Jesus felt power going out of him. He looks around to see who touched him. Mark's account says that the woman came and fell at his feet and, trembling with fear, told him the whole truth.

Here is the amazing part. Despite the important assignment Jesus was on, he stopped and listened to a sick, ostracized woman. His care for her went beyond her physical healing, and he took time to hear her story, to listen to "the whole truth" about her. That was genuine listening.

Stop Stealing Stories

In Garth Stein's novel *The Art of Racing in the Rain*, the narrator—a dog named Enzo—wryly observes, "I never deflect the course of the conversation with a comment of my own. People, if you pay attention to them, change the direction of one another's conversations constantly." He then gives wise counsel (especially for a dog): "Pretend you are a dog like me and listen to other people rather than steal their stories."[2]

Everyone has a story to tell, and every story is a part of God's story. I want to stop stealing people's stories and start listening to them instead. I bet you do, too. I want to follow the wisdom of the earliest Jesuit missionaries, who made it a point to enter new locations and not speak for six months. Instead, they listened. These missionaries recognized the importance of understanding people and not pushing their own agendas.[5] That type of listening requires a long-term mindset.

Each of us enters into a new relationship, workplace, neighborhood, or dorm as a missionary for Jesus Christ. For us, remaining completely silent for the first six months is probably not the most helpful approach, but the point is that many of us feel uncomfortable with silence, ambiguity, or doubt. We are especially uneasy about unanswered spiritual questions. As children and adults, we were trained to give solutions, and we received praise for the right answers—whether they were for math problems in the classroom, Scripture verses in Sunday school, or defenses of biblical truth in public discourse. However, a good listener can handle unresolved emotion or unanswered questions. He or she can leave them as they are for the time being, confident that, in the marketplace of ideas, God's truth will reign.

When we surrender our desire to be experts and our need to resolve differences immediately, we'll see huge barriers to listening dissolve. This is so important because getting to the best answers usually happens through a process of discovering for yourself   and it requires patience to allow that discovery to unfold for someone else. When we give people space to arrive at their own answers, to sort out the questions in their own minds and at their own speed, the result is worth the wait. We may know the answer, but sometimes people don't really want our answer. They want a friend. Listening is an opportunity for each of us to grow in self-control— an underdeveloped quality in our culture and a powerful fruit of the Spirit in our lives.

This is not to imply that we shouldn't engage in conversation. Dialogue is a two-way exchange. Disagreement can happen, but it does not have to result in relational rupture. In fact, if handled correctly, disagreement can increase relational connection and understanding. However, giving someone answers to their questions is not listening. Giving advice often kills dialogue. And telling answers—even right answers—is rarely helpful because it circumvents the very important process of allowing people to discover the truth for themselves.

God Listens

We listen because God listens. It's true; the God of the Angel Armies listens to me—and you. This is a staggering truth. God hears my cry and forgives. He hears my prayer and responds. He humbles himself to care for me enough to hear what's on my mind. God sets the example for us to follow. God listens, really listens, to people—to their doubts, questions, pain, and confusion. What if we listened to people well enough to understand them better and to see where God is at work in their lives?

Listening reflects the attitude of Jesus. In Philippians 2:5-8, the apostle Paul reveals the profound truth that even though the incarnate Jesus was God himself, knowing all things, he didn't use that to his own advantage. He emptied himself and became like us. In his pursuit of people, Jesus gave us the ultimate example of humility and self-sacrifice. When we take the initiative to listen to people around us in our everyday lives, seeking to understand them rather than to explain ourselves, we reflect the genuine care of Jesus. And in reflecting Jesus, we are revealing the heart of God.

Listening requires putting others first, a mind-set of serving that doesn't come easy for most of us. Philippians 2:3 puts it this way: "Do nothing out of selfish ambition or vain conceit. Rather, in humility value others above yourselves." I can display this humility when I accept that I have only part of the truth in a particular conversation, and that only God holds the whole truth in every situation.

Listening Is Love

In 2010, the Museum of Modern Art in New York City mounted an exhibition by performance artist Marina Abramović, titled *The Artist Is Present*. After several months of physical and mental training, Abramović seated herself in a chair facing an empty chair across a small table in the gallery. For the next three months—six days a week, seven and a half hours a day—she focused her full attention on the museum visitors who came to sit across from her.

> In spite of or maybe thanks to the negative media attention for her controversial art, 850,000 visitors came to see her. People slept in the street in front of the museum. At closing time a new line started to form itself for the next morning. The guards were so impressed that after working hours they also joined the line.
>
> The reactions were stunning. People were touched by the sheer possibility that there was someone who would look deeply into their soul without word or movement. Who would only look and listen, without concern for time, without any special reason and without condemnation. . . .
>
> Time and attention [have] become . . . scarce commodit[ies] in our culture. . . .
>
> Abramović understood what people of the twenty-first century need: unique, clean, personal contact—one person being present for the other.[4]

In our culture, listening is often interpreted as love. If I really care about what someone has to say, I listen. Listening calls for an attitude of humility and grace. I surrender my desire to be heard and understood in the interest of understanding the other person—and that takes love. Notre Dame University professor John Paul Lederach puts it this way:

> Listening as a technique takes art and skill, but such
> technical discipline . . . does not in itself lead to a deeper
> level of genuine listening. . . . What leads to the deeper
> level is whether I interact with you as a person about
> whom I care. Listening is a spiritual discipline if, like a
> spring, it bubbles up from genuine love.[5]

When we make an effort to move toward the people who cross our paths and listen to them, we form and deepen relationships. When we demonstrate that we are seeking to understand people and not change their points of view, we create a safe environment for them to open up more intimately. As they feel genuinely understood, they also begin to better understand themselves. People are often ready to listen to us only after they feel understood and heard. In a society full of folks who would rather talk than listen, people are starved for someone who is willing to move into their lives as a listener and learner. Being known as a good listener will cause you to stand out in our self-centered, what's-in-it-for-me kind of world.

In his poem "Loaves and Fishes," David Whyte reminds us that more information is not what people need. People are hungry for connection.

This is not
the age of information.

This is not
the age of information.

Forget the news,
and the radio,
and the blurred screen.

This is the time
of loaves
and fishes.

People are hungry,
and one good word is bread
for a thousand.

With very few words, listening communicates volumes. Through good listening, we can provide people a relational gift, communicate God's love in profoundly real ways, and open up opportunities for further connection. As an opportunity to practice self-control, listening plays an essential role as we come alongside those seeking God. And in the process of listening, we are transformed as well.

Jesus told us to love our neighbor as ourselves. When we listen, we are giving the attention that most of us long to receive. Allowing another person to speak, with the goal of knowing them as an individual, is more than simply hearing or comprehending; it also reveals God's love. In fact, it is "being Christ" to that person. Yet true listening is lacking in our churches, and it is rare in our culture. What Dietrich Bonhoeffer wrote still holds true: "Many people are looking for an ear that will listen. They do not find it among Christians, because Christians are talking where they should be listening."[7]

Driving Blindfolded

Historically, much of the outreach training Christians have been exposed to has said very little about the Art of Listening. Far too many Christ followers have been taught to give gospel presentations rather than to engage in spiritual conversations. These well-intentioned, agenda-driven monologues have left many people with a negative impression of Christianity, sending the message that we think "our religion is better than your religion, so listen to us while we tell you why we're right and you're wrong." Observing this problem, pastor and former director of Alpha USA Todd Hunter said, "I'm willing to bet the farm that in our post-modern Christian society the most important evangelistic skill is listening."[8]

If you want to be a good listener, think of yourself as someone who comes alongside another person—not to give advice, but to learn the other person's real story. True listening is an expression of love and kindness because it does not come with conditions—it is not an attempt to get someone to change their behavior or conform immediately to a certain set of beliefs. Listening is a demonstration of respect that communicates worth. When we listen with love, we hear the person's story without judgment or fear.

Ironically, people are more likely to grow when they can sort out their difficulties in the presence of someone who is committed to them, rather than someone who is focused on a particular outcome. Sometimes people just want to process their thoughts out loud. (If you doubt whether this is of spiritual value, read the Psalms. Page after page of the Psalms contains outpourings of people's feelings, complaints, fears, and frustrations to God.) If you are uncertain what someone needs from you in the middle of an emotional outburst, simply ask, "Do you want my input, or do you just need to talk this out?" More often than not, people just need to say out loud what's going on inside them.

Alice Fryling wisely warns, "If I want to listen well, with love and awe, I need to let go of my need to be right. I need to let go of many preconceived opinions. I need to let go of my own self-consciousness and insecurities. And I need to let go of the need to appear wise, good, or even spiritual."[9]

When we approach people with the intent to tell them what we know and without trying to understand where they're coming from, it is only natural that they will put up defenses. The interaction can easily turn combative. A better approach is to remember James 1:19 20: "My dear brothers and sisters, take note of this: Everyone should be quick to listen, slow to speak and slow to become angry, because human anger does not produce the righteousness that God desires."

Genuine listening can be challenging because it requires self-control, but the good news is that self-control is a fruit of the Spirit. We need to rely on the Holy Spirit to help us keep our mouths closed and ears open. It also takes practice and intentionality to be "quick to listen, slow to speak."

The simple practice of listening to people allows us to identify common ground. It makes us openhearted and outwardly focused. The quality of our listening skills powerfully affects our potential to build trust, engage conversationally, and establish relational credibility. As Doug Pollock, author of *God Space*, explains, "Engaging in a spiritual conversation without listening is like driving a car blindfolded."[10] Not a good idea.

Face, Focus, and Feelings

Wherever you are, whenever you are reading this, you are likely exposed to a variety of sounds. Pause for a few seconds and consider this: *What do you hear right now?* Scientist Seth Horowitz wrote in a *New York Times* article:

> The slight trick in the question is that, by asking you what you were hearing, I prompted your brain to take control of the sensory experience—and made you listen rather than just hear. . . . The difference between the sense of hearing and the skill of listening is attention. . . .
>
> Hearing, in short, is easy. . . . But listening, really listening, is hard when potential distractions are leaping

into your ears every fifty-thousandth of a second—and pathways in your brain are just waiting to interrupt your focus. . . .

Listening is a skill that we're in danger of losing in a world of digital distraction and information overload.[11]

Hearing is an auditory process, but *listening* involves the whole person. To grow as listeners, it would help each of us to target listening in three different categories: our face, our focus, and our feelings.

Face

The face is a channel of our emotions, an instrument of nonverbal communication and a key tool in the listening process. In part, we "listen" with our faces. By tilting their faces forward toward the speaker, good listeners communicate attention and interest. Other ways to listen with your face include watching for nonverbal cues and maintaining alert eye contact. A good listener mirrors the emotional state of the speaker, staying in sync rather than drifting out of the conversation. Position your face and body to convey full attention to the speaker. You want your body language to communicate acceptance, interest, trust, and care.

Focus

Focused, attentive listeners avoid distractions. They don't interrupt or interject lots of their own thoughts or self-referential comments. Their words are few. Any questions they ask are relevant and focused on the speaker, not themselves.

When we listen, most of us fixate on what's literal and obvious; we tend to stay on the surface of what people say. But good listeners pay close attention to clues that reveal the deeper questions beneath a person's story. For example, someone's objections about things like the truth of the Bible or the mystery of pain and suffering may be expressed as philosophical questions, but people rarely think only in theoretical terms. If someone questions God's fairness, it's often because something has happened to him or her that feels unfair (though that person may not feel safe enough to share the specifics). Suffering or hurt caused by another Christian can also be behind the question, and the "objections" may be a smoke screen for the real issue, which often takes trust and time to discover. You may have to build the relational equity to earn the right to dialogue about it. Remember the story at the beginning of the chapter? Unfortunately, I didn't listen or ask clarifying questions to understand the questions *behind* Eileen's question.

Sometimes people's actual words can be a barrier to listening. For example, they might say, "I'm fine," when they really are not. Psychologist Theodor Reik said we listen best when we not only use our sense of hearing, but listen with what he called "the third ear"—paying attention to tone, body language, and other nonverbal cues. People can display emotion in a variety of ways. Even if the words sound calm, you may see subtle incongruities between spoken words and underlying messages: clenched teeth, tight hands, or furrowed brows. A good listener holds loosely to the words and more tightly to the subtext.

Like miners panning for gold, searching attentively for those valuable, shiny nuggets in the watery silt, good listeners focus on the other person to find the gems of truth, understanding, and value in their lives—and to discover where God is already at work.

Feelings

A good listener is empathetic—but most of us have a hard time getting outside of our own frame of reference. When people express emotion or pain, often our knee-jerk reaction is to fix them or give them relief. We find it difficult to join them where they are; we feel discomfort and want to hurry them to a different emotional state.

Empathy offers comfort, not pat answers, and it tries to understand and even experience the other person's feelings. It starts with where the person is and tries to understand rather than change, remembering that only God can change a human heart. Karen Kimsey-House is a coaching expert and the creator of the Co-Active philosophy of relationships. She warns, "When you're not listening well, you're not fully present. You miss what's behind the words, the deep truth that's coming from a person. It's not about hearing the words spoken *per se*; it's about connecting with the heart."[12]

Relational Listening

Listening is a process of communication that extends much further than simply hearing. Listening requires you to concentrate, derive meaning from the sound that is heard, and react to it. Yet there are different kinds of listening. You could separate it into two broad categories—transactional and relational.

Transactional listening is one-way communication. As in a news broadcast or a speech, one person is speaking while another is hearing and trying to understand without the opportunity to interact. In this type of listening, we are seeking information, and accuracy is paramount to us. Transactional listening is characterized by what I get out of it here and now, and it does not include much commitment.

Relational listening allows for interaction between speaker and listener. The person who is listening can ask questions or repeat back what the speaker has said to make sure he or she has heard it correctly. This kind of listening fosters an exchange of feelings between people, not just comprehension of ideas. In this kind of listening, we are seeking connection, and empathy is paramount. Relational listening builds in commitment and trust, so that people in the conversation grow willing to become emotionally involved.

Relational listening involves a variety of listening skills.

Reflecting

One of these skills is sometimes called *reflective listening*. In every conversation you have the opportunity to demonstrate that you've been listening well. A clear way to assure people that you have heard them is to reflect back what you thought you heard them say. *You* become the learner, putting the spotlight on the other person. By paraphrasing your perception of the message you heard and reflecting it back to the speaker for verification, you show genuine interest in understanding what the speaker is thinking and feeling. If you miss the opportunity, the conversation is likely to die out.

Reflective listening, also called *active listening*, helps you go beyond merely hearing the words to really listen for the message. It frees others to share their struggles, their doubts, and even their beliefs about God. As noted by business advisor Ram Charan, "[Active] listening opens the door to truly connecting and is the gateway to building relationships."[13] And while you listen, make it your goal to keep one ear open to God, asking him to supply you with insights into a person's situation. Listen for God's whispers as you listen to your friend, trying to understand more deeply with both human and Spirit-enabled insight.

As you seek to understand people better through reflective listening, you can start with a humble opening followed by a brief paraphrase of the feelings and ideas you thought you heard. Here are some sample reflective phrases to help you demonstrate that you have heard and are seeking to understand.

- So, if I'm hearing you right . . .
- Let me make sure I'm tracking with you. You're . . .
- You're saying you feel . . . Is that right?
- You seem to be saying . . .
- I think I hear you saying . . . [14]

Asking Follow-Up Questions

As you're listening, paying attention to words and meaning and also listening to what God is helping you hear, your next step is to ask a follow-up question. The follow-up question can open the conversation as dramatically as the back of the wardrobe opens to Narnia. Try saying, "Tell me more," "How does that make you feel?" or "What makes you think that?" Then be willing to wait—even in a few moments of silence—for the speaker to share thoughts or even to figure out what he or she thinks, since many people have never actually worked at articulating their feelings or beliefs. Take time to hear the whole story, not just his or her thoughts on spiritual matters. We'll talk even more about the Art of Asking Questions in the next chapter.

Developing Curiosity

Unfortunately, many Christians miss the golden opportunities for follow-up questions because they fail to allow their God-given curiosity to emerge. When we listen actively enough to stir up new areas of curiosity, the description of Proverbs 20:5 can begin to become the reality for us: "The purposes of a person's heart are deep waters, but one who has insight draws them out." When we verbally express our curiosity about what's important to people (their lives, careers, family, and so on), we create an open, safe, and nonjudgmental forum for authentic dialogue. Our questions invite people to search for answers and naturally stimulate them to discover the condition, plans, and purposes of their own hearts.

The cost of curiosity is that we must give up our need to control conversations. Curiosity starts when we unleash our God-given wonder to ponder what we're noticing and hearing. Like the swinging of a pendulum, a good balance of listening and curiosity helps a conversation move along naturally. If we are listening well, our wonder begins to percolate. If we are curious, we'll get plenty of opportunities to listen. As we continue to use these two qualities, only God knows where the conversation might lead.

The good news from this chapter is that high-quality listening emerges through skills that can be learned and practiced. It begins when we act out of genuine care for other people and become curious about their stories and their spiritual journeys. And it continues to improve as we practice listening with our whole self, connect relationally, and ask follow-up questions that lead to greater understanding.

Imagine a world where followers of Jesus are known for being great listeners and learners, with the courage and willingness to engage others. Maybe we are just one listening moment away from a meaningful conversation about God with someone who would never darken the doorway of a church. It's worth listening for, isn't it?

Discover

1. Would those who know you well call you a good listener? Why or why not?

2. Why do you think it is hard for us to refrain from giving advice or from having an agenda when we talk with someone?

Practice

1. Refrain from giving advice for a week. Then think about what it was like to listen and participate in a conversation without offering any suggestions about what others should do. What was their response?

2. Take a sixty-second survey with three people to practice genuine listening. Set it up by simply explaining, "I have a

homework assignment to conduct a one-minute survey by asking someone four questions. Would you be willing to help me with it?" Here are the four survey questions:

- What is the difference between spirituality and religion?
- Which spiritual person do you most admire?
- What would you say to Christians if they would listen?
- Has anyone ever tried to "save" you?

The point is to listen and value someone's opinion, not editorialize. Say *thank you* and let them go without responding.

PART II

Getting Started

THE NEXT GROUPING of The 9 Arts of Spiritual Conversations is called *Getting Started*. These three practices create the engaging, safe, and welcoming environment in which spiritual conversations can thrive and God's love can be on display through you. Like a thermostat that sets the temperature of your home, curiosity, love, and hospitality generate an atmosphere that can thaw a cold heart and invite people to freely explore God's truth without judgment or argument. These Arts include Asking Questions, Loving, and Welcoming.

CHAPTER 6

The Art of Asking Questions

Do nothing out of selfish ambition or vain conceit. Rather, in
humility value others above yourselves, not looking to your own interests
but each of you to the interests of the others. In your relationships
with one another, have the same mindset as Christ Jesus.

PHILIPPIANS 2:3-5

[Curiosity] is not the same as gathering information. Curiosity
is a different way of discovering. . . . When you are curious, you are
no longer in the role of expert. Instead, you are . . . exploring [the]
world with others, not superimposing your world on theirs.

HENRY KIMSEY-HOUSE

FIVE YOUNG MEN were crammed into my (Crilly's) pickup truck. We had just enjoyed some burgers, the music was blaring, and we were talking and laughing loudly above the noise. As I mentioned earlier, over several years' time I had developed a relationship with these young Bantu refugee men. You will recall from chapter 2 that our relationship began when I showed up as a volunteer tutor for them in reading and math, and it quickly morphed into a mentoring friendship. I love these boys, now ages sixteen to twenty-one, and I long for them to know Jesus as Messiah and Lord. Through the years, individually and collectively, we have had profound conversations about life, God, and faith.

We have very different life experiences and faith stories. I was raised in an Irish Catholic middle-class family of four outside of Chicago. They were Muslims raised in Kenyan refugee camps, fleeing tribal violence in their homeland. They boarded a plane in T-shirts and flip-flops and arrived in a new country in the dead of winter carrying all their belongings in a bag. We had hardly anything in common. But because of God, our lives have been divinely woven together as our God of Love pursues each one of these young men.

As we were driving along, one of the boys mentioned something about prayer.

Following a whisper from God and stirred by curiosity, I turned down the radio and asked, "How does a Muslim pray?"

The relational dynamic changed as soon as I asked that question. I wasn't only these young men's tutor/mentor/adult friend in a position of status above them; I was also a person who was interested in learning from them. They were empowered to guide the conversation and share as much or as little as they wanted. They were in control of the discussion.

They started the conversation by telling me about the five "salats" of each day, with each one chiming in as I listened intently. I was fascinated and asked follow-up questions to clarify my understanding and seek to know their lives better. Their experiences were utterly foreign to me. The discussion was rich, as I was able to demonstrate my love for them by hearing their story, learning about their religion, and exploring their world with them.

Then an amazing thing happened.

As we arrived in my driveway, one of them asked me, "How does a Christian pray?"

Curiosity Fuels Questions

The Arts of Noticing, Praying, and Listening have basically been nonspeaking activities that you could practice off the radar. The Art of Asking Questions invites you to directly engage with another person and create an environment for meaningful conversation.

To cross this invisible sound barrier, God has equipped us

with curiosity. Curiosity is the bridge that moves you from listening to asking questions and fully engaging. The word *curiosity* comes from the Latin root *cura*, meaning "to care, to tend, and to heal." When we care enough about a person or a question, we are motivated to know more, understand better, explore deeper. Curiosity, as it relates to relationships, is the humble, sincere interest to know more about another person and his or her thoughts, beliefs, passions, and doubts. As Christians who desire to engage in authentic spiritual conversations, if we can intentionally tap into this God-given bent toward curiosity, we may have the key to discovering excellent questions—questions that communicate to someone how much we really care.

We are not all-knowing and won't always grasp the right question to ask at the right time. If we adopt a policy of peppering our interactions with questions without regard to the reason behind them, our approach can become just as tiresome as monopolizing a conversation. We face the danger of giving our questions an invasive edge that could kill a conversation—or a relationship. But curiosity is a gift that can open the door for questions that are a perfect fit.

We are hard-wired by our awesome Creator to be naturally interested in learning more about people and his creation. That curiosity is the rocket fuel that launches us into the world of discovery. In the land of curiosity, we give up the notion that we must have all the answers. We return to a humble mind-set in which asking, seeking, and knocking are normal. Curiosity helps us move into spiritual conversations authentically, without canned or awkward transitions. After a conversation is started, curiosity is the lubricant that keeps it going.

The brilliant scientist Albert Einstein said:

> The important thing is not to stop questioning. Curiosity has its own reason for existence. One cannot help but be in awe when he contemplates the mysteries of eternity,

of life, of the marvelous structure of reality. It is enough if one tries merely to comprehend a little of this mystery each day. Never lose a holy curiosity.[1]

"Holy" curiosity is an interesting way to say it. Holy curiosity toward another person involves choice. We choose to notice people, allow them to matter to us, and extend love to them. Motivated by this love in the context of a relationship—and with God's guidance—curiosity fuels our ability to ask good questions.

Curiosity focuses our attention on the other person, not ourselves. It reduces our fear of not asking the right question, saying the right thing, or having the right answer. At the end of the day, the reason curiosity has so much potential is because everybody is curious. We all experience emotions like awe, admiration, wonderment, fascination, surprise, astonishment, and amazement.

Proverbs teaches, "Wise men and women are always learning, always listening for fresh insights" (Proverbs 18:15, MSG). But now, perhaps more than ever, our curiosity is hindered by self-preoccupation, selfish pursuits, busyness, and distractions that lead to apathy about the people around us. Once again, it is the apostle Paul's direction to early Christians that calibrates us as twenty-first-century followers of Jesus:

> Do nothing out of selfish ambition or vain conceit. Rather, in humility value others above yourselves, not looking to your own interests but each of you to the interests of the others.
>
> In your relationships with one another, have the same mindset as Christ Jesus.
>
> PHILIPPIANS 2:3-5

Just as Jesus put others' needs above his own, we are called to be interested in others—not for our own sake, but for theirs. This also means that as we tap into our Spirit-led curiosity during a conversation, we will ask questions that are fitting for the moment rather than questions that feel too invasive for the level of connection we have already had in a relationship.

The Natural Order of Curiosity

Scott West heads up a large consulting group that helps financial advisors connect better with their clients. He has discovered, based on research, something called the Natural Order of Curiosity. This is not a rigid structure intended to be formulaic; rather, it's an intuitive process for building deep relationships. The idea is that as we meet and begin to learn about another person, our mutual inquiry will naturally follow a path that includes four categories. When we move through these areas and are mindful of them, we can have conversations that are not invasive but comfortable and appropriate.

HISTORY ("WHERE ARE YOU FROM?")

The first category of questions is History. These questions are about your past and where you have come from. Asking history questions is instinctive when you first meet people, but if you spend a few minutes in this area, you can learn so much more than just their birthplace or schooling. Getting beyond initial introductions, you can express continued curiosity with casual phrases such as "I couldn't help noticing . . . ," "I'm wondering . . . ," or "I'm curious . . ." Curiosity displayed here can reveal significant experiences, both good and bad.

Examples: "So where are you from?" "What did you like most about living there?" (When it is appropriate in the context of a growing relationship, you might be able to ask questions such as "What's your faith background?" "What were your best (or worst) experiences with church, religion, or Christians?" or "Who most influenced your views on God?")

TRANSITIONS ("WHERE ARE YOU NOW?")

When you have a common frame of reference and have shared an understanding of each other's history, Transition questions are appropriate. These questions are focused on where you are at this moment. Lives are always in motion, and this area of inquiry can identify what is most important in someone's life *right now*. You can think of these as "let's get caught up" questions.

Example: "What's going on with you/your kids/your job/your life lately?"

PRINCIPLES ("HOW DID YOU GET HERE?")

The third category of questions is easy to miss. Once you become aware of Principles questions, though, your curiosity can lead you to a much deeper connection with people. These questions seek to discover the principles on which a person builds his or her perspective. Principles can be deeply held convictions based on life experiences that shape our outlook on life and the decisions we make.

Examples: "How did you get to the place you are in life?" "Why did you go into your job field?" "Who is the spiritual person you most admire?" "Whom do you rely on for life or spiritual advice?"

GOALS ("WHERE ARE YOU GOING?")

The final category is Goals. These questions are forward looking and visionary, asking, "How do you want things to be?" The key point here is that goals are not explored until the three prior areas have been discovered.

Examples: "What do you want your faith to look like?" "If you had a million dollars to give to a charity, which one would you want to help and why?" "What is your expectation of life after death?"

Some traditional outreach approaches have prompted Christians to ask questions that leap quickly to the Goals category without building the relational equity of the other categories. While that approach may have been successful in the past or might work in unique circumstances today, our gut sense as ordinary Christians has often been that something doesn't feel right about using that approach in our culture with people we don't know well. For example, if we ask, "What is your expectation of life after death?" or "Where will you go when you die?" shortly after meeting someone, the person is likely to feel that the question is rude and out of line. Our haste may sabotage both a conversation and a relationship.

On the other hand, when we follow the natural order of curiosity in our conversations with people, the level of connection grows, trust is built, and the ultimate questions of life fit into an appropriate place and time. We get to ask these important questions in a way that will be received and seriously considered, not quickly rejected as obtuse.

Good Questions Build Connection

Asking questions from genuine interest builds connection. Connection builds trust. Trust is the bridge that can bear the weight of truth.

Asking appropriate questions invites interaction, showing that you want a relationship rather than an audience. It demonstrates that you value that relationship enough to seek to understand more, to hear another opinion or perspective. Respectful, honoring questions provide people the freedom to choose whether to respond and how much to respond. They also give people the opportunity to wrestle with the truth about life, themselves, and God.

In Mark 10 we read a remarkable exchange between Jesus and Bartimaeus. Jesus was walking out of Jericho in the middle of a clamoring crowd. Bartimaeus, a blind man, was sitting beside the road shouting for Jesus' attention over the din. Others told him to be quiet. But when Jesus heard him, he stopped, told the people to bring the blind man over, and asked him, "What do you want mc to do for you?" (10:51). In this brief interaction, Jesus didn't ask many questions, or even a particularly profound question. His question was simple, but the entire scene reveals that it came from a heart of great love for this man.

First, Jesus was attentive; he heard the cry of Bartimaeus over the crowd's noise. Second, even though the crowd rebuked and disregarded Bartimaeus, Jesus put all of his plans on hold in order to stop and connect with him. Third, Jesus responded in a way that showed that Bartimaeus was not a project but a valued person. Rather than just assuming that this man wanted to be able to see, Jesus asked a question that allowed Bartimaeus the dignity of communicating what he most desired—and in that moment, Bartimaeus also was given the chance to reveal his faith in Jesus.

As authors Jedd Medefind and Erik Lokkesmoe put it,

> Something remarkable happened to people when Jesus— the self-proclaimed answer—began asking questions [over 150 of them are recorded in the Gospels]. . . . [Jesus] invited others to participate in the activity of discovery, to take hold of truth for themselves. . . . His questions invited listeners to embark on a search, candle in hand, rummaging through the attic of their minds for an adequate answer. . . . Jesus' questions were also *decisively clarifying*. They penetrated to the heart of the matter, peeling back layer after layer of what *appeared* to be the real issues so as to address what in all actually *was* the real issue.[2]

When Jesus approached people who were spiritually confused or struggling with what they believed, he asked them questions, often jumping right to the heart of the issue. Jesus seemed comfortable when he was asking questions. But today I wonder whether we, as Christians, are more comfortable with answers than questions. Often we miss the importance of both asking good questions and listening to questions; sometimes, we treat them like they're dangerous.

We can encourage those who believe differently to be open about their questions too. Two buddies and I (Crilly) decided to bring on the questions. We pulled together some friends in our neighborhood who had a variety of beliefs about God. The idea was to create a safe environment where this group of guys could explore together and ask their questions about God. On the night of our initial get-together, eleven of us sat in my living room. Three of us were followers of Jesus, and the other eight guys just agreed to show up.

All we did was ask questions. We started with a few simple ice-breakers, and then we asked, "If you could ask God one question, and you knew he would answer, what would you ask him?"

For the next hour, their questions came flying: "Why couldn't you have made things more clear?" "Why forgive people who do terrible evil?" "What's the end game?" "What's life all about?" "Why punish people for all of eternity for the decisions made in this short life?" As we listened to their questions, we also asked why each question was significant to them.

One of the guys, Dan, had sat quietly for most of the night, so one of my partners, Jeff, invited him into the discussion. "Hey, Dan, we've never seen you this quiet. What's going on?"

Dan replied, "I guess I do have a question, but I have to tell you a story first." He proceeded to tell us about when he was a young teacher and played basketball with some other teachers after school on Fridays. One Friday when he wasn't there, one of his friends, a teacher named Bob, had a heart attack and died on the gym floor. A few weeks later, Dan developed a pain in his side, so he started taking antacids and eventually pain relievers. This went on for two weeks with no real improvement.

One night, he woke up at 3 a.m. from a vivid dream of his friend Bob telling him to get up and go to the hospital. He listened, driving over in great pain. When he got there and the ER staff scanned his abdomen, they found a massive blood clot. The doctors were surprised that he was still alive. Dan concluded his story: "That night, I believe that God saved my life by sending me a sign. My question is, how many other signs have I missed? How can I learn to see God's signs more clearly?"

Dan's question prompted all of us to go on a God hunt—looking for where God was already at work in our lives. That is the power of questions.

Questions help to uncover people's hearts and expose the things that stand between them and God. Questions also create an arena for dialogue where Christians and those who believe differently can ponder life and its mysteries *together*. When we ask a question, we place others at the center of a conversation, and many people find this refreshing and irresistible. Questions help others process and own their decisions. They also help people rethink deeply rooted assumptions and probe unexamined motives and values. Good questions invite people to look in the mirror, wrestle with what they believe, and search for dependable, solid, proven answers.

Humble Inquiry

Culminating fifty years of research as a social and organizational psychologist, Edgar Schein, professor emeritus at the MIT Sloan School of Business, discovered that asking questions is the key to building positive relationships. Schein labels this way of asking "humble inquiry," the gentle art of asking instead of telling. He defines humble inquiry as "the fine art of drawing someone out, of asking questions to which you do not already know the answer, of building a relationship based on curiosity and interest in the other person."[3]

We have to be honest about the unconscious bias we all have about asking questions. It can be scary because we live in a "telling" culture—a society that values knowing the answer, giving advice, having it all together, being the expert. Even if we are open to asking questions, we want them to be the "right" questions. We say, "No question is a stupid question," and then we secretly judge a lot of questions as stupid. Asking questions can be interpreted as exposing my ignorance or weakness, and that feels like a high relational risk.

Asking questions requires humility and vulnerability, but it doesn't have to be intimidating. I love the term that Schein uses to describe our posture about asking questions—he suggests that I "access my ignorance" and allow curiosity to lead me. This is a liberating way of thinking about question asking. I do not have all the answers, so I can be free to access my ignorance and humbly ask a question. Although Schein was focused on communication complexities in the work environment, his research reinforces that asking questions creates a safe climate for building trust, mutual respect, and relational equity.

Joseph Grenny and David Maxfield, known as the Behavioral Science Guys, are acclaimed speakers, authors, and experts in the area of behavioral change. They did a simple study on the power of asking questions as opposed to telling information in order to change behavior. They discovered that asking questions has far greater motivational influence than offering more information.

For their test on the influential power of questions, Grenny and Maxfield targeted a notoriously difficult behavior to change—cigarette smoking. A typical approach to getting someone to quit smoking is to provide them with information about its harmful impact. Think about the scary public-service announcements with the image of the wrinkled old woman on oxygen, the Surgeon General's warning labels on a pack of cigarettes—none of these seem to deter people from smoking.

The Behavioral Science Guys set up a way to test the impact of "telling" versus "asking." For their test they hired two young boys of around ten to twelve years old as their accomplices. In the first attempt, the boys approached people smoking in public and tried to get them to consider quitting by using a "telling" approach. After telling the smokers that "smoking is bad for you," they would ask the smokers whether they'd like information on how to quit. Ninety percent responded negatively, and fewer than half took the information pamphlet on how to quit.

For the second experiment, each boy had a fake cigarette in hand and approached the smokers, asking for a light. The smokers' reactions were fascinating. Not one smoker offered the young boys a light. Instead, the smokers began lecturing the kids on the dangers of smoking!

Then, as part of the test, the boys asked the smokers a second powerful question: "If you care about us, what about you?" In this "asking" approach, 90 percent of the smokers told the boys they would try to quit! Isn't that interesting?

I know what you are wondering: Did the smokers really quit? Well, the study did not provide that information. However, according to Grenny and Maxfield, "when Ogilvy & Mather conducted the experiment in Bangkok, calls to the quit line actually went up 40 percent on the day of the experiment," suggesting a strong correlation between intentions and actions as a result of the test.[4] The bottom line is that questions can be a powerful tool to influence transformation in a person's life.

Characteristics of Good Questions

Asking good questions doesn't mean firing a barrage of inquiries at someone or using a canned formula. Instead, good questions are combined with good listening. The goal is to help people feel safe and heard, not attacked or like a "project." As we listen, we also gain more insight into who they are and where they're coming from, spurring curiosity and follow-up questions. Here are five characteristics of good questions:

1. Good questions originate from curiosity and a genuine interest in another person.
2. Good questions are open-ended. Use classic openers such as *who, what, why,* and *how.*
3. Good questions are concise. Don't ramble; end at the question mark and then listen.
4. Good questions don't come out of nowhere. They connect with what's being discussed and move the conversation forward.
5. Good questions help people feel safe and understood. After others speak, rephrase what they said to be sure you understood their response, and give them a chance to correct you if you didn't.

Good questions help people in the process of self-discovery and God-discovery. For example, a great question to ask is, "How do you think God might have been active in that?" This invites people to consider how God may actually have been present in the story they are telling about themselves. This might be a stretch for a non-Christian, but it helps people to pay attention to what he or she might be doing in the present as well.

It's tempting to ask questions just to get people to give us the "right answer" and then move on. But a spiritual conversation is a dialogue—a two-way exchange. To that end, often the best questions are follow-up questions. When we invite someone to tell us something or share an opinion, we should not move on too quickly. Instead, we can ask questions to clarify, get more details, or have the person elaborate on emotions: "How did that make you feel?" or "Wow, can you tell me more about that?" Avoid follow-up questions that sound accusatory: "How on earth can you think that?" or "Why would anyone do such a thing?"

Practices to Avoid

Remember that a question is something that you do not have the answer to yet. When we ask questions designed to lead someone to agree to our belief, people typically resent the feeling of being "set up." To create good questions, avoid these practices:

1. Don't primarily use yes/no or multiple-choice questions. They tend to kill a conversation.
2. Don't ask leading, coercive, or cornering questions. For example, rather than asking, "Why don't you believe in God when there's so much overwhelming evidence he exists?" you could say, "God is very real to me, and yet at times I have doubts. I'm wondering what doubts you might have." Ask yourself, *Does this question have an agenda, or does it show sincere willingness to understand the life, worldview, perspective, and beliefs of this person?*
3. Don't correct a person's response to your question with the "right" answer, but allow him or her the space to discover the truth as you pray and trust the Holy Spirit to work.
4. Don't ask and then answer your own question. For example: "Why did you stop going to church? Was it the boring sermons?"
5. Don't fill the silence after your question. Enjoy the pause! For example, don't keep adding to your question with pile-on phrases like, "Would you like to meet me for coffee next week? Or maybe you are too busy? Is next week too soon? Would you like to call me instead of deciding right now?"

6. Don't ask formulaic questions. People can tell when they are the recipients of canned questions or a rehearsed approach. Be natural and winsome and consider the context.

Discovering the Story

Good questions allow people to discover—or rediscover—themselves and uncover new truths. Good questions show that we care enough to be curious. And true curiosity—genuine interest in a person and his or her story—flows from the conviction that each person's life matters. Being authentically curious about someone's thoughts and opinions can create a bond of trust that allows more significant conversations to grow. Good questions can also help people wrestle with their beliefs about God.

A not-for-profit organization called StoryCorps provides Americans of all backgrounds and beliefs with the opportunity to record, share, and preserve the stories of their lives. This organization maintains that shared stories "remind one another of our shared humanity, strengthen and build the connections between people, teach the value of listening, and weave into the fabric of our culture the understanding that everyone's story matters."[5] To unearth the incredible stories buried away in the lives of people, StoryCorps asks questions. Here are a couple of examples: "What was the happiest moment of your life?" "Who has been the biggest influence on your life, and what lessons did that person teach you?"

Every person has a story—a lifetime of experiences that have shaped them and impacted their emotions, their spiritual life (or lack thereof), and their relationships. All these little stories make up their big story. When people have some space to tell their stories, they feel loved and empowered. So if you want to show love to people, listen to their stories; to unlock their stories, ask good questions.

When I (Mary) walked into a little storefront near my house,

I had no idea that a life-changing story would unfold before me. Hal, the owner of a small video-editing and production firm, was on the phone when I walked up to the counter. He put his hand over the mouthpiece, said he'd be a few minutes, and asked whether while I was waiting I would mind reading an e-mail he was getting ready to send. He felt that his grammar and syntax needed refinement. As he turned his computer screen in my direction, I began reading a very personal e-mail to a woman he had hurt by his bad choices over the past several years. He asked for her forgiveness and wanted to see her again.

What do you say to a complete stranger when he gives you this intimate glimpse into his life? I asked God for immediate help and wisdom. When Hal got off the phone and turned his attention to me, I responded with a simple question—I asked him to tell me more about what was going on. He explained that the woman he was writing to was his estranged grown daughter whom he hadn't seen in many years. He'd had a messy divorce with the girl's mother and had been banned from seeing his daughter. Now he had finally gotten clean and sober from substance abuse and wanted to make amends.

Not knowing what else to say, I said, "It sounds like you have a God-sized problem!" He replied, "Oh, don't mention God to me! There's no way he'll ever forgive me for what I have done. I can never turn to God for help."

Since I was asking Hal to edit a video for my ministry, I was able to tell him a little bit about what we do at Q Place, including inviting people into small groups to question, discover, and grow in their relationship with God. I asked if he would like to join a group like that, and he said yes! I put him in touch with a couple of Christian guys nearby who were starting a group, and he joined them. He obviously needed both community to work through life's challenges and a place to figure out more about God. Within a few years, through his experience with that group, Hal chose to follow Jesus because he knew that he was forgiven and loved by God, in spite of his difficult past. He was even able to reconcile with his daughter.

We may never know the stories of people around us unless we ask questions. Becoming a good question-asker depends on having the right heart and right motives when engaging others in conversations. We are at our best when we align our hearts and motives with our leader, the greatest questioner ever, Jesus.

Certainly, we as Christ followers have a message to share. But the apostle Paul, in Colossians 4:5-6, counsels us to *be wise* in the way we interact with outsiders, "[making] the most of every opportunity." Our conversation should "be always full of grace, seasoned with salt." Salt makes food appealing; it causes us to desire more. And asking good questions has the same effect in a conversation.

Discover

1. Can you recall a time when someone was sincerely curious about your life? How did you know? How did it make you feel? What was your response?

2. What do you think hinders us from being curious about others?

Practice

1. Keep a log of good questions you hear this week. What made them good questions? What are some of the not-so-good questions you heard?

2. Think of three questions that might open up a spiritual conversation with someone in a natural way. Try asking those questions of someone on your list of people with whom you think God may be calling you to engage. How did it turn out?

CHAPTER 7

The Art of Loving

*Jesus replied, "'Love the Lord your God with all of your heart and
with all your soul and with all your mind.' This is the first and greatest
commandment. And the second is like it: 'Love your neighbor as yourself.'"*

MATTHEW 22:37-39

*What we need is not intellectual theorizing or even preaching, but
a demonstration. One of the most powerful ways of turning people's
loyalty to Christ is by loving others with the great love of God.*

ELTON TRUEBLOOD

I (CRILLY) DID NOT LIKE MY GRANDMOTHER, and she did not
like me. I thought she was as mean as a snake, selfish, and uncom-
passionate. She thought I was rude, disrespectful, and disobedient.
She called me a drunk. Then, when I was twenty-two years old,
Jesus got through to me and radically transformed my life.

The apostle Paul puts that transformation into words in
2 Corinthians 5:17: "Therefore, if anyone is in Christ, the new
creation has come: The old has gone, the new is here!" This became
my life verse after Jesus came into my life and turned it inside
out. He transformed me from a discourager, who looks to identify
and criticize people's weaknesses, to an encourager, who looks for
positive attributes to highlight in others. He changed me from a
self-absorbed young man to a lover of people. Praise God for his
forgiveness and his provision of a new start and a new heart—a
big heart of love and compassion to replace that small, shriveled,
self-centered heart of stone.

When Jesus reclaimed my life, he changed my heart toward my grandma. I found myself becoming interested in her life. I would take her out for dinner and ask questions about her upbringing and family history. I burned with curiosity about her life experiences and her view of God. Through this growing relationship, Jesus slowly gave me the capacity to love my grandmother. He gave me a desire to be with her. He gave me a willingness to listen to her and to understand the hardships of her life—an immigrant childhood without a father, a very young marriage, an abusive husband who broke her nose, a divorce at a time when that was taboo, and many other heart-hardening trials.

I started to have great compassion for this woman. My heart became tender toward her, even while she did not really change much. She still called me an idiot when I didn't show up on time to pick her up. When she was in the assisted-care home, she was known for throwing punches at the nurses, and they threatened to kick her out a few times. One time, when I arrived to visit her with my wife, Danielle, she cursed at us, asking, "Where have you been and who is she?" But I still loved her because God loved her, and he had implanted his capacity to love her in me. As she came near to the end of this life, my visits consisted mostly of holding her hand and gently stroking her greasy, matted hair, telling her of the Father's great love for her. When I left, I would whisper in her ear, "I love you, Grandma." And I meant it.

The Art of Loving is the all-encompassing attitude that pervades each of the other practices. Love binds all facets of our relationships together. This idea is reinforced in Colossians 3:14: "Above all, clothe yourselves with love, which binds us all together in perfect harmony" (NLT). The Art of Loving is the thread woven throughout the other practices, holding them together. If we do not love when we notice, pray, listen, and ask questions, our attempts will fail. If we do not love when we welcome people, facilitate well, serve with others, and share God's story, our attempts will crumble. Love is the glue. Loving people, especially those who are different from us, can be difficult. But when God's love is poured out in us, it overflows into the lives of everyone around us. Noticing people, engaging them in conversation, asking meaningful questions, listening empathetically, serving with them, and inviting them into relationship are not only powerful expressions of God's love; they are also dependent on his love in order to be authentic, meaningful, and compelling.

God Loves Us

Love describes God. He is loving; he acts on his love; he loves each of us. But at the core, love is God's identity. It is who he is, and he cannot be something other than love. The apostle John described God this way in 1 John 4:16: "God is love. Whoever lives in love lives in God, and God in them." God expresses his identity by pouring out his love on people. I always enjoy the beautiful image of God's love adapted from a thousand-year-old Jewish poem and captured in the third stanza of the hymn "The Love of God." It reminds me of the immensity of his love:

> *Could we with ink the ocean fill,*
> *And were the skies of parchment made,*
> *Were every stalk on earth a quill,*
> *And every man a scribe by trade;*
> *To write the love of God above*
> *Would drain the ocean dry;*
> *Nor could the scroll contain the whole,*
> *Though stretched from sky to sky.*
> *Oh, love of God, how rich and pure!*
> *How measureless and strong!*
> *It shall forevermore endure—*
> *The saints' and angels' song.*[1]

These lyrics provide an artistic expression of God's love as immeasurable. God's love is not scarce or about to run out. He is not stingy with his love, parceling it out in tiny bits. He is not controlling with his love, holding it back to punish us. God is an ardent and exuberant lover. He first communicated love through his creation—a vibrant sunset, a warm puppy, a juicy apple. But God's incredible expression of sacrificial love for us culminated in the birth, death, and resurrection of Jesus. John quoted Jesus himself when he wrote, "Greater love has no one than this: to lay down one's life for one's friends" (John 15:13).

Scripture uses a variety of metaphors to paint a picture of God's love, such as a parent's love for a child or a husband's love for his wife. Though helpful, each metaphor falls short of fully capturing the vastness of God's love. Any way you look at it, his love is extreme. This sacrificial, boundless, and deep love is worth investigating, understanding, experiencing, and sharing. And it is this incredible love that Paul implores us to grasp in Ephesians 3:18-19: "May you have the power to understand, as all God's people should, how wide, how long, how high, and how deep his love is. May you experience the love of Christ, though it is too great to understand fully" (NLT).

It is this love that we are compelled to share with those who do not yet know him. Because we have experienced this lavish love, we are motivated to spread it in tangible ways to people in our world who are burdened with guilt and judgment, without God and without hope.

We Love because He Loves Us

My nutritional intake provides fuel for my body. If I take in calories without using them, my body accumulates that fuel as fat, and I grow less and less healthy. Similarly, my soul is not designed to take in the spiritual nutrition of God's love without then turning it outward in loving action toward others. But I cannot expect to love others purely if I am not being nourished by God's love. I must tap into the source of love—in fact, into Love himself. That is the essence of the Great Commandment in Matthew 22:36-38.

God doesn't command me to try harder to get my cold heart to love more. Instead, he invites me to have my heart transformed by loving him, so that love for others follows as the natural outflow. When a bucket is filled to overflowing, and water keeps pouring in, the bucket doesn't have to try to make everything around it get wet; it can't help but spill all over whatever is nearby.

If I truly appreciate God's love, I increasingly love what he loves—other people, both those who are close to him and those who are separated from him. As a result, my focus realigns to include loving and caring for others as a way of life. Paul's instruction in Galatians 5:13-14 reflects Jesus' teaching: "Do not use your freedom to indulge the flesh; rather, serve one another humbly in love. For the entire law is fulfilled in keeping this one command: 'Love your neighbor as yourself.'"

This is not a suggestion to take under advisement. Loving your neighbor is foundational to the Christian faith. What if Christians were known all over the world for this love?

Despite our shortcomings, God is still madly in love with each of us. He considers us his treasure, his beloved children. He dotes over us as our loving heavenly Father. So what are we to do with this outlandish love from God? The answer is evident in 1 John 4:19: "We love because he first loved us." Musician Aaron Niequist explains it this way in his song "Changed":

We have been blessed—
now we're going to be a blessing
We have been loved—
now we're going to bring love
We've been invited—
We're going to share the invitation

We have been changed—
to bring change[2]

We are called to love the down-and-out and the up-and-coming, the wallflower and the gadfly, the atheist and the religious, our friend and our enemy. Jesus showed us how to do this. He was called a "friend of sinners" (Matthew 11:19).

Love Pursues on Purpose

When we talk about how we came to know Jesus, we often describe ourselves as "seekers" or "explorers," as if our spiritual journey is all about us—that we are the ones who are active and God is out there passively waiting to be found (maybe even *hiding*). We may think that God is far off and disinterested or that he only cares about us if we initiate a relationship with him. But the truth is that God pursues each one of us. We are less the seekers and more the sought-after ones (Isaiah 62:12). God's love is an active love; the thread running through Scripture reveals that God actively seeks us.

From Adam and Eve to Abraham, from Moses to Ruth, from David to a virgin girl named Mary—God sought them out. He demonstrated his love personally to each of them while he worked in their lives to carry out his plan, motivated by love for the whole world. And then Jesus came from heaven to earth as God in the flesh:

> This is how God showed his love among us: He sent his
> one and only Son into the world that we might live through
> him. This is love: not that we loved God, but that he loved
> us and sent his Son as an atoning sacrifice for our sins.
>
> I JOHN 4:9-10

Jesus' mission was "to seek and to save the lost" (Luke 19:10). God has always earnestly sought his people. That is his nature. God pursues us intentionally and sacrificially, seeking us out because of his fervent love and deep desire for connection. God is the one initiating, the one who takes the first step, even if we are not aware of it. He longs for us to respond to his promptings and invitation—and to seek him in return.

God has been wooing us to himself since the beginning. In *The Sacred Romance*, Brent Curtis and John Eldredge describe God as "the hero in love" and us as the "Beloved" or the "Pursued."[3] Here's how God's story is described in *The Message*:

> Long before he laid down earth's foundations, he had us in mind, had settled on us as the focus of his love, to be made whole and holy by his love. Long, long ago he decided to adopt us into his family through Jesus Christ. (What pleasure he took in planning this!) He wanted us to enter into the celebration of his lavish gift-giving by the hand of his beloved Son. . . . Long before we first heard of Christ and got our hopes up, he had his eye on us, had designs on us for glorious living.
> EPHESIANS 1:4-5, 11, MSG

Long before the beginning of time, God had his eye on you and me as the focus of his love. And yet Psalm 14:2-3 reminds us that we do not reciprocate that interest: "The LORD looks down from heaven on the entire human race; he looks to see if anyone is truly wise, if anyone seeks God. But no, all have turned away" (NLT).

In his book *No Wonder They Call Him the Savior*, Pastor Max Lucado uses a story about a runaway girl to describe God's passionate pursuit of us:

> Longing to leave her poor Brazilian neighborhood, Christina wanted to see the world. Discontent with a home having only a pallet on the floor, . . . she dreamed

of a better life in the city. One morning she slipped away, breaking her mother's heart. Knowing what life on the streets would be like for her young, attractive daughter, Maria hurriedly packed to go find her. On her way to the bus stop she entered a drugstore to get one last thing. Pictures. She sat in the photograph booth, closed the curtain, and spent all she could on pictures of herself. With her purse full of small black-and-white photos, she boarded the next bus to Rio de Janeiro. Maria knew Christina had no way of earning money. . . . Maria began her search. Bars, hotels, nightclubs, any place with the reputation for street walkers or prostitutes. . . . And at each place she left her picture—taped on a bathroom mirror, tacked to a hotel bulletin board, fastened to a corner phone booth. And on the back of each photo she wrote a note. . . .

It was a few weeks later that young Christina descended the hotel stairs. Her young face was tired. Her brown eyes no longer danced with youth but spoke of pain and fear. . . . Her dream had become a nightmare. A thousand times over she had longed to trade these countless beds for her secure pallet. . . . As she reached the bottom of the stairs, her eyes noticed a familiar face. . . . There on the lobby mirror was a small picture of her mother. Christina's eyes burned and her throat tightened as she walked across the room and removed the small photo. Written on the back was this compelling invitation. "Whatever you have done, whatever you have become, it doesn't matter. Please come home." She did.[4]

Like the Brazilian mother who pursued her daughter, our God lovingly pursues you as well as your friends, neighbors, colleagues, classmates, and relatives. He is the Shepherd who pursues the one lost sheep, and we can follow in his steps by proactively seeking out the people who are living desperate lives without him. We are called to notice with compassion, pray purposefully for people, initiate the conversation, reach a hand out, take the first step, listen patiently, extend an invitation, welcome warmly, and intentionally seek others out.

Love Pursues with Sacrifice

In the aftermath of the 2011 earthquake, tsunami, and subsequent nuclear-plant meltdown in Japan, a massive cleanup of the hazardous site was required. A retired Japanese physicist invited other retired scientists to join him in offering their services to help clean up the Fukushima Daiichi nuclear plant. Within four months, four hundred men and women signed up. This "Skilled Veterans Corps" wanted to go in the place of young workers. In an effort to protect the younger generation from radioactive exposure, these individuals were willing to face perilous radiation levels.

God's love is expressed in an even more heroic sacrifice. Jesus, God the Son, left the comfort of heaven and the presence of the Father and became like us, willingly entering our contaminated world to save us from sin's fallout.

These days, the word *love* has lost its value. Saying we love someone, or even feeling kind thoughts about him or her, is not really love. Love may sometimes *feel*, but it always *acts*. "God demonstrates his own love for us in this: While we were still sinners, Christ died for us" (Romans 5:8).

That word *demonstrates* is important. God doesn't just talk about love. He acts on it—with a huge sacrifice! He proves his love, not *after* we prove our worthiness but *before*. While we were still stuck in our sinful actions, he loved us enough to die for us. Today he offers his love to Muslims, Buddhists, atheists, hedonists, communists, terrorists, and anarchists. To your coworkers, relatives, neighbors, and classmates. To everyone who will come to him. His love says: "Whatever you have done—whatever you have become—it doesn't matter. Please come home."

Loving People Who Are Different from You

Action accompanies real love, but action can take very different forms as we interact with people unlike us. The apostle Paul gives us a clear description of the action of love in 1 Corinthians 13:

> Love is patient, love is kind. It does not envy, it does not boast, it is not proud. It does not dishonor others, it is not self-seeking, it is not easily angered, it keeps no record of wrongs. Love does not delight in evil but rejoices with the truth. It always protects, always trusts, always hopes, always perseveres.
>
> I CORINTHIANS 13:4-7

In his book *The Magnificent Defeat*, theologian Frederick Buechner provides this perspective:

> The love for equals is a human thing—of friend for friend, brother for brother. It is to love what is loving and lovely. The world smiles. The love for the less fortunate is a beautiful thing—the love for those who suffer, for those who are poor, the sick, the failures, the unlovely. This is compassion, and it touches the heart of the world. The love for the more fortunate is a rare thing—to love those who succeed where we fail, to rejoice without envy with those who rejoice, the love of the poor for the rich, of the black man for the white man. The world is always bewildered by its saints. And then there is the love for

the enemy—love for the one who does not love you but mocks, threatens, and inflicts pain. The tortured's love for the torturer. This is God's love. It conquers the world.

It may be helpful to think about the five ways Buechner breaks down loving our neighbors. Loving our neighbors means loving those who are lovable, those who are like me, those less fortunate than I am, those more fortunate than I am, and also my enemies.

Let's face it—loving those who are lovable or who are like us can be much easier than loving someone different from us. I confess that my lifestyle insulates me from the poor and desperate. But rather than absolving me, God calls me to deliberately put myself in settings, neighborhoods, or social gatherings where I can get to know and love those who are not like me.

I am sad to admit that I am more prone to judge, avoid, or ignore people less fortunate than I am. But Jesus challenges me to be generous with my time and resources to those in need—whether this is a person who is lacking basic necessities or a person who has plenty but is spiritually bankrupt. As followers of Jesus, we are called to love people across every economic, spiritual, and ethnic spectrum.

Loving people more fortunate than we are is not easy either. How can we love the person who was promoted when we were overlooked; the person who is healthy when we are struggling with chronic pain; the person who scored higher than we did on the exam; or the person who has the newest clothing, technological device, or electronic gadget? How can we love people who look as if they have it all, and love them without judgment or critique? Only with God's help will you and I be able to celebrate their good fortune without envy, jealousy, malice, or ulterior motive.

Finally comes the most challenging and courageous love of all: loving your enemies. Picture Jesus speaking to the crowd: "Love your enemies, do good to those who hate you, bless those who curse you, pray for those who mistreat you" (Luke 6:27-28). Are you kidding me? Jesus is asking us to love the people who do us harm? This command seems impossible to practice. Yet history records many stories of Jesus' followers making the sacrifice to obey this teaching—martyrs through the centuries, Holocaust prisoners, underground church pastors in China, Muslim converts to Christ, and many others with less dramatic examples of this self-sacrificial love. Author and speaker Bob Goff encourages us to "love everybody always. Start with the ones you don't get." That's a less intimidating way to think about loving our enemies. Who are the people you just don't get? This is an easier place to begin.

Pastor Francis Chan challenges us: "There has to be more to our faith than friendliness, politeness, and even kindness. . . . True faith is loving a person after he has hurt you."[6]

Consider the story of Charles Carl Roberts IV. He was a milk truck driver who in October 2006 tied up and shot ten Amish schoolgirls between the ages of six and fourteen in their Pennsylvania classroom, killing five of them before turning the gun on himself. Shortly after the massacre, the same Amish community donated money to the gunman's widow and said they wanted to forgive him. To the watching world, this kind of love elicits questions, curiosity, and amazement. It demands an explanation.

Most of us don't directly experience dramatic scenarios of tragedy and evil. But we do experience conflict and internal resistance when we engage in conversation with people whose beliefs or worldviews are in opposition to ours, especially if they are hostile to our views. We have a simple choice to make in these interactions. We can choose to love people with differing opinions, listen to them, and seek to understand—or we can devalue them, creating an enemy. Gabe Lyons states it clearly: "Followers of Christ in a pluralistic society must be willing and able to engage those they disagree with in constructive conversations. . . . How can we love someone we don't know or understand?"[7]

It is only by God's love filling us and enabling us that we will be able to freely love our peer neighbor, our less fortunate neighbor, our more fortunate neighbor, and our adversarial neighbor. But by this love, we will distinguish ourselves as followers of Jesus who live counter to the cultural norm.

Love the Hurting

Finally, we can't talk about love without talking about suffering. Love means being present for people who are hurting. Lurking under the surface of many people's veneer are grief, pain, and heartache. Jesus experienced sadness, sorrow, pain, and suffering. He chose to come down from heaven to be with us in our broken world as "Immanuel, which means 'God is with us'" (Matthew 1:23, NLT). Jesus also entered into these emotions when other people experienced them.

The apostle Paul reminds us to "rejoice with those who rejoice; mourn with those who mourn" (Romans 12:15). Jesus mourned with those who mourn, modeling a loving response to grief. For example, when Jesus arrived at Bethany after his friend Lazarus had died, he was deeply moved in spirit and troubled when he saw Mary and her friends weeping. Then, in grief himself, he wept. As author Peter Kreeft puts it:

> He didn't give us a placebo or a pill or good advice. He
> gave us himself. He came. He entered space and time
> and suffering. He came, like a lover. Love seeks above
> all intimacy, presence, togetherness. . . . Remove Jesus
> and the knowledge of God becomes questionable. If the
> knowledge of God is questionable, trusting this unknown
> God becomes questionable. . . . Suffering is the evidence
> against God, the reason not to trust him. Jesus is the
> evidence for God, the reason to trust him.[8]

I (Crilly) still remember the people who came to the memorial service and hugged me and shed tears with me when I lost a good friend in a tragic motorcycle accident in 2003. I remember my friend Victor, who sat at the back of the room for hours not saying anything, just wanting me to know that he was present. Showing up for the hurting is powerfully healing. As followers of Christ, we can be there for hurting people.

Grief, disappointment, and trauma can all be profoundly disorienting, numbing a person's consciousness and clouding his or her ability to think clearly. In his helpful book *When the Bottom Drops Out*,[9] pastor Rob Bugh speaks personally about the grief he experienced in the illness and death of his wife, Carol. Pastor Bugh shares that the "practical ministries" extended to him were of incredible value. Hurt shuts down people's ability to cope. Forgetful, preoccupied, and reeling amid the strain of the emotional situation, hurting people need practical help—Jesus with dirty feet.[10] "My friend Steve cut my grass week after week. Dan kept our older cars and anything mechanical running. Chuck and his wife, Pat, prayed and prayed. . . . Jeff basically ran our house, keeping track of our kids and paying all our bills."[11]

Like Jesus, we can be bearers of hope to the hurting. We can recognize our own feelings of discomfort, helplessness, and vulnerability in these situations and choose to push past them in love. We can run toward hurting people, not away from them.

Time does not heal all wounds. There are hurts that a person may never get over. And God chooses to use us, his people, as the primary agents to minister to hurting people. Coming alongside those who are hurting can be one of the most significant things you will ever do.

Here are five practices that will help you love a person struggling through a difficult time in life—experiencing grief, divorce, job loss, chronic or terminal illness, or some other life crisis.

1. DON'T SPEAK, JUST LISTEN.

Silence dignifies a person's hurt because sometimes pain is too deep for words. This is the ministry of presence, being with someone listening a lot, speaking a little, and bringing the presence of Christ in you alongside the person who is in pain.

When Job suffered a succession of disasters, his friends came and sat with him in silence. "Then they sat on the ground with him for seven days and seven nights. No one said a word to him, because they saw how great his suffering was" (Job 2:13). Ancient Jewish tradition refers to this act of mourning as "sitting shiva." True compassion is expressed through presence, silence, and human companionship.

When you are empathetic, you identify with the other person, coming alongside him or her gently and quietly. Studies have concluded that the two most helpful listening behaviors when interacting with the bereaved are (1) providing the opportunity for them to vent and (2) just being there.[12]

2. WHEN YOU DO SPEAK, USE GENTLE, SENSITIVE WORDS.

Speak from your heart, not from your head—don't try to offer nuggets of wisdom. One of the best things you can say to someone who is struggling is simply "I'm sorry." Ask good questions; don't offer trite answers. Hurting people need you to acknowledge that their pain is real, giving them permission to grieve and allowing them to move forward with healing. Follow the wisdom from Proverbs 25:11: "A word fitly spoken is like apples of gold in a setting of silver" (esv). "Fitly spoken" words are gentle, informed, timely, and appropriate. Measure your words and avoid careless, inappropriate comments or questions.

Here are some useful guidelines for when you do feel that it is right to speak:

- Use phrases like "I don't know what to say," "I can't imagine how difficult this is," or "This must be awful."

- Do not offer platitudes (examples: "You have so much to be thankful for" or "It's time for you to move on").
- Don't minimize the problem (examples: "You can always have another one" or "You had many good years together").
- Do not give unsolicited advice (examples: "Now that your husband is gone, you should consider getting a dog" or "In ten years you will not even remember this").
- Do not claim to know how the person feels.[13]

3. AVOID THEOLOGICAL PRONOUNCEMENTS.

Be very careful about what spiritual words you say. Do not offer pat Christian answers to a tragedy ("God needed him more than you did" or "He's in a better place now"). Hold on to impressions from God loosely ("God told me that . . .") and let time prove them right or wrong. Statements that may be true can come across as heartless, thoughtless, and trite in tragic circumstances. (Ever heard someone quote, "God works all things together for good" in the midst of suffering?) A time will come when theological truth from Scripture may bring comfort, but not when the pain is intense. And even when sharing Scripture becomes appropriate, be sure that's not all that you say or do.

4. SHOW UP!

Pastor Bugh encourages us to "err on the side of involvement for the hurting." Show up for them again and again and again. If you don't show up, they will never know you care. "Love never gives up"—it shows up. "It never loses faith"—it gives faith. "Love . . . is always hopeful and endures through every circumstance" (1 Corinthians 13:7, NLT).

Love by going to the funeral home and sitting quietly in support. Love by visiting the hospital and offering a prayer. Love by stopping by the house and providing a meal or offering to watch the kids. Love by dropping by the office and expressing your concern.

By showing up in physical and practical ways, we incarnate Christ's love to hurting people, helping to heal their pain and ease their burden in Christ's name. Your quiet and consistent witness will speak volumes about his love to those who are seeking God and longing for his comfort.

6. LOOK TO JESUS.

We can have faith in God's goodness when our hurting friends cannot. We can bring hope to them when they feel hopeless. We can bring hurting people to Jesus figuratively just as the friends of the paralyzed man in Luke 5:17-20 did literally. In that remarkable story, "when Jesus saw [the friends'] faith" he forgave and healed the paralyzed man. By our presence, kindness, and careful words, we get the privilege of ministering to hurting people and escorting them to Jesus' care.

As Hebrews 12:1-2 says, "Let us . . . [fix] our eyes on Jesus, the pioneer and perfecter of faith." We first must look to Jesus ourselves, trusting that he is capable to restore the hurting and that he "is close to the brokenhearted and saves those who are crushed in spirit" (Psalm 34:18). Pastor Bugh tells us, "Gently remind yourself and others of God's sovereignty . . . as a balm to heal the wounded. Pray and ask the Holy Spirit to help you know when to remind people of these truths."[14] You can direct your thoughts and theirs to Jesus by offering to pray that they would be able to sense God's nearness.

Grief is inevitable in this fallen world filled with pain and loss. Often, we want to push it to the fringes. We tend to avoid it as much as possible. Yet grief properly expressed is good and necessary. Pain, suffering, grief—these are probably the most common of human experiences. Like Jesus, we can show love in practical and profound ways to hurting people and introduce them to his love as we walk with them.

God loves people more than we can fathom. He initiates a relationship with us as a model for us to follow. When we begin to grasp his purposeful, passionate, sacrificial love for us, this understanding moves us to intentionally seek out people far from God and to let them experience his love through us. When Jesus was asked to describe the greatest commandment, he made it clear that the core value is love:

> Jesus replied, "'Love the Lord your God with all your heart and with all your soul and with all your mind.' This is the first and greatest commandment. And the second is like it: 'Love your neighbor as yourself.'"
>
> MATTHEW 22:37-39

Although the Great Commandment is not normally considered to be related to evangelism and the Great Commission, it is the starting point for sharing the good news about Jesus. In fact, loving God and loving others will galvanize our involvement in the Great Commission. If we strive to love others as God loves us, we can begin to build trusting friendships and to earn the right to engage in spiritual conversations with people outside of our churches. God invites ordinary men and women in their everyday lives to make an extraordinary impact with an extraordinary message. What's the message? God extravagantly loves *all* people. Do we?

Discover

1. How have you viewed the relationship between the Great Commandment (to love God and love others) and the Great Commission (to go and make disciples)? What new insights do you have now?

2. Now that you've been reminded of God's love for you, what would you like to change in your life to make loving God and loving others a higher priority?

Practice

1. Think of people in your life who are like you, who are less fortunate than you, who are more fortunate than you, and who are more like enemies. Plan to do something this week that will bless (not judge) a person from each of these categories.

2. Think about someone you know (maybe from the list you developed in chapter 1) who is hurting right now. Consider how you could reach out to that person using one of the five practical ways described in this chapter.

CHAPTER 8

The Art of Welcoming

Now the tax collectors and sinners were all gathering around
to hear Jesus. But the Pharisees and the teachers of the law
muttered, "This man welcomes sinners and eats with them."

LUKE 15:1-2

Hospitality, therefore, means primarily the creation of a free space
where the stranger can enter and become a friend instead of an enemy.

HENRI NOUWEN

AS MY WIFE AND I (CRILLY) prepared to buy our first home, we
prayed that God would place us in a neighborhood where we could
intentionally love our neighbors like Jesus. The initial awkwardness of being the "new people on the block" soon gave way to
friendly connections, but we yearned to build deeper community.
We prayed for our neighborhood and wanted to extend Jesus' love
to those who lived around us.

One day, I surprised my next-door neighbor by mowing his
front lawn. It only took me a couple of extra minutes, but when he
and his wife noticed, you would have thought I had rescued their
kids from a burning building. The whole neighborhood buzzed
with gossip about the "new guy" who mowed the neighbor's lawn.
Shortly after, my neighbor across the street ribbed me one Saturday
afternoon by calling, "Hey, why don't you mow my grass too?" So

I did! Within a year, the couple next door asked us to be the god-parents of their fourth child.

When Danielle and I moved in, the neighborhood already had some connection points in place, such as the summer block party and a women's book group. But to extend our own ties in the neighborhood, we came up with the idea of hosting an open house. Partnering with some friends who also lived in the area, we invited everyone in the neighborhood to come over for a few hours late on a Sunday afternoon. We made a pot of chili and encouraged everyone to bring some food to share. We paid some local high school students to care for the children and ordered some pizza for them too.

We had no agenda except to welcome and love our neighbors. And that's what we did! We made the open house a once-a-month event, calling it Second Sunday so folks would remember which Sunday to plan on coming over. Clever, huh? By staying regularly connected with the people in our proximity, we noticed more ways to be intentionally involved with their lives and extend Christ's love in tangible ways.

Danielle and I decided to give our small Cape Cod home a nickname: "The Cape of Good Hope." This name reminded us of our vision to create a safe, welcoming environment where people would find hope. We wanted our home to be a place where anyone could explore matters of faith openly in the company of true friends. We have been fortunate to experience this, as neighbors have confided in us about their family difficulties, marriage struggles, and spiritual challenges. Danielle and I pray nearly every day that our neighbors would experience the love and grace of Jesus.

We try to extend welcome beyond the limits of our physical habitat and cultivate community wherever we go. This will look different for each of us based on our personalities and preferences. Your approach may be very different than mine. Some folks welcome by intentionally placing a candy jar at their desk to bring more opportunities to connect with coworkers. Some folks take welcoming mobile and walk the dog to connect with their neighbors. Some folks look for opportunities to include others in things they are already doing—like a fantasy football league, an evening at the fire pit, a woodworking hobby, a reading group, or a fitness activity. Some folks love hosting book clubs and parties. Welcoming is not just about inviting; it's about bringing a warm, appealing presence to others wherever you are. It is a way of living.

It is hard to overstate the impact that a genuinely warm welcome can have in a person's life. Welcoming someone brings him or her from being a vulnerable outsider to being connected with others. When you include someone, you lay the initial groundwork that will help a relationship to thrive. Conversely, by not including someone, you shut down his or her willingness to engage relationally. Welcoming provides a safe environment where wrestling with matters of faith for more than just one quick conversation is acceptable and where dealing with the hardships of life without being judged is allowed. It is what everyone desperately needs as they make their way toward faith.

Welcoming is not the same as entertaining in your home. It's opening your heart and creating a safe place of love and acceptance wherever you may be. One of the most practical ways to step into another person's world—and to make him or her feel comfortable enough to step into yours—is simply to offer the gift of attentiveness.

In our "two-screen" culture, giving our attention to only one thing at a time is rare; we've allowed multitasking to become normal. But people don't feel welcomed if we are checking our mobile devices, allowing our minds to wander, or even just thinking about what we're going to say next. And the opposite also is true: If we stop what we're doing to listen and give our full attention, people will feel welcomed by us. When you set aside your agenda to focus on others, you communicate that you value them and that you're glad to spend time with them.

Even a casual reading of the Gospels shows how often Jesus gave individuals his full attention. For example, in John 4 we read the story of Jesus' meeting with the Samaritan woman who came to the well to draw water. Although Jesus was a visitor in the Samaritan woman's neighborhood, we see him deliberately creating a safe environment for spiritual conversation through his attentiveness.

We often think of "welcoming" as inviting people into our home, our church, our turf—asking them to come to us. Jesus turned that upside down by bringing that welcoming space into the woman's environment—he went to her. I'm fascinated by the way the story begins in verse 4: "Now he *had* to go through Samaria" (emphasis added). Jesus had Samaria on his mind. Though the Jewish culture shunned Samaritans and pious Jews purposefully avoided Samaria when traveling from northern Israel to Jerusalem, Jesus determined to go through this region. What's more, Jesus stayed two days in the town of Sychar itself. His heart was open to the townspeople as he accepted their hospitality.

Welcoming is simply the act of showing unconditional acceptance to people without any expectations of reciprocation. When you welcome people into your life and activities, you are reflecting Christ's love and acceptance. When people experience the warmth of your welcome, they are drawn to it, as they would be to a light in the darkness or a fire on a chilly night. When they have a taste, like a sample of savory food, they want more. This is an action that speaks to any culture and across any language, race, or religious divide. In this way, we are following Jesus' instruction in Matthew 5 to be light and salt to people we know.

How about you? Have you ever had someone in your life who made you feel welcome no matter where you were? Can you think of ways you might extend welcome to those around you? Following this practice of Jesus is especially valuable for creating a safe place to allow people to be themselves, and ask questions about matters of faith.

God Welcomes Us

Our God is a welcoming God, constantly pursuing, seeking, and inviting people into his loving community. By practicing the Art of Welcoming, we can extend God's welcome to others so they feel invited into friendship with him. Examples of God's abundant welcome flow throughout Scripture. From the Creator's lavish preparation of the Garden of Eden for Adam and Eve, to the Shepherd's inviting presence in Psalm 23, to the Savior's open-armed readiness to gather in the excluded, God takes the initiative to draw people near. His ultimate welcome, of course, came by means of his sacrifice on the cross, so that we could come into relationship with him even though we had gone our own way.

Luke 15:1-2 reveals a fascinating scene: "Now the tax collectors and sinners were all gathering around to hear Jesus. But the Pharisees and the teachers of the law muttered, 'This man welcomes sinners and eats with them.'" In response to the Pharisees' criticism and in defense of his relentless welcome, Jesus told three stories, culminating in the powerful parable of the prodigal son. In each story something is lost, and first its absence is recognized and then an urgent search follows. In each story something is found, and first a joyous reunion and then a wild celebration follows.

In the prodigal son story, a young man had demanded his inheritance and had become a disgrace, squandering the entire amount. Yet when he came to his senses, he found his father waiting for him:

> While he was still a long way off, his father saw him and was filled with compassion for him; he ran to his son, threw his arms around him and kissed him.

The son said to him, "Father, I have sinned against heaven and against you. I am no longer worthy to be called your son."

But the father said to his servants, "Quick! Bring the best robe and put it on him. Put a ring on his finger and sandals on his feet. Bring the fattened calf and kill it. Let's have a feast and celebrate. For this son of mine was dead and is alive again; he was lost and is found." So they began to celebrate.

LUKE 15:20-24

The robe, ring, sandals, and feast all indicated the father's acceptance and his restoration of the son's position. We can imagine that the robe was a long robe of distinction, the ring was a signet ring of authority, the sandals represented sonship (slaves went barefoot), and the fattened calf indicated the momentous occasion—all part of the father's abundant welcome. But the story was not complete. In a final clever plot twist to address the Pharisees' accusation— that he was welcoming sinners—Jesus added intrigue to the parable by including a character who does not represent the heart of the father. The older son's attitude was not at all welcoming (see 15:26- 32). He did not receive his brother back but instead resented him. Jesus was connecting the Pharisees' behavior (15:1-2) with the older son's and was contrasting it to the father's welcoming response. The Pharisees resented that Jesus welcomed sinners, and they didn't realize that his approach, not theirs, reflected God's character.

Aspects of Welcoming

God the Father extends a welcome to everyone. When we are willing to welcome like the Father, we reflect his unconditional acceptance. The challenge we face is in knowing *how* to welcome others, communicating genuine acceptance while expecting nothing in return. Welcoming may come naturally to some people based on their personality or the home they grew up in, but for most people it requires practice and intentionality. Some key, common "ingredients" that create a welcoming environment might include honesty, authenticity, common interests, a flexible plan, food that is generously shared, good conversation, genuine listening, empathy, fun, and humor. However, even with the best of these ingredients, the foundation of welcoming into community is the acceptance of the risk to open up our hearts.

How can you become one of those people who provides the kind of full welcome we all desire in new situations? To keep it simple, consider welcoming as something that happens best when you are keenly aware of maximizing four welcoming aspects—your *face*, your *space*, your *place*, and your *grace*. Let's briefly unpack each one.

1. YOUR FACE

Welcoming starts with your facial expression. Have you ever heard the sarcastic comment, "If you are so happy to see me, why haven't you told your face?" Your face is the first indicator of a welcoming spirit. It is the first impression people receive when they meet you. A smile and warm eye contact go a long way toward helping someone feel welcomed. When this is the way you greet the people you frequently encounter, they will begin to remember your face. Facial recognition lays the groundwork for the connection to deepen. In conjunction with your facial expression, your body language also supports or contradicts how welcoming you are. Crossed arms or a tense posture can convey that you don't have time for others right now, while a relaxed, open stance is more inviting.

2. YOUR SPACE

This is the impression of openness you express to others. Do you make people feel at ease? Do they feel you are happy to see them and eager to spend time with them? To limit relational awkwardness and build rapport, look for common ground, such as stage of life, hobbies, or enthusiasm for a sports team or a musical group. Asking open-ended questions encourages people to share their stories. In a casual group setting, look for ways to connect people with each other. Each year at our neighborhood St. Patrick's Day party, we pack the house, and when each guest enters, I interrupt the whole group and publicly announce the new arrival. The whole room full of people greets them with a cheer! The person immediately feels welcomed, valued, and personally connected to everyone. How can you, in your own way as an introvert or extrovert, create a welcome space for people to be generously received?

3. YOUR PLACE

This is the physical environment—your home, office, or car, for example—where you welcome others, and the condition of the space matters. I'm not talking about the area being clean but about it seeming warm and inviting. Whether you are in your living room, kitchen, dorm, coffee shop, or local park, think through what will help the person you're connecting with feel most welcome. When you provide a comfortable place, people feel more relaxed and accepted. Do the physical spaces that you control provide a way for people to feel instantly comfortable and welcomed? For example, think of how "white-glove" neatness, an orderly space, or a more casual setting might impact your ability to welcome someone. When is the television or music distracting, or when can it help break the ice? How can sharing food and drink with others help build community?

4. YOUR GRACE

Most people long to go beyond relational superficiality and to find a person who is safe, who accepts them as they are, and who will allow them to process the significant questions of life without expecting anything in return. It takes prayerful insight to foster vulnerability at an appropriate pace. As you get to know a person over time, be willing to ask questions that encourage deeper discussion. Keep it safe for people to share transparently by encouraging them rather than by giving advice or communicating a judgmental attitude. As you reflect Christ's welcome, model vulnerability, and show interest in meaningful conversation, people will pick up on your gracious offer. Relational grace characterizes a welcoming spirit willing to discuss difficult questions, share hard topics, avoid trite responses, and explore answers together.

Welcoming grace is willing to walk alongside others, admit that you don't have all the answers, and allow life and faith to be messy and mysterious. This aspect of welcoming leads you to be intentional about taking relationships deeper, allowing conversations about God to occur naturally.

Prayer is important in each aspect of welcoming, but especially here. When inviting someone to spend time with you, pray before, after, and during your time with them (not necessarily out loud with people who aren't used to that). While you're together, you can silently ask God for wisdom to deepen the conversation as well as for discernment about what needs to be said and what needs to be left unsaid for now.

How's your grace factor? Do you extend grace freely and generously, allowing people the open space to discover truth for themselves with the work of the Spirit?

Of these four aspects of welcoming, only one is restricted to a place. The others we carry with us. In other words, we can bring a welcoming space with us wherever we go. That's good, because according to the US Bureau of Labor Statistics, the average American between the ages of twenty-five and fifty-four spends over 50 percent of his or her waking hours at work.[1] So the place for most of us to begin creating a more welcoming space may be at work, where we spend so much of our time.

For some of my (Crilly's) career in the marketplace, I worked in the construction contracting field, specifically in high-voltage electric utility work. The job was fast paced and high risk, and an error could get someone seriously injured or killed. If an incident on the power lines interrupted electricity, people would be without power, which is disruptive and frustrating. As a result, workdays were often quite hectic and stressful. My typical day was filled with frequent interruptions as my project managers, general foremen, project accountant, and other colleagues regularly stopped by my office to discuss issues and ask questions. It was challenging to get my work done with so many distractions, but I am not proud of what I did to deter these frequent visitors.

To try to send the clear yet unspoken message "I'm busy; don't bother me," I positioned my desk so that my back was facing anyone who entered my office. After a while, I heard the Holy Spirit's insistent, convicting whisper asking whether this desk arrangement demonstrated the Father's welcoming heart. It took me a while to listen and obey, but I eventually rearranged my office. With the desk facing the door, I intentionally greeted folks who came by and tried to create a more inviting office space and posture.

Welcoming can be practiced everywhere. In our daily activities inside and outside work, we can choose to create patterns that allow us to get to know people. We can keep going back to the same stores or coffee shops so that we develop relationships with the people who spend a lot of time there. With our welcoming spirit, we can extend God's grace and love to others wherever we go. We've been graciously welcomed by God to be his children, and he wants us to extend that same welcome to others in our everyday lives—at the job site, on the train, at the office, in the yard, on the bus, in the store, at the laundromat, at a restaurant, and in our homes. We have countless opportunities each day to share a warm presence both with the people we know best and with those we don't know at all yet. However, we need to be aware of common obstacles to welcoming, or we will too easily fall into the pattern of an unwelcoming attitude in our lives.

Barriers to Welcoming

I don't aspire to be unfriendly or unwelcoming. Few people do. In fact, it would be a tragedy for Christians to be known as rude, cold, or unwelcoming. And yet, we don't always invite others in, particularly when those "others" are different from us. At the heart of it, most barriers to welcoming others are fear based. By identifying the barriers that keep us apart, maybe we can begin to overcome the fears that support them, allowing us to create an environment in which people feel welcomed. Let's take a look at five common barriers.

1. BUSYNESS

The words "I'm busy" are often code for "I'm important." How much of your busyness is driven by your desire for significance? Do you fear missing out on an opportunity, accomplishment, or experience? Busyness tends to push out the margin in our lives. Without margin, we may view people as interruptions. It will take humility and intentionality to slow down and make space to welcome others.

Take a good look at your schedule. To what have you said "yes" that is keeping you from taking time for people who need to know God's love? How much do you involve the Holy Spirit in decisions about what to commit to, and how much margin have you built into your schedule? What tasks can you delegate (or simply stop doing)? Are you willing to put aside your agenda to be interruptible or to intentionally choose activities where you will get to know people who believe differently?

2. SHALLOWNESS

Many of us have become accustomed to surface-level relationships, which are what we may experience in the workplace, at school, with our neighbors, and sometimes even among our friends. We may wish for deeper connections, but we're not sure how to get there. Perhaps because we've been burned before or because no one ever modeled authentic community for us, we skim the surface of relationships. Frankly, we lack relational depth ourselves—or we fear it—so we're unable or unwilling to show vulnerability, especially toward spiritually curious people.

What is a relational risk you can take to overcome this obstacle? Can you tell someone that you appreciate him or her? Share something that might be misunderstood? Share how you are feeling? Not everyone is ready to go deeper with you, so pray for opportunities to build safe relationships. The goal is to experience why relational risk taking is worth it.

3. COMPETITIVENESS

Like the other barriers to welcoming, competitiveness is often driven by fear. Afraid that we won't measure up, we adopt a win-or-lose mentality and try to beat or outsmart others in some way. We push people away instead of welcoming them in. Our competitiveness comes out in conversation with spiritual seekers when we think that because we know the truth, we are somehow better than they are. Competition and comparison destroy the potential for community and connection.

To remedy this inclination, be intentionally curious and open. You can learn something from people who believe differently from you. Consider the possibility that other people's questions or opinions might cause you to think more deeply and might help your faith grow. Before you even start a conversation, consciously choose to let go of the need to win. Ephesians 4:29 can serve as a key guide for us: "Do not let any unwholesome talk come out of your mouths, but only what is helpful for building others up according to their needs, that it may benefit those who listen."

4. DEFENSIVENESS

When we feel defensive, we typically don't engage in open dialogue. Around people who believe differently, we may fear they will judge us, misunderstand us, or look down on us for our faith. When we lack a firm foundation of identity in Christ, we'll be vulnerable to defensiveness, and it will push people away. To overcome this obstacle, relax! Trust in God and develop *your* relationship with him. Intentionally spend time with people who are not followers of Jesus to get past the stereotypes you have. They are not "out to get you" but are full of fears and doubts—just as you are. Take yourself less seriously. You don't have to prove anything.

5. SELFISHNESS

The default mode of every human being is to ask, "What's in it for me?" We fear that God is not on our side (or worse, not in control), so we take things into our own hands, looking out for ourselves. We often choose relationships based on what we can get, rather than what we can give. If we think engaging with people who believe differently is too much work, we won't do it. Perhaps we're afraid that if we spend time and energy welcoming others, we'll miss out on good things for ourselves. But as people who are loved by God, we're called to serve others and show them that same love.

The antidote to selfishness is to serve others. Here's a little-known secret about serving selflessly: It brings joy! When you discover an opportunity to serve someone, do it.

Accept People Where They Are

When we're talking to people engaged in behaviors we find particularly offensive, it is tempting to focus on their lifestyle choices. Even though we may not appear to do this outwardly, we may inwardly harbor judgments about them and even hold them in contempt. When we do this, we set up barriers that keep us from welcoming. By judging people (even subtly), we play God. By not accepting where people are, we're also communicating that we don't trust God to get them where he wants them to go.

Returning to Jesus' conversation with the woman at the well (John 4), we see a great example of how Jesus interacted with someone full of moral failures without getting hung up on them. Initially, Jesus found a point of common interest—water—and then responded casually to the woman's questions in the conversation that unfolded. By the time he brought up her current sinful lifestyle, he did so with grace, also allowing her to change the subject to a topic that she found more comfortable.

For us, one of the keys to avoid judging people is to take the time to listen. Once we hear more of a person's story and situation, it becomes easier to be empathetic. The simple phrase "Tell me more about that" creates space for a person to feel welcomed and accepted. When you open up your heart to someone who believes differently, you become an ally and not an adversary, providing a safe place to honestly explore matters of life and faith.

For several years, my (Mary's) husband, Paul, headed up an airplane manufacturing company in the Pacific Northwest that was building a bush aircraft for mission and commercial applications. Most of the employees and contractors also had a strong faith in Christ.

On one occasion, we invited an out-of-town consultant and his wife over for dinner. We'd assumed that they were Bible-believing Christians, but halfway through the meal it came out that they were actually Jehovah's Witnesses. My discovery that our core beliefs about Jesus were different made it difficult for me to know how to relate to this couple, and I found myself tempted to judge them for having beliefs that didn't line up with the Bible and orthodox Christianity. I asked God to show me how to move forward in the evening, given what I now knew. He guided me to start asking questions about the area that I knew must be important to them and was also important to me: witnessing.

Because neighborhood witness is mandatory for all Jehovah's Witnesses, I was able to focus my queries on *their* experiences and ask how easy or difficult sharing their faith was for them. Hearing their views and struggles related to that core requirement of their faith was a great learning experience, and I tried to put myself in their shoes. I asked God to show me how to communicate grace and welcome to my guests as we moved forward in the evening.

While they have different beliefs than I, their religion takes sharing their faith more seriously than many of my fellow Christ followers. I admired their commitment and courage. I found myself empathizing with their personal witness challenges as we started to discuss more tender subjects about what they believed. By the time the husband and wife left that night, I had a genuine love for both of them and prayed in the upcoming months that they would know the full truth about Jesus.

In speaking of welcoming as hospitality, Henri Nouwen, internationally renowned priest, professor, and beloved pastor, offers helpful insight and inspiration:

> In our world full of strangers, estranged from their own past, culture and country, from their neighbors, friends and family, from their deepest self and their God, we witness a painful search for a hospitable place where life can be lived without fear and where community can be found. . . . Hospitality, therefore, means primarily the creation of a free space where the stranger can enter and become a friend instead of an enemy.[2]

When you welcome people who believe differently rather than shunning them, your winsome friendship as a follower of Jesus creates a place where God can work to bring about eternal life change. Creating that kind of environment is a challenge—how easy it is for defenses to go up when worldviews clash! But Jesus modeled the value of welcoming people together in community, to experience his care and interact with his words together. As he rubbed shoulders with people from all walks of life and varied spiritual backgrounds, he was intent on keeping the environment around him open to people with baggage of all kinds.

Think of a "Samaritan" in your life. How have you considered yourself superior to this person (morally, aesthetically, vocationally, socioeconomically, racially) in your heart or with your words? I encourage you to take a moment right now to confess and surrender your conclusions and judgments to God, asking him to forgive you for not loving and welcoming this person, and to replace your criticism with love and acceptance. Ask God to reveal this person's good attributes to you and to reveal Jesus to him or her through your actions.

God Is Responsible for the Results

We all long for places that feel like home even if they're not. In those places, we experience what it means to be valued, to be known, and to be loved. Whether you have welcomed someone by inviting her to eat a meal with you, by getting into an informal conversation in the break room at work, or by gladly entering his home, the spiritual result of your interaction must be left in God's hands.

Sometimes just being together and building a friendship has a greater net effect than anything you might say about the Bible or your relationship with Christ. We are not suggesting that sharing the truths of the Bible and being upfront about your personal faith are not important. However, without a welcoming environment people will not as easily be able to receive those words. Your job is to create a safe space to allow others to honestly explore matters of faith with you, as a true friend. Where it goes from there is ultimately between them and God.

Discover

1. How has Jesus extended his welcome to you in tangible ways? What impact has this had on your life?

2. What simple, doable welcoming practice fits your personality? How can you incorporate that into your everyday life?

Practice

1. In the next few days, practice welcoming through one of the four aspects: your face, your space, your place, and your grace.

2. Review the list of people you developed in chapter 1 and choose someone from it who is different from you. How have you considered yourself superior to this person in your heart or with your words? Take a moment to surrender your conclusions to God, asking him to forgive you and to show you how you can be more welcoming. Act on that insight and pray for that person in the upcoming weeks.

PART III

Keeping It Going

THE FINAL THREE Arts of Spiritual Conversations are called *Keeping It Going* because they help us to maintain ongoing faith-based discussions with a small-group community. We're building on the relationships we've established through consistently practicing the first six Arts and moving into regular conversations about spiritual topics.

To review, the first three practices—Noticing, Praying, Listening—are *Getting Ready* Arts, with no expectation for you to say anything. The next three Arts, called *Getting Started*—Asking Questions, Loving, and Welcoming—are interactive Arts to help you initiate a meaningful conversation. These first six Arts can be exercised well with just one other person.

The Arts for *Keeping It Going* transition from primarily one-on-one spiritual conversations to arts that can keep the conversation fresh on an ongoing basis in one-on-one interactions or in a small-group community. They include the Arts of Facilitating, Serving Together, and Sharing.

CHAPTER 9

The Art of Facilitating

And Jesus turned and saw them following, and said to them,
"What do you seek?" They said to Him, "Rabbi . . . where are
You staying?" He said to them, "Come, and you will see."
JOHN 1:38-39, NASB

One who learns through the process of honest questioning, objective
thinking, and respectful challenging is more apt to know in the end
what is really true. And he will also know "why" he believes it.
RANDALL ARTHUR

MY (MARY'S) FRIEND BILL loved leading his small group, which
was made up of several couples from his church. Leading gave him
opportunities to teach others what he was studying in his Sunday
school Bible class, and he learned a lot by preparing for his regular
presentation to the group. Meetings didn't include much dynamic
discussion or diversity of opinion. It wasn't necessary with Bill in
the room; he had almost any answer that people needed. The other
group members didn't always agree with Bill or get to talk much,
but he made it so clear that he was the expert that they were afraid
to speak up with a differing opinion.

Then one day Bill was sick with the flu, and his wife, Sally,
volunteered to lead the group in his place. Sally didn't consider
herself a Bible expert, but she knew how to draw people out. She
brought a discussion guide that asked good questions about the

Bible passage. She made sure everyone got a chance to talk and share their perspective, even if it didn't agree with hers or others' in the group. By the end of the meeting, the group had experienced more laughter and lively discussion than on most evenings. Everyone asked whether Sally would mind leading more often. They couldn't quite put their finger on how her leadership was different from Bill's, but they knew they liked it and wanted more.

Flipped

A relatively recent phenomenon in education is called the *flipped classroom*. A traditional classroom approach involves listening to lectures and taking tests in the classroom, while problem solving and interacting with the concepts you are learning both occur at home. A flipped classroom is a reversed instructional model where students learn content at home, watching online video lectures about the subject, and then do "homework" in class, with teachers and students discussing questions and solving problems in their prime time together. Relational interaction between students and teachers significantly increases, and teacher interaction with students is more personalized. The role of the teacher is to *guide* or *facilitate* learning, rather than only to deliver content in a lecture.

Greg Green, the principal of Clintondale High School in Clinton Township, Michigan, a financially challenged school near Detroit, had seen his school's failure rates—the percentage of students failing each class—compete for the highest in the country year after year. His staff thought the situation was hopeless, given no clear solution from the experts and inadequate funding available to address problems. Yet after only eighteen months of "flipping" classrooms at Clintondale, discipline problems decreased dramatically, the English failure rate decreased from 52 percent to 19 percent, the math failure rate decreased from 44 percent to 13 percent, and the science failure rate decreased from 41 percent to

19 percent.[1] A complete paradigm shift had been needed, and it worked at almost no new expense to the school! Thanks to Internet and video technology, students watched lectures outside of class and then worked closely with their teachers and fellow classmates at school to discuss and problem-solve.

With those impressive results in such a short period of time, educators all over the world began watching what was happening at Clintondale and wondering what it could mean for them. Those involved in the flipped-classroom movement say that it changes the teacher's role from a "sage on the stage" to a "guide on the side."

I can't help but wonder what relevance this might have to the church. Do any aspects of how the church functions need to be flipped? A fascinating article titled "Flipping the 40-Minute Sermon" appeared in the May 2013 issue of *Christianity Today*. Contributing writer Karen E. Yates points out that we are all so busy with jobs, parenting, and extracurricular activities that we hardly have time for each other, resulting in crowded loneliness. Christians come to church to connect with God and one another, and yet most Sunday church services rarely give them a chance to relate much.

Yates cites an expert and pioneer on interactive learning, Harvard Professor Eric Mazur, who believes that the greatest learning occurs when people engage in dialogue about a topic with their peers. Yates points out that evolving academic structures could have big implications for the church at large. Even though instructional teaching holds an important place in the church, she doesn't think the forty-minute sermon given by the pastor is what makes the church the church. Rather, it's the interaction of the congregation and the formation of community around the Word of God that are most important. She writes, "When we hear a lecture we receive information into our short-term memory, but to learn, we also need to assimilate the information we've received; meaning, we need to engage and apply the information."[2] Should we incorporate more opportunities to interact with one another during the Sunday service to address our need for community and to help us better engage with what we're learning?

Scottish theologian William Barclay pointed out that "it is only when truth is self-discovered that it is appropriated. When a man is simply told the truth it remains external to him and he can quite easily forget it. When he is led to discover the truth for himself, it becomes an integral part of him and he never forgets it."[3]

The Unit of Transformation

If it is true that people learn best through facilitated discussion rather than a lecture format, then we must consider how we can implement more strategies where people can seek God in small-group communities led by facilitators rather than experts. As the church becomes more intentional about forming communities to interact with one another not only at church but also where people live, work, and play, the Art of Facilitating becomes an important practice to cultivate. We will need hundreds of thousands of *initiators* who can form safe places where ongoing spiritual conversations can flourish.

Peter Block, author of *Community: The Structure of Belonging*, calls a small group the ideal "unit of transformation." While his book is written for a secular audience, its discoveries can be applied to any small-group community. He explains why it is worth investing in authentic transformative communities:

The small group is the structure that allows every voice to be heard. It is in groups of 3 to 12 that intimacy is created. This intimate conversation makes the process personal. It provides the structure where people overcome isolation and where the experience of belonging is created. . . .

In the small group discussion we discover that our

own concerns are more universal than we imagined. This discovery that we are not alone, that others can at least understand what is on our mind, if not agree with us, is what creates the feeling of belonging. . . .

The power of the small group cannot be overemphasized. Something almost mystical, certainly mysterious, occurs when citizens sit in a small group, for they often become more authentic and personal with each other there than in other settings.[4]

Block identifies questions as the essential tools of engagement because questions create the space for something new to emerge. They promote freedom of expression. On the other hand, ready-made answers by an expert in the group can shut down the discussion and the future possibilities of what could be said. While good questions are important for dynamic discussion in one-on-one conversations, they are *critical* in small groups.

Guide on the Side

As we discussed in chapter 1, there are two general approaches to learning: the *telling* approach and the *asking* approach. In the telling approach, sometimes referred to as didactic or *deductive* learning, one individual acts as the expert, telling listeners what he or she has learned about a selected topic. In this approach, the listeners are passive receivers of information, and the teacher is the active giver of information.

In the asking or *inductive* approach, facilitators create an environment in which the participants can all be active discoverers. The facilitator is a guide, not a teacher or information dispenser. The definition of *facilitate* is "to make easier or less difficult" or "to help forward." A facilitator's role is to help someone learn. The focus is on the learner, not on the one with more knowledge.

Several years ago, I ran across a book by educator Maryellen Weimer called *Learner-Centered Teaching*, which provides a foundation for why facilitating is generally more effective than lecturing in the learning process. While reading the book, I came to the conclusion that Jesus was a learner-centered teacher. He seemed to meet people where they were in their understanding of God and their own personal spiritual journey, rather than expecting them to grasp advanced principles that he knew would be over their heads or that they were not ready to receive. For example, after Jesus' resurrection, he came to some of the disciples as they were fishing on the Sea of Galilee. (See John 21:1-19.) He talked to Peter, who had just betrayed him, and through a simple repeated sentiment—"Feed my sheep"—showed Peter that he was forgiven and could still be counted as Jesus' disciple. Jesus worked within Peter's frame of reference rather than beginning with complicated teaching.

When we talk to people about God, do we, like Jesus, meet them where they are—in their brokenness and current understanding of faith? Or do we expect them to know what we know about God and the Bible?

Weimer's premise is that traditional classrooms are *teacher centered* rather than *learner centered*. She points out that teachers do most of the work when learning is teacher-centric; therefore, they are learning more than the students. Could this also be true of those delivering sermons and Sunday school lessons and leading small groups? Those doing the teaching might be the biggest benefactors of this learning approach.

Acting as a facilitator to others' learning challenges everyone to be more engaged in the process. In learner-centered teaching, students develop skills for *how* to think, rather than just absorbing the content. This approach encourages learners to reflect on what they are learning and how they are grasping it. Learners are challenged to accept responsibility for their own understanding by reflecting on, analyzing, and critiquing new content rather than passively accepting it.

Learner-centered teaching motivates learners by giving them some control. Weimer believes that teachers have been making too many decisions about what students should learn, how they learn it, the pace at which they learn, and the conditions under which they learn. Then they also determine whether students have learned. In contrast, Weimer sees people in a classroom (much like a church gathering or a small group) as communities of learners. People learn from and with each other.[5] Perhaps giving faith learners a chance to determine what they want to learn, how they'll learn it, whom they'll learn it with, and the pace at which they learn it could increase the likelihood of behavioral change and more gradual and consistent choices to follow Jesus.

Given all of this, why don't we become learner centered in how we approach making new disciples? One reason is that facilitation, or guiding someone's learning, is more difficult than teaching through content delivery because you do not control the process. And let's face it: We all prefer to be in control. Facilitation is messy; it takes more time, and it requires patience. But in another way facilitation is easier for the ordinary Christian who does not have a seminary degree, teaching gift, or pastor credential because you don't have to have all the answers! You are walking alongside someone as a fellow learner, learning together as an initiator of the process but certainly not as an expert. It gives you permission to say, "I don't know the answer. What do the rest of you think? Let's discover the answer together."

A facilitator guides learners who are active in the process rather than supplying information to passive recipients. Encouraging active learning is important in matters of faith if we want to see disciples whose hearts are truly transformed rather than those who merely give nominal assent to Christian principles. Because our traditional approach to discipleship has been more teacher centered than learner centered, sadly, it has often been more about *us* than *them*. We focus on what we want to tell people rather than on what they want to know.

Jesus' actions in first-century Israel reveal the timeless value of facilitation. Even Jesus' public ministry required people to wrestle with the meaning of what he said; it's easy to imagine people dialoguing about one of Jesus' parables as they walked home after hearing his teaching. But Jesus' primary focus was to facilitate learning and growth in a small group of twelve. Again and again, Jesus took his small band of followers aside and helped them think through what he had just said or done. He often asked them many more questions than he gave answers.

Consider the account in Matthew 16 when Jesus asked his disciples a simple but profound question: *Who do people say the Son of Man is?* (16:13). This was a chance for the disciples to share what others thought about Jesus after seeing him perform many miracles, teach about the Kingdom, and model a life that glorified God. Interestingly, Jesus started out with a lighter, less intense question by first asking who *others* thought he was. Then, when he heard the disciples' answers, he asked who *they* thought he was (16:15). I am sure they had discussed this among themselves many times in the months leading up to this particular conversation, as Jesus was probably such a mystery to all of them. They were already asking this question themselves. As facilitators, do we know how to ask the questions that people are already asking—the questions that are on their minds and that beg for answers? How do we improve at this? I think the short answer is intentionality and practice.

With Jesus as our model, we can learn to become more intentional as we make new disciples through small groups in which we are guides (not teachers) to those seeking God. In the past few decades, small groups have become common in many churches. However, often they have been led in a way that does not result in vibrant discussions and growth for all of the participants. Some small-group leaders try to follow the approach of a preacher or a teacher, bearing the weight of studying and then dispensing the information they have discovered. Other leaders simply are present in the group, but have no idea how to spark a discussion and keep it going. Either way, the group does not flourish.

In the past fifteen years I've led a number of spiritual conversation groups, and I'll share stories about them both in this chapter and in chapter 12. The first time I invited people to join a spiritual conversation group in my community, they were a little surprised when I told them that my job was to *facilitate* discussions about God and the Bible, not to *tell* them what to believe. I explained that, even though I was in my first year of seminary at the time, I had a lot of holes in my own theology and I was still learning what it meant to have a relationship with God. I said that I was willing to walk alongside them as they discovered what was true, because the search for God was important and we all were continually growing in our understanding of God.

I love how much I learned from the participants in the groups I cofacilitated, even from those who did not have an active and fully informed faith in God. For example, one day our small group was talking about why God would wait four thousand years to send a savior after Adam and Eve sinned. Once he knew a savior was needed, he could have sent his Son right away. My friend Kate, who was not yet a Christian, wisely observed that God waited because people had to realize their need for a savior over time and history before God would send one. They had to see time and time again that people couldn't save themselves from their own sin. Kate's comment was the single most profound contribution to our discussion that day, and it came from someone who had chosen, at least for that time period, not to believe in Jesus.

Bill Mowry, on staff with The Navigators, wrote an important practical book called *The Ways of the Alongsider*, providing ten simple ways we can make disciples like Jesus. He writes:

Jesus does the unthinkable. He invites us in our weakness and inexperience, to be his helpers in the Great Commission. He recruits ministry amateurs to come alongside friends to model behaviors such as how to love God, build friendships, read the Bible with others, tell stories, ask questions—and encourage application.[6]

Could it be so simple? Is God looking for ministry amateurs to walk alongside those who don't yet know him personally? Can our friendship with God enable us to guide others to have a relationship with him?

Up to this point in the book we've been talking about using the building blocks of the first six Arts of Spiritual Conversations to develop one-on-one relationships with people who believe differently. Here we're transitioning some of those same skills to a group environment. If you want to pursue your relationships with non-Christians in a small-group setting—and our experience shows that's a highly effective approach—then you need to know how to be facilitators.

Individual interactions affect just one other person. When you facilitate a conversation group where people who believe differently can explore their questions about faith, you have the potential to multiply your efforts. Not only do you have ongoing, planned opportunities for spiritual conversations, you can also join forces with other followers of Jesus and open up the possibility for God to work among different combinations of people.

As mentioned earlier, a small-group community of two to twelve people, where the majority of the participants are not Christians, is a great place for people to figure out what they believe about God and the Bible. Whether you're aiming for an organized weekly Q Place or you find yourself in a conversation about God with three moms at school or with friends at a bar after a sports event, facilitating well is important and will help determine whether the experience is positive or negative. It will also have an effect on whether people will want to continue having these highly sensitive discussions.

Beacons of Light: Core Values

Spiritual transformation in a small group requires more than just getting a group of believers or skeptics together and having conversations about God and the Bible. And it looks far different from a lecture scaled down to a small-group monologue. Several key foundational elements will help a small group of people with diverse beliefs thrive, including clarity on the core values that undergird the formation of the group, the way the group starts out and functions, and the guiding principles for choosing the topics to discuss. We'll look at some of these elements here and then in more detail in chapter 12, "Starting a Q Place," where we'll walk you through the key issues involved in beginning a spiritual conversation group.

Core values are an important building block for facilitating a small group. The following four core values establish the foundational DNA of a spiritual conversation group that will enable people who are curious about God to get on a journey of discovery. For easy memory recall, all of these values begin with the letter *s*:

Self-Discovery: People learn best when they discover truth for themselves through discussion and study.

Safe Place: An ideal environment for spiritual growth is a small group where personal dignity is valued and leadership is shared.

Spirit: God's Spirit will guide those who are spiritually open.

Scripture: The Bible and the life of Jesus are worth serious examination.

The introduction of *Encounters with Jesus: Unexpected Answers to Life's Biggest Questions*, by well-known author and pastor Tim Keller, contains a story about a spiritual crisis he had when he was in college. At the time, Keller was questioning his faith even though he had grown up in a Christian home. He describes how he ended up in a Bible study where the leader didn't take the role of teacher or instructor but instead would facilitate the entire group's reading and interpretation of the chosen Bible text. Keller's description of this small-group experience beautifully illustrates all four of these core values and the resulting impact the group had on his future faith.

Keller explains his small-group community's values and "ground rules": You didn't have to believe the Bible was true; you just had to believe it was worth serious study because of its historical roots and widespread use. No single interpretation was to be the final conclusion, but all participants were given a chance to share their thoughts about the text.

We sought to mine the riches of the material as a community, assuming together we would see far more than any individual could.

Before I was even sure where I stood in my own faith, I was asked to lead a group and was provided with a set of Bible studies entitled *Conversations with Jesus Christ from the Gospel of John* by Marilyn Kunz and Catherine Schell. It covered thirteen passages in the book of John where Jesus had conversations with individuals. Those studies helped my group uncover layers of meaning and insight that astonished us all. Moving through these accounts of Jesus' life, I began to sense more than ever before that the Bible was not an ordinary book. Yes, it carried the strange beauty of literature from the remote past; but there was something else. It was through these studies of encounters with Jesus that I began to sense an inexplicable life and power in the text. These conversations from centuries ago were inwaanally relevant and incisive to me—right now. I began to search the Scriptures not just for intellectual stimulation but in order to find God.[7]

The authors of the discussion guide he used, Marilyn Kunz and Catherine Schell, were the founders of Neighborhood Bible Studies, which is now Q Place.

Keller's description is strong evidence of the impact that the inductive process can have on doubters and skeptics when these core values are on display. Participants were discovering for themselves what the Bible said. The group was a safe place where every participant was valued and leadership was shared. God's Spirit was guiding them as they studied the Scriptures and the life of Jesus with an understanding that the Bible was valuable. As participants like Keller continued to sense these values lived out in the group, they engaged more fully, took risks, and experienced God's work in their lives. These core values become beacons of light when you initiate this process with people who are seeking to know God.

Facilitating as a Team

While we practice most of the 9 Arts individually, Facilitating is best done with other followers of Jesus. When I (Mary) started my first small group for spiritually curious people in 2002, I invited two Christian friends, Kristin and Judy, to help me facilitate it. I think I knew that I would never want to do something like this alone in the very secular community where I resided, as leading a spiritual conversation group was totally new to me. While I was more entrepreneurial than most, I needed the wisdom of a few other people to start a community where the majority were not Christians. And although Jesus sent his disciples out two by two when he was giving them their first taste of spreading his message (see Matthew 10:1-42 and Luke 10:1-23), my instincts at the time were that *three* might be a stronger team in order to create a sustainable community to talk about God with people who believed differently.

Later I learned how good it was to start a group like this with two other facilitators. Together the three of us created a Christ-centered community that remained at the core in our group, even when the group went from three to twelve and included participants who had a variety of beliefs about God.

The demands of facilitating can be overwhelming, especially when the majority of group participants have diverse beliefs. Solo facilitation casts the facilitator as a small-group superhero who has X-ray vision into group dynamics, heroic power to invite people to the group, and the ability to leap over discussion-ending comments in a single bound. But who facilitates the group when the leader is out of town or sick or is backed into a corner on a theological point that is way over his or her head? What happens when the leader starts to burn out or has to work late? How can the leader invite people into the group beyond his or her social circle?

There's no such thing as a perfect group facilitator—everyone has strengths and weaknesses. A facilitator may be great at inviting people to the group yet struggle to lead discussions. He or she may have great empathy yet shy away from addressing deep issues for fear of group conflict. A facilitator may be great at asking questions yet be weak at waiting to hear answers. And whatever their gift mix is, all facilitators have good days and bad days, moments when they lead well and moments when they don't.

A team of facilitators can support each other both inside and outside the small-group setting. When the group discussion bogs down, one of them may offer a new question or point the group back to its guidelines. Outside the group, facilitators can debrief, offering each other specific affirmation and constructive suggestions for future group sessions. The co-leadership approach allows each facilitator to use his or her strengths and look to others to compensate for weaknesses. As a result, each of them will feel more at home in the facilitating role and better valued for what he or she brings to the group.

A team of facilitators can share encouragement, prayer, ideas, support, and wisdom, living out the idea that we can do more together than we could apart.

Effective group facilitators strive to provide an environment that is conducive to exploration and discovery, where people who believe differently can explore, discover, and share with transparency while the Spirit of God works through Scripture. As they create this environment for others, they need it also for themselves.

As the adage goes, "You can't give away what you don't have." If a facilitator isn't being discipled in a loving community, he or she is ill equipped to disciple others in a loving community. A group of three or four facilitators live out the idea of peer-discipleship, of iron sharpening iron (see Proverbs 27:17).

Jesus modeled this community-within-a-community approach. While investing in all twelve disciples, he gave extra attention to three of his closest followers: Peter, James, and John. Jesus exclusively invited them into specific highs and lows of his ministry—the resurrection of a little girl (Mark 5:37-42), the Transfiguration (Matthew 17:1-13), and his night of prayer at Gethsemane (Mark 14:32-34). Surely Peter, James, and John talked together about these experiences. That processing-in-community perfectly captures the essence of a group of three—meeting together to work through our responses to Jesus and partnering together in the Kingdom work Jesus gives us to do. Facilitator meetings outside of small-group meetings offer a rich discipleship environment.

Jesus Chose to Invest in Twelve

We are living in times when the Western world has increasingly rejected institutional Christianity. An invitation to explore God and the Bible with a few others is a great first step for people who are unlikely to step through the doors of a church. It's also a rich, holistic approach for Jesus followers of all levels of maturity.

Jesus is our model for creating God-honoring, life-changing community. When he began his earthly ministry, he could have spent all of his time preaching to thousands. This might seem like the most efficient method of gathering followers. Instead, Jesus invited twelve ordinary Jewish men into a community to learn and grow together as they followed him. Rather than mass-producing disciples, Jesus chose to invest deeply in a handful of people, thereby developing committed followers.

We've identified four simple stages that are essential in starting a small group for spiritually curious people—stages that mirror what Jesus did in building his group of disciples.

Stage 1: Preparation. Jesus spent focused time in prayer to discern which people he would disciple. Notice how he prayed all night before he chose the Twelve (see Luke 6:12-13). Prayer is also crucial for us as we prepare to begin a small group. In addition, preparation involves finding two other followers of Jesus who will pray and plan together, building relationships with people who may accept your invitations.

Stage 2: Invitation. Jesus extended compelling invitations to those he chose to follow him. See John 1:35-50, Luke 5:27-32, and Luke 6:13-16. For our invitations to be compelling, we need to pray for those we will invite and follow the Holy Spirit's guidance in the way that we invite them.

Stage 3: Trial Meeting. Jesus invited potential followers to "come and see" (John 1:38) where he was staying and spend the day with him, almost as a sample of what it would be like to follow him. A trial meeting allows people to come and check out what it would be like to be in a discussion group where people aren't being told what to believe but can safely discover things for themselves. In a trial meeting, participants see that initiators are there to listen and create a welcoming, safe place to discuss life, God, and the Bible together.

Stage 4: Growth. Jesus cared for the Twelve—day in and day out—through three years of their limited understanding, encouraging them to watch his life and wrestle with his words so that the truth would penetrate them completely. When we follow his lead, faithfully walking alongside the participants in our group and helping them experience God's Word for themselves, the Holy Spirit uses his Word to work in their hearts, and we can be assured that everyone will grow (including us!).

Jesus is our model for facilitating spiritual conversations and starting small groups. He prepared well by praying about whom to invite; he extended compelling invitations; he encouraged those he invited to check it out; and those who accepted his invitation grew in their understanding of God. Jesus knew the Kingdom of God was all about relationships with each other and with him. We can follow his pattern for starting small groups today.

When you start a small group for ongoing spiritual conversations with people who believe differently, it is important to know where your group is going and how to get there, always being attentive to the Holy Spirit's guidance and the group participants' freedom along the way. Twenty-first-century small-group guru Bill Donahue notes:

Small groups were an integral part of the early church structure. They were small enough to allow individual members to minister to one another, use their spiritual gifts, and be discipled in the teachings of Christ. In addition, they were vibrant and life-giving communities where evangelism could take place as unchurched people watched a loving and compassionate community in action.[8]

Facilitating these small-group communities well is an honor and a privilege for all followers of Jesus.

Discover

1. What are the major benefits of facilitating a discussion rather than coming across as an expert or teacher? What are the challenges?

2. Why do you think facilitating a spiritual conversation group with a team of two to four Christians is more effective than facilitating alone?

Practice

1. Try facilitating a group discussion with two to five people you already know on a topic where there is a diversity of opinion. Your goal is to get everyone talking and respectfully engaged. What did you learn?

2. Ask some of your friends how they learn best: through listening or discussion. Did you notice a difference in response from your Christians friends and those who believe differently? Why do you think that is the case?

CHAPTER 10

The Art of Serving Together

You are the salt of the earth. But if the salt loses its saltiness, how
can it be made salty again? . . . Neither do people light a lamp and put
it under a bowl. Instead they put it on its stand, and it gives light to
everyone in the house. In the same way, let your light shine before others,
that they may see your good deeds and glorify your Father in heaven.

MATTHEW 5:13-16

Today's typical outsiders aren't likely to be reached through
persuasive argument but instead through first experiencing
an authentic Christian: someone who is willing to roll
up his or her sleeves and restore alongside them.

GABE LYONS

MY BUDDY SCOTT AND I (CRILLY) invited four of the teenage
African refugees we were mentoring to come with us and pack beet
seeds for people living in poverty in Zimbabwe. As we drove to
the packing location, we talked about the privileges and blessings
we have in our lives compared to the struggles these young men
experienced in their home countries and in refugee camps. When
we arrived, we entered a room bustling with people of all ages.
Together we watched a compelling video about the people who
would receive the seeds, listened to the instructions, and formed
our team to start packing. As energetic music played in the background and the host announced which group was ahead in filling
seed packs, our team pushed harder and harder.

Finally the ending bell rang, the seed packs were counted,
and our team went wild at the announcement that we won! The

guys were exuberant. Together we had accomplished something meaningful.

During the drive home, I asked the guys some questions about the experience. Soon I discovered what they enjoyed, what they learned, and what they found most meaningful. I asked them about their religion's beliefs on compassion and serving, and in turn, they began to ask me about my faith. They wanted to understand who Jesus was to me as a Christian compared to who he was in their religion. I shared parts of my story with them, emphasizing that I began my spiritual search when I was about their age and needed to understand my beliefs for myself, not as the faith of my parents or my peers. At the end of the discussion, I encouraged these young men to explore their faith for themselves as they entered adulthood, and not just to view beliefs as cultural or biological.

As the conversation naturally moved to other topics, I marveled at how God had opened up this exchange. I was convinced he would use it to continue to work in the hearts of these young men. Serving together had easily opened up this conversation, one that nudged them closer to understanding who Jesus (*Isa* as he is known to them) really is: their Rescuer and Leader.

The Medium Is the Message

Marshall McLuhan was one of the most influential communication theorists of the twentieth century. Regarding media, he coined the phrase "The medium is the message." What exactly did he mean by that?

A medium is a vehicle through which something is conveyed. Video, print, and radio are all different ways to communicate a message. McLuhan believed that the *means* or *medium* of communication is intimately related to how the message is perceived. He believed that the way a message was communicated had as much to say as the message itself. Therefore, the same message would be perceived differently if it were received through television versus through a person you knew.

This concept becomes profound when you consider the medium that God used to communicate his message to mankind: the Incarnation. Jesus was the perfect medium—God in the flesh, dwelling among us, full of grace and truth—communicating God himself in everything he did.

What a paradox that the medium God now uses to share the good news of Jesus to the world is *us*! In all of our imperfections and failings, we are God's choice for communicating himself to people who are not yet in relationship with him.

What does this have to do with serving together with our spiritually curious friends and neighbors? So often we think of sharing the gospel as an oral exercise. But God didn't just redeem our mouths, he redeemed all of us. And our relationship with God speaks most clearly when every part of our lives is involved, not just our speech.

The idea of serving people in order to communicate God's grace is hardly novel. "Bringing the whole gospel to the whole person" marks both contemporary missional churches and longstanding mission organizations. Yet, if we limit ourselves to serving people in order to demonstrate God's love for them, we may be ignoring an even more loving, relational, authentic, and dynamic approach—serving *together with* people who believe differently.

Together is the key word. The dynamic changes when people are doing something *together*; the rules change when you are in relationship. When I was in grade school, I played multiple sports against a lot of the same kids. One boy from a rival school I regularly competed against was named Jimmy. Jimmy was good and was one of my most difficult opponents. I couldn't stand to play against him. But he and I ended up at the same high school, playing two sports together, and soon I loved having him on my team.

Jimmy was passionate, scrappy, and competitive. Because we were together on the same team, I learned a lot more about Jimmy and liked him for who he was, not just for his athletic talents. Jimmy became a great high school friend. The rules changed when I got to know him through our shared experience.

A special bond is formed when you pursue a common cause with someone, and people who seem the least interested in discussing God and the Bible may jump at the chance to come with you to serve at a food pantry, assist in disaster relief, or join a community recycling project. Serving together invites people into a relational environment where they can belong so that they may see and feel the gospel being lived out. The shared experience also provides something worthwhile to talk about.

When you welcome someone to serve with you, your experience fosters new relational dimensions, increasing common ground, activating mutual curiosity, and opening up the potential for meaningful conversations about God. There's a natural debriefing time after a service project that may organically open up into a conversation about life and God. The medium of service gives you opportunities to ask questions about the experience, share your perspective, talk about God's work in your life, and interpret the experience from your worldview. And when you spend worthwhile time *together with* people who may share little else in common with you, they just may catch a glimpse of Jesus.

Jesus Modeled Serving Together

In several memorable scenes throughout the Gospels, Jesus asked people to participate *with* him in the work he was doing, even though they did not yet understand who he was. He asked wedding servants to fill thirty-gallon pots with water when the wine had run out. He asked a Samaritan woman, in the heat of the day, to give him a drink from a well. He told a lame man to carry his mat, a blind man to go wash clay from his eyes, and mourners to remove a stone from a cave and unwrap the dead man who came out of it.

Why did Jesus ask people to take part in the action *with him* when he was about to reveal more of the grace, power, and love of God? Clearly, people's obedience to his commands reveals their faith, and throughout the Gospels, Jesus acts in response to faith. But taking action on Jesus' behalf may also prepare people to understand more of who he is. I know this is often the case for me; I learn better by doing. Maybe you are the same. As the saying goes, "Tell me and I forget. Teach me and I remember. Involve me and I learn."

Like me, Jesus' disciples also seemed to benefit from hands-on experience. They regularly showed that they didn't understand who Jesus was and what he was calling them to. They argued about who would be the greatest, they misunderstood Jesus' purpose, and they were frequently annoyed with the crowds of people, even once sending away children who had come for a blessing. So Jesus involved them *with him*.

As you read the following account, notice all the ways that Jesus involved these imperfect followers *with him*, even though they were still uncertain about who he was:

> When Jesus looked up and saw a great crowd coming toward him, he said to Philip, "Where shall we buy bread for these people to eat?" He asked this only to test him, for he already had in mind what he was going to do.
>
> Philip answered him, "It would take more than half a year's wages to buy enough bread for each one to have a bite!"
>
> Another of his disciples, Andrew, Simon Peter's brother, spoke up, "Here is a boy with five small barley loaves and two small fish, but how far will they go among so many?"

Jesus said, "Have the people sit down." There was plenty of grass in that place, and they sat down (about five thousand men were there). Jesus then took the loaves, gave thanks, and distributed to those who were seated as much as they wanted. He did the same with the fish.

When they had all had enough to eat, he said to his disciples, "Gather the pieces that are left over. Let nothing be wasted." So they gathered them and filled twelve baskets with the pieces of the five barley loaves left over by those who had eaten.

JOHN 6:5-13

Jesus had a more profound purpose in mind than filling the stomachs of a multitude of people. He made the feeding of this crowd a hands-on experience of serving together and a significant instructional moment for his disciples, who gained a new understanding of his power and identity. This is evident through the last half of John 6, when Jesus reveals a message so difficult that it becomes a point of decision for many who turn away and leave. The message begins with "I am the bread of life" (6:35) and culminates when Peter speaks for most of the Twelve, expressing a new understanding and faith: "Lord, to whom shall we go? You have the words of eternal life. We have come to believe and to know that you are the Holy One of God" (6:68). I can't help but speculate how the tactile experience of serving together helped Peter come to the conclusion he did about Jesus.

Flavorless Salt and Hidden Light?

When the Communists took over Russia in 1917, they vigorously persecuted the church but did not make Christianity illegal. In the Constitution of 1918, Article 13 guaranteed freedom of religion. But Article 16 established that only the Soviet Republic would render "material and all other assistance to the workers and poorest peasants,"[1] effectively making it illegal for Christians to do any good works. In their book *The Externally Focused Church*, Rick Rusaw and Eric Swanson note that because the church in Russia could no longer feed the hungry or take care of the sick or the orphans, within seventy years it was irrelevant. "Take away service, and you take away the church's power, influence, and evangelistic effectiveness. The power of the gospel is combining its life-changing message with selfless service."[2]

In Romans 15:17-19, the apostle Paul was full of enthusiasm about all that Christ Jesus had done through him, "bringing the Gentiles to God by my message *and* by the way I worked among them" (NLT, emphasis added). The Spirit of God worked through Paul's words *and* actions as he "fully presented the Good News of Christ." Similarly, Paul explains in 1 Thessalonians 1:5 that the "gospel came . . . not simply with words but also with power, with the Holy Spirit and deep conviction." The gospel is not just spoken, it's modeled. Our actions give substance, meaning, and credibility to our words. Paul is a powerful example of what Jesus told his followers—that they would be like *salt* and *light* for people around them—"that they may see your good deeds and glorify your Father in heaven" (Matthew 5:16).

Now, in twenty-first-century America, are people experiencing Christians as salt and light? Researcher Brené Brown, a popular TED Talk presenter, talks about the "disengagement gap"—the space between what we *practice* on a daily basis and what we *profess*.[3] In other words, when people who believe differently observe us, as Christians, being out of alignment with the core values we profess, such as loving and serving our neighbors, they conclude that we do not have integrity or credibility. If we don't close this gap, we will continue to turn people off from the gospel. Gabe Lyons suggests that "today's typical outsiders aren't likely to be reached through persuasive argument but instead through first experiencing an authentic Christian: someone who is willing to roll up his or her sleeves and restore alongside them."[4]

Serving together is a powerful way to live out our values in the presence of spiritual explorers and to close the gap so that the impact of our message increases. Imagine if Christians' actions shone a bright light, illuminating the beauty of the gospel, sparking curiosity, and opening up the opportunity for the exchange of life-giving words. And what if we invited people who believe differently to join us in serving, and they got the opportunity to see Jesus up close, in action through us? They would taste the salt and see the light shining, and they would probably want more.

Barriers to Serving Together

Inviting individuals to serve with us is a loving and welcoming act. Opportunities abound for us to serve others and to serve alongside others; we aren't living under legal restrictions from serving. But we still face barriers that hinder us from getting started and from serving together well once we've begun. As you plan to invite someone to serve together with you, check your tendency toward the three biggest barriers to serving together: *individualism, materialism,* and *consumerism.*

You might refer to these barriers as "Me, Mine, More." Resolving to move beyond them requires taking some risks and challenging our cherished comfort, security, safety, and convenience. Serving, in itself, requires us to move out of our comfortable routines to be touched by the needs of other people. Minimally, it's inconvenient. Frequently it involves uncertainty, discomfort, and a steep learning curve. Yet if we face these challenges and dissolve the three barriers with effective antidotes, serving together can become a doorway to fulfilling our purpose—as lights pointing people to God.

The first barrier to serving together is *individualism.* Our society's "me first" attitude and the ever-expanding technology that supports isolation rather than community reinforce this barrier. The antidote to this "me" focus is humility and relational engagement. Pursuing humility remedies the tendency to want personal recognition, to take credit, and to pass blame, and engaging relationally means that *we* replaces *me*. Instead of asking, "What's in it for me?" we ask, "How can we do this *together*?"

Serving with people who believe differently means that we're on a team with blended worldviews and varying approaches to life. We have to surrender the desire for any personal glory and focus on what the team can accomplish together. We value the ones we're serving with and become dependent on each other, caring for each other and the people we serve. Church-planting expert Ed Stetzer, paraphrasing Neil Cole, maintains that "you win people *to* what you win them *with*." If we hope to draw people to Christ through service, we need to show them what the loving, caring community of his people can look like. Gabe Lyons puts it this way:

> When communities serve together, they experience connection and purpose, and are reminded that this life is not about them. Serving is one of the clearest ways the concept of restoration begins to manifest itself in our world.[5]

The second big barrier is *materialism*. It is easy to think that your value is measured by what you own. This may be true in our culture, but it is not true in the Kingdom of God. By focusing our lives on what we possess, we lose out on the vital connection that happens when we find our value in what we give and in how rich we are relationally. Materialism is a barrier to any kind of serving, but we can overcome it when we share our time, talents, or treasures and inspire others to break the hold these things have. Embarking on a massive development project to support Solomon's future construction of the Temple, King David understood that if he gave of himself, his generosity could inspire many others to surrender their treasures to God for his purposes. David gave from his own resources to galvanize others to do the same, and the action rippled throughout the community:

> "Besides, in my devotion to the temple of my God I now give my personal treasures of gold and silver for the temple of my God, over and above everything I have provided for this holy temple. . . . Now, who is willing to consecrate themselves to the LORD today?"
>
> Then the leaders of families, the officers of the tribes of Israel, the commanders of thousands and commanders of hundreds, and the officials in charge of the king's work gave willingly. . . . The people rejoiced at the willing response of their leaders, for they had given freely and wholeheartedly to the LORD.
>
> I CHRONICLES 29:3, 5-6, 9

The antidote for our tendency to focus on "stuff" is generosity: giving our time, talent, and treasures. We begin to wonder not how to get the best but how to give the best. *Ours* or *yours* eventually replaces *mine*. Our focus can shift from what we have to the value of relationships and to serving and growing together.

Consumerism is the third significant barrier to serving together. When we value life for what we can get out of it, we become self-absorbed, measuring material goods, experiences, and even people by how they serve us. The antidote for a consumeristic mind-set is to live a sacrificial life: giving our lives away, showing up for others, and focusing on what they need. It's to live daily asking the question, "How can I let go of my agenda to benefit everyone else?" *Sacrifice for others* replaces *more for me*. Speaking of the impact of people engaged in service together, Lyons writes:

When serving together—whether ministering to one another or those outside their community—[people] are forced to sacrifice, be inconvenienced, and demolish walls. They get to know one another in ways they wouldn't have to if they just sat around in a friendly circle talking. It is in the *doing* that they come alive, their gifts are exposed, and their hearts are opened to one another. Serving others together is the key ingredient in creating community.[6]

Once we become convinced that the rewards are worth the risks, we will make the effort to join with others, give more freely, and joyfully sacrifice whatever it takes so that serving with others is a regular part of our lifestyle as followers of Christ. In humble dependence on God, we will find that we start to "believe differently"; our *me, mine, more* mind-set will dissolve, and our hearts will come into alignment with God's design for us. Our own discipleship, becoming more like Jesus, happens in the doing.

Making It Meaningful

Jesus made it crystal clear to his disciples that they would be powerless to produce good results unless they were constantly relying on him, just as a branch must be connected to the vine to get its nourishment and power (John 15:4-5). If you want people to see Jesus in your life, you need to continually rely on God. As you serve with them, they will then experience the fruit of his Spirit—love, joy, peace, patience, kindness, goodness, faithfulness, gentleness, and self-control—coming through you. That fruit brings real blessing and makes people curious about its source. But only by being in communion with Jesus will you have that ability to pique others' curiosity. A boring, lifeless, critical, or stress-filled Christian is hardly going to make an outsider thirsty for that kind of life!

When we're dependent on Christ, relying on him to help us

be salt and light, we can begin to look for opportunities to serve together with others. Serving together is a powerful way to engage with different people, forging strong relationships over a common cause. Taking many different forms, this Art involves welcoming people to join us in purposeful, beneficial activities. Meaningful conversation flows more naturally as the task at hand is in the spotlight—not our differences. Winsome interactions about God can be a very natural part of the shared experience. In the process, Jesus is on display. As we serve together with people who believe differently, we can maximize the impact both on those being served and on those who are serving.

Practically speaking, effective service begins with a useful plan, including elements such as choosing the right opportunity, making a meaningful invitation to your nonbelieving friend, casting a compelling vision for your serving, organizing the logistics, and bathing the time in plenty of advance prayer.

Choosing the right opportunity. One of the ways you can deepen relationships among people around you and find common serving areas is to discover what they are passionate about. You may be able to identify a mutual interest. As you consider an option to suggest serving together, be willing to put others' interests and desires above your own. Here are a few questions that could open a conversation about serving together:

- If your employer offered you an opportunity to take eighty hours of work time to do paid community service, serving anywhere in the world, what would you do? Why would that be your choice?
- What causes have you donated money or given time to (e.g., modern-day slavery, racial discrimination, sex trafficking, homelessness, illiteracy)? What makes you so passionate about that particular issue?

- During your childhood, what experience did you have in serving someone that meant a lot to you? What made it meaningful?

As you read through these questions, I suspect that you thought about your own responses. In light of that, who is someone you know who is far from God and may have preferences or passions similar to yours?

Making an invitation. Here are some tips to think through as you prepare to make meaningful invitations to your serving opportunity:

- *Build a bridge.* Invitations are more readily accepted when people know and trust you. Practicing The 9 Arts of Spiritual Conversations as a natural part of your life will open up opportunities to invite.
- *Pray first.* Pray for each person you plan to invite. Follow God's leading as he prompts you to invite others that you may have not planned to ask.
- *Make it fun.* When you make your invitation, show your enthusiasm to serve and your interest in doing it with them. There is power in being chosen. You are handpicking others to serve with you! Let them know that you thought about them when you considered this opportunity.
- *Make it solid.* In a winsome way, communicate clearly what you are inviting them to, providing the details (who, what, where, when, how) and including well-defined time parameters. Don't leave it open-ended, but make your invitation specific. Don't say, "Do you want to pack food for starving kids with me sometime?" Instead, give them the details: "Next Saturday I am planning to go and pack food for starving kids in Haiti. It'll be about two hours,

THE 9 ARTS OF SPIRITUAL CONVERSATIONS

from 9 to 11 a.m. The organization is called Feed My
Starving Children. It's simple and fun, and I always leave
feeling like I made a difference in the lives of children. I
know you have a heart for this, and I think you would love
it. I'll leave at 8:30 a.m. Will you join me?"

- *Make it face-to-face.* It is preferable to extend the actual
  invitation in person, as it may be your best option for a
  positive response. E-mail, texting, and social media are all
  less personal ways to make this invitation.
- *Don't say "no" for them!* By not inviting them, you're saying
  "no" for them. By inviting them with an uninspired, negative
  invitation, you are expecting a "no." So ask with a positive
  expectation that they will come. Don't answer for them.

Casting vision. In Luke 9, Jesus casts a clear vision for his disciples
as he sends them out: "When Jesus had called the Twelve together,
he gave them power and authority to drive out all demons and to
cure diseases, and he sent them out to proclaim the kingdom of
God and to heal the sick" (Luke 9:1-2). To focus everyone's energy
in the right direction, make sure you're all in agreement about what
you're trying to accomplish. If necessary, include clearly identified
roles and responsibilities. The details will not be a distraction when
everyone knows who is doing what for how long.

Praying before you begin. Use discernment and sensitivity about
praying with people you have invited who believe differently. Some
may be comfortable joining you in prayer, others may not. Let
your relationship guide your judgment. Whether you decide to
pray beforehand with the Christians involved or during the experience with everyone, ask God to multiply your efforts so that your
actions will introduce people to our God of love and will open a
way for the Good News to be known.

Organizing the logistics. Some key logistical elements may include the following:

- *Asking permission of the people you are going to serve.* Be respectful in your service of others. What we think needs to be fixed or cleaned up might not be all right with someone else. Make sure to talk with the people you are planning to serve, and tune in to their vision so that what you do really benefits them.
- *Plan for safety.* Sometimes in our excitement to serve, we put ourselves in dangerous situations or take unnecessary risks. Make sure to think through what it looks like to keep everyone safe while you do the work.
- *Have the right supplies ready.* It is frustrating to have a crew of passionate workers waiting for someone to come back from the hardware store. Make sure to acquire all of the equipment you need in advance so that momentum stays strong as you serve.

Don't allow your planning to paralyze you. Sometimes we get so hung up on the planning that we never serve. As Jesus sent his disciples out, he told them to take nothing with them—no staff, no bread, no money, and no extra shirt. He wanted them to get going and to trust God for what they needed. As we serve in areas that do require preparation, we still need to depend on God and not get bogged down in the planning process. When you begin serving with another person, you'll learn a lot about each other. Those you're serving with will be watching you, both in how you plan and how you carry out plans. *How* you serve sends a message of credibility—or lack of it—especially for the people you work alongside.

What's Going On Here?

The people of ancient Israel would set up stones in places where they had encountered God in meaningful ways. When someone came upon the site later, the standing stones would then prompt the question, "What happened here?" If a person wasn't present to explain what had occurred, the stones served only as a silent marker to the event.

Scripture describes followers of Jesus as "living stones" (1 Peter 2:5). We serve the same purpose as the standing stones of biblical times. But unlike those stones, we can give witness to what Jesus has done in our lives. We are literally "living" markers of God's work in the world.[7]

Going out to serve among and with the people of our communities gives us a great opportunity to be living stones. Our actions can cause people to ask, "What's going on here?" And then when we communicate God's personal love and care for people, our message resonates with authenticity.

Service in the name of Jesus is set apart from service provided for social welfare or personal altruism. We are identified by how we love. Service motivated by intentional love is what differentiates us. When our service is rooted in love, it is rooted in Jesus. Christ-centered service has the potential to transform both those serving and those being served. Jesus calls this transformation *fruit*. Kingdom fruit includes changing lives, breaking down spiritual barriers, and discrediting the enemy's lies. All this can happen when we pay attention to some simple principles while we are serving:

1. MEANINGFUL INVOLVEMENT

We want everyone to feel that they have contributed to the work in a meaningful way. This means paying attention to gifts, abilities, and skills. (Don't hand a chain saw to a person who has never used one and doesn't have the strength to operate it.)

2. CONTINUOUS PRAYER

Paul tells us in 1 Thessalonians 5:17 to "pray continually." Encourage each of the Christians to keep praying while they are working—for safety, team unity, strong relationships, opportunities for spiritual conversations, and protection from the enemy. Notice how God answers prayers, and as appropriate, share personally with group members as you see him at work.

3. SPIRITUAL AWARENESS

When we are serving, we need to stay aware of what is going on in the spiritual realm. Evidence of God's activity can open up significant conversations, while conflict could arise from the enemy. As we seek God in each situation, he gives us power to break down spiritual barriers erected by the enemy and to enter into life-changing interactions led by his Spirit. For example, one autumn, a buddy of mine (Crilly) pulled together a group to serve in his community. As they raked leaves in an elderly woman's front yard, the owner of the adjacent house came out and angrily rebuked the crew for blowing leaves into his yard. Instead of engaging in a dispute, they simply apologized. After the man went inside, the team recognized the enemy's desire to destroy God's work and decided to rake this man's yard as well, pack his leaves, and pay to have them removed. When he came out again, the only words he could utter were "Thank you."

4. COMPELLING QUALITY

When a group serves someone but fails to do the job well, the experience leaves a negative impression and is a poor reflection of God's excellent handiwork. When we delight in serving God himself, doing the best job possible, then both the people we serve with and those we serve may be compelled by our service—and by our God. Colossians 3:23-24 instructs us, "Whatever you do, work at it with all your heart, as working for the Lord, not for human masters, since you know that you will receive an inheritance from the Lord as a reward. It is the Lord Christ you are serving."

5. GENTLE ANSWER

While you are serving with no strings attached, people may ask you why you are doing this. First Peter 3:15 tells us, "Always be prepared to give an answer to everyone who asks you to give the reason for the hope that you have. But do this with gentleness and respect." Remember, you are a living stone. In advance, think through what your relationship with God means to you, how it affects what you do, and how you would communicate that to individuals serving with you. Thinking this through ahead of time will help you to handle questions when they come and to communicate how deeply God loves and cares for people.

Debriefing the Experience

In Luke 9:10, Jesus welcomes back his followers who have been driving out demons, healing the sick, and preaching the message of the Kingdom. When they return, the disciples report what they have done. Similarly, after you serve together with people of different beliefs, you have an opportunity to intentionally open up a dialogue about what you each learned and experienced.

Debriefing can happen very naturally; for example, you could simply stop together for a meal or for coffee before heading home and throw out a good question such as the following:

- What part of the experience did you enjoy the most?
- Who is someone new that you met? What did you learn about him or her?
- What ideas do you have for serving more effectively the next time?
- Did you learn anything about yourself today?

- Did you learn anything about God today?
- Would you say that you were changed? If so, how?
- What do you think was most helpful or meaningful for the people we served?

When you take time to reflect and discuss your experience, you can more clearly see what transforming work is being done (or not being done) in those around you. Discussing your experience together helps everyone to take notice of things that you learned and to grow—both individually and in your relationships with each other.

Serving together with people who believe differently has the potential to raise curiosity about what makes a Christian's life different. Serving together can be a great equalizer: Both those who serve and those being served are humbled by the presence of God through loving one another as Christ loves and serves us. As we serve alongside people who don't yet know Jesus, they get to experience the difference that Jesus has made in our lives. By God's grace, they will see his character shining through us. What an impact we could have if our salt made people thirsty and our light made people look. Let it be so.

Discover

1. How might the act of serving together have helped Jesus' disciples come to the right conclusion about who he was?

2. What's the most fruitful act of service you have ever been a part of? What made it rewarding? What did it teach you about God?

Practice

1. In the next few weeks, identify a need in your own community, neighborhood, or workplace that people you know can meet.

Pray for one or two Christians to join you, and pray for God to show you a few people who believe differently, who could help too.

2. What impact did meeting the need have on those relationships? On your own faith?

CHAPTER 11

The Art of Sharing

In your hearts revere Christ as Lord. Always be prepared to
give an answer to everyone who asks you to give the reason for the
hope that you have. But do this with gentleness and respect.

1 PETER 3:15

If you really believe in the redeeming and transforming power of
God's presence in a person's life, then the single greatest gift you can give
someone is an explanation of how to be rightly connected to him.

BILL HYBELS

ONE OF THE MOST WIDELY ACCLAIMED movies of 2014 was
Boyhood, which is about a young boy named Mason growing up
in Texas in a broken home. By the time Mason is a teenager, his
formerly deadbeat dad has turned in a positive direction and now
has a new wife and baby. For Mason's fifteenth birthday, his step-
grandparents give him a Bible engraved with his name. He smiles
politely and thanks them. In the next scene, you see Mason holding the Bible on his lap unopened as he and his older sister sit in
a church—probably for the first time ever—along with the dad,
stepmom, and step-grandparents.

Later that day, when the conversation turns to the upcoming
baptism of his dad's new baby, Mason asks whether Mason had
been baptized when he was a baby. His dad laughs, saying he hadn't
given any thought at all to Mason's soul back then. It's obvious that
Mason is slightly curious about spiritual things but that his dad is

not prepared to have a conversation about God, even when the subject comes up naturally. Mason and his sister, Samantha, both wonder out loud if their dad is now one of those "God people."

As I (Mary) watched the movie, I found myself wanting to contribute some of the plotline. What I desperately wanted the dad to say was that he now *was one of God's people*, and that Jesus had made a huge difference in his life. I wanted him to tell his story of redemption—how he used to be an absentee father and broken man but now was becoming the man God wanted him to be. These two adolescent kids saw a stability and joy in their father's new life that begged for an explanation. Because they had seen so much of his poor parenting and brokenness, they might have been open to hearing about the faith component that had changed him. The love and acceptance they received from the step-grandparents and step-mother (who were obviously Christ followers) had to have made a strong impression on them too. Sadly, the dad let the moment pass. He missed an opportunity to share his faith story. How true is that of so many of us?

Let's face it—our culture is deteriorating. Broken families. Addictions. Abuse. Absent fathers. Struggling single parents. Failing schools. Violence in the home. Sexual promiscuity. Pornography. Hostile politics. People moving frequently and having no stable community of friends and family.

Problems are everywhere, but as followers of Jesus, we can offer hope. We need to share the stories of how God has worked in our lives. Getting a better understanding of the Art of Sharing in a post-Christian society is highly relevant as the final practice in The 9 Arts of Spiritual Conversations. If we have experienced the power of the gospel, the priceless value of our own relationship with God through Jesus, and genuine love for those we know, we will be compelled to share our faith with others. If we believe that Jesus can meet the deepest needs of people we know, isn't it possible that our simple redemptive story and God's story can intersect their story?

International evangelist Luis Palau's research shows that 75 percent of all those who come to Christ do so through a relationship with a Christian friend, relative, or coworker. The Institute of American Church Growth reports an even higher percentage, with almost 90 percent of the 14,000 Christians recently polled saying they came to Christ through "a friend or relative who invested in a relationship with them."[1]

Why share our faith? As you are in relationships or intentionally develop new ones with people who are different from you—people who may not yet know Christ—I'd encourage you to honestly ask yourself these questions: Do you want the best for them? Are you convinced that knowing Jesus will give them not just assurance for eternity but the most fulfilling life right here and now? Do you care deeply for them, and do you want to spend eternity with them? If the answer is yes, our response is clear. The question is, *how* can we share our faith effectively and for the right reasons? We must first look at our motives.

Love Compels Us

The first and most important reason to share your faith in Jesus should always be genuine love for the other person, not your own agenda or a sense of obligation. If we share our faith because we think we're supposed to or because we think, perhaps subconsciously, that we'll earn God's favor or some sort of divine credit, we will alienate people when they detect our tainted motives. Sharing our faith is not like closing a sales deal. Out of love, we are sharing our experience and understanding of who Jesus is and how someone can relate to him. We are not "selling" Jesus.

Let's mine an illustration from another movie. In *The Big Kahuna*, Phil, a salesman, confronts his young, zealous Christian coworker, Bob, about his motives for heavy-handed proselytizing on the job:

It doesn't matter whether you're selling Jesus or Buddha or civil rights or "How to Make Money in Real Estate with No Money Down." That doesn't make you a human being; it makes you a marketing rep. If you want to talk to somebody honestly, as a human being, ask him about his kids. Find out what his dreams are—just to find out, for no other reason. Because as soon as you lay your hands on a conversation to steer it, it's not a conversation anymore; it's a pitch. And you're not a human being; you're a marketing rep.[2]

We as Christians need to treat others as humans, not as objects of a sales and marketing ploy. As we get to know people and genuinely care about them, we are able to help make the authentic connection between their humanity and the message of Jesus. The goal of what we share is not "Let's get you to heaven!" The goal is "I would love for you to meet Jesus because he really loves you and so do I." We are introducing people to him. He is real life, meaningful life, abundant life, hope-filled life. Jesus is not a way to heaven. He is the Way to God. We share Jesus because he is real life now and for eternity. As Colossians 3 teaches, "Your real life is hidden with Christ in God. And when Christ, who is your life, is revealed to the whole world, you will share in all his glory" (Colossians 3:3-4, NLT).

Jesus Has Met Our Deepest Need

The second reason to share our faith in Christ is that we sincerely believe the gospel has met our deepest need and will meet others' deepest need. What makes us willing to take the risk of sharing our story and God's story? Why face our fears and risk rejection or criticism? It's simply that we've come to the conviction that the gospel is not just true for us but that it is "good news that will bring great joy to all people" (Luke 2:10, NLT).

The gospel—that Jesus died for our sins, that Jesus rose from the dead, and that Jesus is Lord of all things—defines the Christian faith (see 1 Corinthians 15). Of course, the gospel isn't just about knowing these things; it is about responding and accepting for ourselves what Christ has done. The gospel is the incredible message that God has provided us a way to be in relationship with him now and always through Jesus Christ, and that all things will be brought under the sovereign authority of our good God.

An important part of sharing Jesus with people who believe differently is to be aware of how God might be at work in their current circumstances to bring them to himself. They may trust you enough to open up about a health issue, a problem at work, or a difficult relationship. And while you may have both a listening ear and wise counsel for those issues, you can also share, if the Spirit leads you, about how God has met a similar need in your life. Share simply, honestly, and transparently. Be attentive to Scripture that God may reveal to you for that specific situation, and prayerfully and sensitively share it with your friends.

As you walk alongside your friends, God may show you specific ways in which he has prepared them for the message of the gospel. You may also begin to see evidence of emptiness in their lives—emptiness that they are not even likely to recognize. This was so obvious in the characters in *Boyhood,* who seemed "harassed and helpless, like sheep without a shepherd" (Matthew 9:36). The fullness of your life in Jesus will increase your compassion for your friends and your desire for them to know Jesus as well, so that their own deepest need might be met—and that's a great reason to share your faith!

It's Our Greatest Treasure

The third reason to share your faith in Jesus is that you are convinced that God is worth knowing. Have you ever taken part in a "white elephant" gift exchange? The beautiful wrapping paper on each gift hides an object someone actually wants to get rid of. The intent is to re-gift a useless item you have previously received, and everyone at a party can have a good laugh at the ridiculous things they unwrap.

Compare that kind of "sharing" to giving the gift of a personal relationship with God. Unlike the re-gifted hand-crocheted beer can hat, having God's presence is something we cherish and want to give away. Of course, as we give that gift, we don't lose it; our faith is actually strengthened and increased by sharing. It multiplies.

Furthermore, we sincerely want the person to have this gift. We know the priceless value of forgiveness, of new life, of having God as a part of every moment. We have found "the pearl of great price"—that treasure that makes all others seem like worthless trinkets—and we're glad to show its beauty and value to the world. This was true in my life. I (Mary) became a Christ follower at age sixteen at a weekend retreat led by a group of charismatic Catholics who were part of the Cursillo movement. Although I had gone through eleven years of Catholic schooling, somehow I had missed the central concept of believing and following Jesus. It all became clear to me in one weekend when I was a junior in high school. My mother was in the hospital with a nervous breakdown for an entire year, and our whole family was in crisis. I didn't think I could make it through life on my own. On the first night, the speaker shared that God loved me and wanted a relationship with me.

Admitting I was a sinner and needed a Savior seemed so obvious to me after years of unsuccessfully trying to keep all of God's rules! I decided that if Jesus had paid the price for all I did wrong and was willing to forgive me if I believed and followed him, I couldn't refuse such a good gift. I invited him into my life. I can't imagine living each day without the love and forgiveness that I found in Christ. It gives my life meaning and purpose. I want others to have that peace, joy, and love that only God can give. It is my greatest treasure!

The Value of Story

From an early age, we all love stories. Ever-expanding numbers of children's books reveal the hunger children have to hear stories—but they're not the only ones who crave a good tale. New books and movies are released each month to an expectant adult population of all ages, stages, backgrounds, and ethnic groups. I confess that I would rather hear a personal story than an educational principle or a doctrinal statement, and a fitting story helps me understand how doctrine applies in real life.

Each of us has a compelling story worth sharing—the story of how God intersected our lives and offered us his free gift of salvation, transforming our lives here and now and for all eternity. As American literary scholar Jonathan Gottschall puts it, "We are creatures of story, and the process of changing one mind or the whole world must begin with 'Once upon a time.'"[3]

When you share your faith story, you connect with the listener's story and with God's story. Your faith journey is a real experience of the power of God—not an abstract idea—and it can generate questions, move others, and inspire action. Your story captures both the head and the heart of the listener and can move people to consider ideas they never have considered before.

Jesus was well aware of the power of a good story. His parables of the Prodigal Son, the Good Samaritan, and the seeds planted in different types of soil all painted pictures in people's minds and allowed truth to penetrate their hearts. Over time, as they thought through what they'd heard, they could discover more and more what the stories revealed about God and themselves.

The parable of the two sons in Matthew 21:28-31 is short but profound: A father owns a vineyard and asks his sons to go out to work in it. The first son says he won't, but later he changes his mind and goes. The second son says he will, but he doesn't go to the vineyard.

Jesus closed this short story with a question to the chief priests and elders who heard it: Which of the two sons did what the father wanted? They answered, of course, that it was the first son—the one who initially said he wouldn't go but later changed his mind and obeyed. Jesus went on to tell his listeners that the scum of society (tax collectors and prostitutes), though they had said no to God, were now repenting, doing the Father's will, and entering into his Kingdom. By contrast, the religious leaders had said yes to God but never obeyed his teaching, and therefore they were failing to enter his Kingdom. What a clear picture Jesus painted through this simple parable of how he wants us to respond to God's message of repentance!

In addition, every day Jesus created new stories as he interacted with people around him. Stories about blind and sick people being healed. Stories about thousands being fed with a few loaves of bread and fish. Stories of Jesus interacting with his followers, with religious leaders, and with "sinners." The four Gospels are filled with real stories that help us know what Jesus is like.

People who are just beginning to explore the life of Jesus may be willing to read a little of the Bible or hear a story or two about him. But the story of how Jesus has impacted *your* life makes a radical statement that he is living and active today—that he is a personal, integral part of your life now.

Jesus says he came "that [his followers] may have life, and have it to the full" (John 10:10). The apostle Paul reveals in 2 Corinthians 5:17 that as soon as we belong to Jesus, we become new people. We are not the same anymore; our old lives have gone and a new life has begun. Our personal faith stories key into this reality and answer this basic question: *What difference has Jesus made in your life?* In other words, what were you like before knowing Jesus, and what was your life like without him? How did you make your decision to follow Jesus? And finally, what are you like now, after you have had a relationship with Jesus for a while?

Telling Your Story Well

When you are at the point in a relationship of explaining God's story, you already have done the hard work of building trust and have earned the right to explain the gospel message. This is a high-risk, high-trust interaction. Your relational investment in the person you are about to share with makes it much more likely that your story will be warmly received.

We don't get numerous opportunities to tell our faith stories to people God has placed in our lives. Consider it a great privilege when it happens. This is a chance to share something of tremendous value with someone else. It is a humble, genuine moment, not a time to "download" a memorized strategy on someone without discretion. If you are willing to share what God has done in your life, he will orchestrate a time and place for a conversation. Learn to listen to the prompting of the Holy Spirit to know when it's appropriate to share your faith story.

When that opportunity comes along, here are four simple guidelines to help you tell it well. They are adapted from Willow Creek Church pastor Bill Hybels's sermons and his book *Just Walk across the Room*:

1. Be brief. Tell the whole story in less than two to three minutes, or ideally in fewer than one hundred words. This may seem very short to you, but to your listeners it will seem like a long time. You are much better off leaving them wanting more rather than wishing you had never started talking. If they want to know more, they will ask follow-up questions. Keep the follow-up discussion more of a dialogue than a monologue. In this way your listener has more control in determining the length of the conversation.

2. Be clear. Don't tell weird or complicated storylines. People don't usually have the tolerance or interest to make sense of things that might have great meaning to you but are hard to understand or can quickly categorize you as a "religious nut."

3. Use common language. Try to use ordinary language in your faith story. Compose your story in such a way that it can be understood both by Christians and by people who believe differently. Terms like "born again" and "accepting Jesus" are not phrases typically used outside of a church context. If you have to use words that you don't think will resonate with your listener, then define them casually within the conversation. (For example: "Then I realized that my problem was sin—I did wrong and selfish things all the time in a way I couldn't change on my own.")

4. Be humble. Often Christians come across as superior when they tell their stories. Avoid criticizing the church, organizations, or other people. It's probably better not even to mention church denominations in your story. What's important for us to understand is the main difference between people who have found a relationship with Jesus and those who haven't. Christians know they are sinners in need of someone to save them, which means they recognize their continuous need for God. This understanding should produce a deep humility in us as we interact with everyone—Christians and non-Christians alike.[4]

Simplifying Your Story

A simple structure and a clear focus will enable you to share your story in a compelling way that will help people see the reality and power of Jesus in your life and can potentially lead them to desire a relationship with him. In telling your story, you are attempting to answer these three simple questions: (1) What were you like *before* knowing Jesus? (2) How did you end up placing your trust in Jesus? (3) What are you like now *after* becoming a follower of Christ?

If you grew up in a Christian home with a very early belief in Jesus, the way you approach these questions may be a little different. You might not remember what you were like before you knew Jesus, but you can see how he has changed you over the years. You may not know what your life was like without him, but you can imagine what your life would be like now if you weren't in a committed relationship with him.

Jesus transforms each of us, but sometimes when we try to describe specifically what he has done, it takes thought to put the change into words. Be honest about your own process—don't make up something that sounds more dramatic than it is. It's also helpful to share the uncertainties and struggles that still remain. No Christian is perfect. But if you are a true follower of Christ, he has certainly made some difference in your life, and that is what you need to share.

To understand the strength of this approach, consider how the weight-loss industry leverages the "before" and "after" portraits of people who joined their programs. "Hi! I'm Sheila and I used to wear a size 18. Now after the best-ever diet, I wear a size 6." The transformation that happens in us when we come to know Jesus is a much more profound gift than any weight-loss program can provide! The question here is, how can we communicate that life-changing story well to others?

Try to find one word or phrase that easily identifies who you were before you met Jesus or fully trusted him, and another that describes who you are now that you have a relationship with him. We see several good examples in the Bible. One of the simplest faith stories is found in John 9:25, when the blind man has been healed by Jesus and is being questioned by the Pharisees. They grill him with questions: Was he born blind? Can he now see? How did this happen? With all eyes on him to answer, the former blind man says to them, "One thing I do know. I was blind but now I see!"

His transformation was clear—from blindness to sight. For you it might be a "before" life consumed with guilt and shame, changed to one that is filled with grace and freedom "after" you received the forgiveness and power of Jesus.

When my friend Colin was asked what difference Jesus really made in his life, he was ready with his simple story:

> Throughout high school, I was proud—and to be honest, pretty selfish. I had grown up in a churchgoing family, and I knew about Jesus; but for me Jesus was a Sunday idea. My youth leader sat me down for nachos when I was a senior in high school and said, "When are you going to quit thinking about Jesus and start following him?" I hadn't made him the leader of my life. Right there, I prayed to Jesus and accepted his gift of forgiveness and new life. There weren't any fireworks, but I knew that my life would never be the same.

As Colin concluded his personal story, he briefly shared what his life is like now.

> Now I know that I'm a child of God. Jesus isn't an idea to me—he's the leader of my life. My focus is to love and serve God.

Colin's short story could read like this: Before, I was self-focused. Then I met Jesus personally, and now I am God-focused.

Sharing God's Story

If you have simplified your own story, how can you share God's story in a way that is also simple and compelling and leaves listeners wanting more? For some of us, the tendency is to tell more than people are ready to hear. For others, the tendency is to shy away from the conversation and say very little. What if there was a way to share God's story that would pique the listener's interest to hear more?

Every year, movie producers filter through hundreds of screenplays to find the next great film. To get their attention, writers create a simple plot description with an emotional "hook." It's called the "logline." Here's an example: "A young man and woman from different social classes fall in love aboard an ill-fated voyage at sea" (*Titanic*). Screenwriters have found that a clear, concise logline is essential to stimulate interest in their story so that studio executives will give the pivotal invitation: "Tell me more."

How can our approach to sharing God's story be more like a logline and less like a lecture? What if it took only fifteen to thirty seconds to share? What if we told the story of God's incredible offer of love, grace, and *real* life in such a concise, compelling way that seekers burned with curiosity and wanted us to tell them more?

In 2011, *Christian Century* invited some Christian authors to summarize the gospel in a maximum of seven words. Here are some samples:

- "God, through Jesus Christ, welcomes you anyhow" (Martin Marty).
- "Divinely persistent, God really loves us" (Donald Shriver).
- "In Christ, God's 'yes' defeats our 'no'" (Beverly Roberts Gaventa).
- "God is love: This is no joke" (Kathleen Norris).[5]

These statements are likely to intrigue a listener by virtue of their brevity, provoking thought and inviting further conversation: "Tell me more . . ." or "So what do you mean by that?" But you can't say something in a few words if you're not clear on the essence of the message.

Most of us have a big gap between understanding the gospel and being able to explain it to someone else. We "get it" when it comes to God's story, facts of Christianity, and themes of the Bible. We may know the right answers to a list of multiple-choice questions. But could we actually teach Christianity 101 from memory? And if a listener were hostile, would we be completely at a loss to defend our ideas in a compelling, convincing way?

The first step is to know the essence of the Christian message so that we can explain the truth clearly and concisely to someone who wants to understand. With brevity that doesn't sound condescending, what is the simple message God wants us to share with people?

Just as Jesus modeled teaching through storytelling, it's a good idea to know several simple analogies and illustrations to help you tell God's story clearly. However, filter them into a conversation rather than presenting them as a monologue. While you're sharing, continue to notice, pray, listen, and ask questions so that you're in tune with the person you're sharing with. It's much more than a quick presentation; it's a dialogue. Be sure to choose illustrations carefully, paying attention to what might resonate most with your listener and his or her questions about God.

These may seem familiar or even too simple, but a straightforward analogy can still communicate powerfully when you share it with someone with whom you've developed a relationship over time. Here are a few simple, time-tested illustrations.

1. God as a Good Judge

We know from the Bible that God is both loving and just. We've discussed his tremendous love for us throughout this book, but he is also the God of justice, who will one day judge every person. How do we reconcile that? This simple story might help explain it.

Suppose you rob a bank, get caught, and are brought to court. You are clearly guilty when you go before the judge—who, as luck would have it, turns out to be your father. The judge, needing to be impartial and uphold the law, must declare you guilty of the crime and sentence you to time in prison. But because he loves you so much as his child, he then takes off the judicial robes he is wearing, comes around to the other side of the judge's bench, and agrees to take the jail sentence in your place. You don't have to pay the price for your crime, because he is choosing to pay it for you.

The apostle Paul says that "all have sinned and fall short of the glory of God" (Romans 3:23) and that we will be accountable to God, our ultimate judge who views our sins against his perfect standard of holiness. Paul goes on to explain that "God presented Christ as a sacrifice of atonement, through the shedding of his blood—to be received by faith. He did this to demonstrate his righteousness, because in his forbearance he had left the sins committed beforehand unpunished—he did it to demonstrate his righteousness at the present time, so as to be just and the one who justifies those who have faith in Jesus" (Romans 3:25-26).

In the powerful movie *Courageous*, police officer Nathan Hayes talks to a fellow officer about God as a good and righteous judge:

> Okay. Suppose [your mom] was brutally attacked and murdered in a parking lot. The guy was caught and put on trial. But he says, "Hey, Judge, I've committed this crime, but I've done a lot of good in my life." If the judge let him go free, would you say he was a good judge or a bad judge? . . . The Bible says that God is a good judge, and He will punish the guilty, not for what they did right, but for what they did wrong. Because He loved us, He sent His son, Jesus Christ, to take the punishment that we deserved, and put it on Himself, and that's why He died on the cross. But it only applies if you accept it. That's

why I asked for His forgiveness. I asked Him to save me. And I'm a new man because of Christ.[6]

This presentation was simple and natural, and the timing of Hayes's sharing was appropriate.

In telling your own personal story of why you asked for God's forgiveness and accepted his atoning gift of grace, you could reference these other important verses in John 3:16-18:

> For God so loved the world, that He gave His only begotten Son, that whoever believes in Him shall not perish, but have eternal life. For God did not send the Son into the world to judge the world, but that the world might be saved through Him. He who believes in Him is not judged; he who does not believe has been judged already, because he has not believed in the name of the only begotten Son of God. (NASB)

2. The Bridge

The Bible tells us: "For the wages of sin is death, but the free gift of God is eternal life in Christ Jesus our Lord" (Romans 6:23, ESV). On a piece of paper, you could draw a stick figure on the left side. Write *us* under it. On the right side, write *God*. Draw a horizontal line above each word, with lines extending down so it looks like there are two cliffs with a wide gap between *us* and *God*. Explain that because each of us has moral failures (what the Bible calls "sin"), we have all "earned" separation from God, or spiritual death. (Write *death* at the bottom of the paper.) There's a gap between us and God. We can't jump across the gap or earn our way across it; trying to cross it ourselves leads to death. The only thing that can bridge the gap is Jesus. (Draw a cross that connects the two cliffs, connecting *us* to *God*.) He made a connection possible; now all that remains is for us to walk across the way he's given us by accepting Christ as the forgiver and leader of our lives.[7]

The bridge is one of the most common illustrations seen on gospel tracts handed out on street corners, and some would claim it has outlived its usefulness. However, I (Mary) think it still has great merit—if used when people are ready to see it. For example, Alice, a woman who had been coming to my first spiritual-conversation group for several months, had heard me say that I had a personal relationship with Jesus. Alice had started coming to the group when she lost her executive job with a large company and her husband left her for another woman. She had attended church on and off for most of her life, but she had not understood the core message about Jesus and his forgiveness of our sins when we believe in him. She hadn't understood that we as humans have a sin problem that separates us from God. She also was not desperate for God—until this season of her life when things were going much differently than she had expected.

Living without a close relationship with God was increasingly problematic for Alice, especially when she saw people like the group facilitators who were in close communion with God, living with peace and joy. She wanted that for herself. After one of our discussions, I showed Alice the bridge illustration, and it enabled her to know what she needed to do. The following week, she came to me privately and asked if she could become a Christian, knowing that Jesus would forgive her and be the leader of her life.

3. Do versus Done

On a piece of paper, you could write the word *DO*. Explain that a common misconception about Christianity is that it (like all religions) consists of a set of rules to be obeyed or practices in which to engage, all so that we can earn God's approval. This frame of reference sees religion as *DO*; it is all about our activity, self-improvement, and hard work. Now add an N and E at the end to spell *DONE*. Explain that becoming a Christian is about accepting what *Christ* has done—not about *our* own actions. The new birth Jesus talked about (see John 3) actually comes from ceasing to do anything we think would earn God's favor (which is, if you think about it, spiritual pride masquerading as "good character"). Like children, we are to accept that it is "done" and there's nothing we can add to Jesus' finished work on the cross. We don't earn forgiveness through a life of dos and don'ts—that would be impossible, even if we tried. Instead, salvation is already *done*, completed; so we simply accept God's grace as a gift, and we experience a new life by faith.[8]

Two women named Chelsey and Pam began attending a spiritual conversation group a few years ago in the Pacific Northwest. When they joined, they were convinced from their experience with churches that they were not good enough to become Christians. They thought they had to get their act cleaned up before God would love them and accept them. They learned in their group— by studying the Bible and talking about what it meant to be a Christian—that they would never be good enough to please God on their own merits. Jesus paid the ultimate price for sin by dying on the cross so that we can be right with God when we admit that we are sinners and need God's unmerited favor, called grace. Both women decided to put their faith in Jesus, knowing that they didn't have to *do* anything but repent and believe. The work of salvation was *done* through Jesus' death and resurrection.

Sharon, one of their group facilitators and a friend of mine, explained the beauty of God's grace by reading *The Message*'s rendering of Ephesians 2:1-10 in their group:

> It wasn't so long ago that you were mired in that old
> stagnant life of sin. You let the world, which doesn't know
> the first thing about living, tell you how to live. You
> filled your lungs with polluted unbelief, and then exhaled

disobedience. We all did it, all of us doing what we felt like doing, when we felt like doing it, all of us in the same boat. It's a wonder God didn't lose his temper and do away with the whole lot of us. Instead, immense in mercy and with an incredible love, he embraced us. He took our sin-dead lives and made us alive in Christ. He did all this on his own, with no help from us! Then he picked us up and set us down in highest heaven in company with Jesus, our Messiah.

Now God has us where he wants us, with all the time in this world and the next to shower grace and kindness upon us in Christ Jesus. Saving is all his idea, and all his work. All we do is trust him enough to let him do it. It's God's gift from start to finish! We don't play the major role. If we did, we'd probably go around bragging that we'd done the whole thing! No, we neither make nor save ourselves. God does both the making and saving. He creates each of us by Christ Jesus to join him in the work he does, the good work he has gotten ready for us to do, work we had better be doing.

We cannot brag or take any credit for this saving act by God. Reading this simple passage to people who are ready to hear it can help people understand the amazing gift of grace God has given us through Jesus Christ.

4. God in the Driver's Seat

Almost everyone understands the difference between driving a car and riding along as a passenger. Another simple illustration is to suggest that putting Jesus, rather than yourself, in the "driver's seat" of your life will give him the authority to steer your life in the direction he wants to take it. When we direct ourselves, we tend to make mistakes and focus more on ourselves than God. That often results in self-induced suffering and pain, harming others around us and negatively impacting our own lives. But when we trust Jesus to take over the steering wheel, he guides us to the destinations God has for our lives.

My husband, Paul, is a private plane pilot. Several years ago, we were flying back from a resort community with my nephew Tim, who was actively seeking God at the time. We had engaged in several spiritual conversations with him over our family vacation, which was now concluding with a flight home in Uncle Paul's plane. Due to some bad weather and slippery conditions on the runway, it was a rocky takeoff from the resort airport, and even I was feeling a little anxious about our safety. As Tim and I sat in the back seat of the plane after takeoff, I asked him whether he was nervous about our departure. He said no, because he fully trusted Uncle Paul as a pilot. His response prompted me to say that faith in Christ was like that too. When we trust Jesus as the pilot flying the "plane" of our life, we know that he is worthy of our faith in him.

At the time, I thought this might be a little cheesy for my twenty-year-old nephew, but he said he got it. I asked if he would be ready to invite Jesus into his life as Lord, and to my surprise he said yes. At 22,000 feet above the ground, with our Piper Malibu airplane noise surrounding us, Tim prayed a simple prayer to do just that.

5. Believe + Receive = Become

Following a simple Scripture—"Yet to all who did receive him, to those who believed in his name, he gave the right to become children of God" (John 1:12)—you can write the above equation on a piece of paper to explain the simple steps to accepting Jesus.

First, explain that it is necessary to *believe* Jesus is who he said he was—the Son of God. But belief is not enough. You also must *receive* that truth into your heart and soul. Once you have done that, you will *become* God's child, adopted into his family, forgiven of your sins and promised hope and life at its fullest now and into eternity.

My father believed almost all his life that Jesus was the Son of God, and he had been a regular churchgoer since his youth. But it wasn't until he was in his late seventies that he began to *receive* the truth about the saving power that Jesus gives. He let that truth start to transform him as we began regularly talking about spiritual matters. Dad could become easily irritated by aggressive drivers or people he thought were trying to cheat him in some way. He also had some irrational fears and guilt that went way back to his childhood. His little sister Betty was only four years old when my dad, who was only a year older, walked her across a busy street. She let go of his hand, ran in front of an oncoming car, and was killed. He carried that guilt and shame around all of his life. Yet decades later, when Dad and I lived in different parts of the country, we started to read the Bible together weekly on the phone. As he slowly began to *believe and receive* the truth of God's Word and apply it to his life in new ways that healed him, Dad *became* one of God's children and was more joyful, knowing he was fully forgiven, accepted, and loved by God.

Ready to Follow?

Telling someone about Jesus is different from asking them to open themselves up to him—either by way of investigation or, if they are ready, to receive his forgiveness. Just knowing God's story is not enough; after all, the devil knows lots of biblical truths!

God wants our hearts; we need to respond and surrender our lives to him. If you're in conversation with a person who is ready to do that, you can lead him or her in a simple prayer, either to ask that Jesus make himself real to the person or to invite Jesus to be their leader (Lord) and forgiver (Savior). One way to structure this prayer is with the simple outline *Help, Sorry, Thanks*: Help, I need your forgiveness, God. Sorry for the way I've shut you out of my life. Thanks for what you did for me through Jesus.

Young Life expresses it this way: Coming into a relationship with Jesus is as easy as *ABC*: *Admit* that you are a sinner, *believe* that Jesus died for your sins and is God, and *commit* to follow Jesus as the leader of your life. I really like this one for its simplicity. When someone is ready to follow Jesus, using this model seems to lead naturally to praying with that person and letting them use words that have meaning to them.

Overcoming Obstacles

To engage with people who believe differently and to share our story and God's story, we must identify and overcome three primary hurdles in sharing our faith: (1) We're unclear about our understanding of the gospel and how to explain our experience with God, (2) we are afraid we'll receive a negative response, and (3) we think that evangelism is the job of the professionals. By facing and understanding these barriers, we can intentionally overcome them.

The apostle Paul recognizes the first hurdle. He asks the church at Colossae to "pray that I may proclaim [the gospel] clearly, as I should" (Colossians 4:4). If we sincerely want help, God loves to answer that prayer! With the guidance of God's Holy Spirit and some intentional practice of the simple suggestions given in this chapter, anyone can share his or her story and God's story in a winsome manner.

Another hurdle to overcome is our fear of receiving a negative response. At some level, we all want to be liked, and most of us avoid offending or bothering others. The fear of being ostracized or rejected is a powerful force. Our culture has a negative stereotype of people who proselytize, and we don't want to be labeled as intolerant, narrow minded, or "one of those people"—even if we do have something we believe our world desperately needs. I love the reminder in 2 Timothy 1:7 (NLT): "For God has not given us a spirit of fear and timidity, but of power, love, and self-discipline." It's also helpful to remember that "there is no fear in love. But perfect love drives out fear" (1 John 4:18).

Finally, our third hurdle is based on the thinking that sharing the good news about Jesus is a job for pastors and those with the spiritual gift of evangelism. We have adopted the mentality that we should bring our friends to someone more qualified (pastors, evangelists, Bible experts), and they will "deliver the goods and close the deal." Hopefully, these 9 Arts of Spiritual Conversations have given you a different perspective on this. Anyone can notice, pray, listen, ask questions, love, welcome, facilitate, and serve together. Sharing is natural in the context of a trusting relationship.

The apostle Peter wrote, "Always be prepared to give an answer to everyone who asks you to give the reason for the hope that you have" (1 Peter 3:15). We are all—and always—called to be prepared in advance for an opportunity to give a reason for our hope in Jesus. And if God wants us geared up at all times, he must plan to send many opportunities our way to share our faith.

My (Crilly's) buddy Dan was sitting on the bleachers, waiting for his men's flag football game to start, when he met Johnny. They connected quickly over sports and Italian food. After the game, Dan told me about this bleacher connection, and we began praying for Johnny. Within a couple of weeks the conversations between Dan and Johnny transitioned naturally from sports to more substantive spiritual topics. Johnny had questions about his religious upbringing, and he wondered about this Jesus whom Dan talked about. What the sidelines didn't allow, the local restaurant did: food and an opportunity to talk more deeply.

With Johnny's permission, Dan took his best stab at summing up what the Bible teaches about Christ, why he had to come, and what it all means for our lives. Using two water glasses and a straw, Dan laid out the classic bridge illustration in full 3D: The glasses represented us and God; the distance between the glasses, the separation caused by our moral failure. But thank God for the straw—that is, Jesus, who alone bridged the gap through his life, death, and resurrection.

Feeling bold because of his deepening friendship with Johnny, Dan issued a challenge. "Johnny, there are just two kinds of people in the world: those swimming around in this glass without God, and those on this side who've crossed over and are now swimming in this glass with God. Which one are you?" Johnny indicated that he had never asked Christ to be his Savior and Leader, and politely declined Dan's invitation. "Not ready!" Johnny said. Dan replied, "Fine. Then you can pay the bill."

After a good laugh, the two parted with the understanding that Johnny's decision wouldn't affect their relationship. Two weeks later, Dan got a call. "Yo, Dan . . . I did it." Dan knew right away what that was about. Johnny had walked over "the straw," the bridge connecting him to God, and now, through Jesus, he was on God's side!

Discover

1. What is the biggest obstacle for you when sharing God's story?

2. Why do you think people are afraid to tell their personal stories about becoming a Christ follower?

Practice

1. Get together this week with someone who will role-play with you, and explain God's story of redemption as you would to a non-Christian.

2. Practice sharing your personal faith story with a friend in under two minutes. Ask for feedback on how it was received.

PART IV

Ongoing Spiritual Conversations

GOD HAS PLACED people in your life who might not attend a church but would be willing to talk about spiritual matters in a small-group community if it feels safe for honest discussion and discovery. Starting an ongoing spiritual conversation group is an effective way to engage others in the big questions about life, God, and the Bible. It begins when three or four Christians join together to facilitate a discussion and learn along with the group participants. No one is an expert. Everyone is a learner. At the heart is the inductive learning approach, because people learn best when they discover truth for themselves through dialogue—as the early followers of Jesus did with him.

CHAPTER 12

Starting a Q Place

Then Jesus came to them and said, "All authority in heaven and on earth has been given to me. Therefore go and make disciples of all nations, baptizing them in the name of the Father and of the Son and of the Holy Spirit, and teaching them to obey everything I have commanded you. And surely I am with you always, to the very end of the age."

MATTHEW 28:18-20

Who is to bring the knowledge that will answer life's great questions to our world today? That would be you. If you are a follower of Jesus . . . you have a calling far more important than you may know.

JOHN ORTBERG

MY (MARY'S) FAMILY LIVED in Portola Valley, California, for nineteen years. During that time, Paul and I coached our three kids' sports teams, volunteered in many school functions, and led several community groups. We knew a lot of people there. Most of them were not regular churchgoers.

In late 2001, I spoke to two of my Christian friends, Kristin and Judy, about the possibility of starting a spiritual discussion group for friends in our community. We started praying about whom to invite and when to start. Most of the people we considered inviting would have told you at the time that they were not actively seeking anything spiritual. They were more skeptics than seekers. But God placed them on our hearts as potential participants in our big experiment to have ongoing spiritual conversations with our friends.

We invited thirty women to come to my house to check out the possibility of a spiritual discussion group, which we described as "a nonthreatening place to have conversations about God." Fourteen women came that first day, and they eventually brought friends. Each person who came back in the subsequent weeks and years has been profoundly touched by this life-changing experience, including me. I believe that God guided us through our discussions about faith-related issues, and as a result each person's understanding of him deepened. Concurrently, we came to genuinely love and respect one another and had a ton of fun through these weekly authentic conversations about God.

Many participants had not known what it meant to be a Christian, even though they had grown up attending Catholic, Protestant, Christian Scientist, or Mormon churches. Others had no background at all in Christianity, describing themselves as agnostics, atheists, or New Age. It was a pretty diverse group!

One of the regular participants was Denise. She and I had become friends when she was a Brownie troop leader and I volunteered at the troop meetings each week. When I started this group, she was one of the first people I invited because I sensed that she was spiritually curious and I thought she'd trust me enough to check it out.

An attorney who worked part-time, Denise enjoyed our discussions so much that she regularly arranged her work schedule around our group meetings. After several months of discussing difficult faith questions and considering Scripture in our group, Denise stayed around to talk with me after one of our meetings. In the process of responding to one of the questions that day, I had briefly shared that I had a personal relationship with Jesus. Another participant had shared with the group that the previous week she had made a decision to become a Christian.

These comments were on Denise's mind. She told me that even though she had gone to church most of her life, she didn't think she had a relationship with Jesus, and she wanted to know how she could. I shared with her a simple way to invite Jesus into her life, and she chose to do so right there in my living room that day.

Denise was eager to share the good news about Jesus and invite others to explore faith the way that she had. Over the next few years, she brought several women to our group, including her sister-in-law, Monica. Monica had been struggling with infertility, and every week Denise asked our group to pray that Monica would conceive. When Monica did end up getting pregnant, she discovered she was going to have twins! Our group celebrated with a baby shower. Overwhelmed by the love and prayers of this group, Monica decided she also wanted to have a personal relationship with this God who had provided such a miracle.

Denise's husband, Brad, was another person affected by her growing faith. In between our Tuesday group meetings, Denise shared with him what she was learning about God and the Bible. Before long, Denise *and* Brad were attending church again and getting fed spiritually. Two years later, at age forty-six, Brad was in a fatal ski accident. This was tragic for Denise and her family, but she was confident that a few months before he died, Brad had figured out what was true about Jesus and had made a decision to follow him. "While his death is devastating news to all of us, I am at peace knowing that Brad was finally on a spiritual path, getting to know Jesus, right before his death," she said.

The previous chapters describe practices that equip you to engage in meaningful conversations about God. However, without intentionality to create an ongoing opportunity, your conversations may be hit-or-miss. In chapter 9 we looked at the value of small groups and facilitating them well. When safe, meaningful conversations get started, the most natural next step is to keep them going by gathering a group of spiritually curious people who are interested in learning more about God and what they believe. The result will be ripple effects in everyone's lives. New disciples make more new disciples.

It's All about Relationships

Greg Ogden, pastor and author of several books on disciples and leadership, says, "If the mantra regarding the value of real estate is 'location, location, location,' then the core ingredient in making disciples is 'relationship, relationship, relationship.'"[1]

As Christ followers, we know that being a Christian is not about following rules but about having a relationship with Jesus because of what he did for us on the cross. Yet as we've discussed throughout the book, so often our approach to making new disciples misses that very point. Rather than being in a relationship with followers of Jesus who talk naturally about God, most people have experienced the gospel message as a one-time hit from a stranger or a download of information from a speaker—or they have never heard it at all. The ministry example that Jesus himself gave us is one of relationship—of pouring his time and energy into a small group of twelve. He prayed fervently in choosing his disciples, and over three years' time he experienced life with them, engaged them in discussions, and challenged them to take action as well as to observe, think, and draw conclusions about who he was.

Jesus' life contains an even more profound illustration of relationship that is readily taught as doctrine, yet so easy to miss in significance: the Trinity. Luke records the event at Jesus' baptism: "While He was praying, heaven was opened, and the Holy Spirit descended upon Him in bodily form like a dove, and a voice came out of heaven, 'You are My beloved Son, in You I am well-pleased'" (Luke 3:21-22, NASB).

In everything Jesus did during his earthly ministry, as well as throughout time and eternity, he was in a perfect relationship with the Father and the Holy Spirit. In the most perfect community ever, there are *three* persons, and each one is in constant fellowship with the other two. This divine triad is equal in all ways, equally expressing the fullness of the attributes of God—his love, grace, truth, holiness, and power. What can we learn from this beautiful illustration of a triad that is relevant to disciple making?

Finding Twelve through Three

When Jesus led his closest followers, he wasn't acting independently but in perfect communion with the Father and the Holy Spirit. If we follow his example in making disciples, we'll set out not by ourselves but with the community of a triad of like-minded believers.

No matter the strengths and weaknesses of individual facilitators, triad leadership fosters greater success and greater synergy through the power of partnership. The writer of the book of Ecclesiastes describes this power and highlights the unique advantages of three working together:

> Two people are better off than one, for they can help each other succeed. If one person falls, the other can reach out and help. But someone who falls alone is in real trouble.
> . . . A person standing alone can be attacked and defeated, but two can stand back-to-back and conquer. Three are even better, for a triple-braided cord is not easily broken.
> ECCLESIASTES 4:9-10, 12, NLT

Any discussion of triads warrants considerable study of Greg Ogden's work regarding *making disciples a few at a time*, which is the subtitle of his book *Transforming Discipleship*. Ogden addresses the assumption that the best biblical paradigm for making disciples is the Paul-Timothy model, with an older, wiser follower of Jesus making a disciple of a teachable younger person in a teacher-student or parent-child kind of relationship. Ogden maintains that this one-on-one relationship sets up a hierarchy that tends to result in a dependency of the disciple on the discipler, a false perfectionism on the part of the discipler, and too much primary influence on the new disciple that limits his or her development as a follower of Christ.[2]

Ogden proposes an alternative biblical model: a side-by-side relational approach to disciple making that reflects the nature of the Trinity and involves three people (or four at most). This shift from the hierarchical relationship of two to an "alongside" relational approach of a triad creates a "mutual journey" in which the focus is not on one discipler as much as it is upon Christ as the teacher through God's Word and his Spirit.[3]

Ogden identifies several *shifts* that take place when three (or four) people work together rather than just two:

- From unnatural pressure on the discipler to his or her natural participation
- From hierarchy to a side-by-side personal dynamic
- From dialogue between two to a dynamic interchange among three
- From limited input by one to wisdom in numbers
- From addition to multiplication when all three reproduce the discipleship process

Ogden is careful to clarify that he is not attacking one-on-one mentoring relationships. In fact, he affirms the great value of three types of such relationships: spiritual director, coach, and sponsor. But as a primary strategy for discipleship, he sees triads as "hothouses" of Christian spiritual growth. Just as a hothouse maximizes the environmental conditions for living things to grow at an optimal rate, discipleship through triads can create a hothouse effect when specific "climatic conditions" are built into the relationship:

Condition #1: *Transparent trust*—the ability of people to open their hearts to one another.

Condition #2: *Truth of God's Word*—a focus on Scripture to transform us.

Condition #3: *Mutual accountability*—a willingness to be accountable to each other.[4]

When a group of three followers of Jesus cultivates these conditions in their relationship, they grow together spiritually, and they have a community that can easily expand to include others who don't yet have a relationship with Jesus.

Church planter Neil Cole has designed a similar strategy for "micro groups" of two to four that he calls "Life Transformation Groups" (LTGs). These groups place a high value on "accountability that consists of three essential disciplines for personal spiritual growth: a steady diet of Scripture, confession of sin, and prayer for others who need Christ."[5] No experience or training is necessary to be in one of these groups, as they are highly organic.

Jesus also demonstrated this model of forming a smaller circle of disciples with a greater level of accountability, transparency, and sharing in the revelation of truth. As mentioned in chapter 9 of this book, Jesus prayerfully selected twelve individuals to follow him closely. He invested even more of himself in three men: Peter, James, and John. In one instance, related in Mark 9:1-12, Jesus took these three to be alone with him on a mountainside to witness the Transfiguration—to get a glimpse of Christ's radiant glory and his interaction with Elijah and Moses! How amazing that must have been! And then the three were told not to tell *anyone*, including the other nine disciples, until after "the Son of Man had risen from the dead."

From biblical example and also from personal experience, we believe that a powerful way to make disciples relationally is to start with a triad of three committed followers of Jesus who are transparent, accountable to each other, and centered in Scripture. When these three followers spend time in prayer together, grow together in the Word of God, and take action to serve others, they can select and walk alongside nine others in a small-group community to discover who Jesus is. This is what we are calling the *Jesus 3:12 strategy*. It's modeled by Jesus, in community with the Trinity, walking alongside a handful of people and letting them see who he is. The strategy is simple but profound, and it's easily reproducible.

It starts with three Christians we call *initiators*, who are willing to be discipled by Jesus as they walk with each other. He is still at the center of this group when they invite nine more to join them—people who are not yet ready to follow Jesus but are curious about him at some level. When the group of three Christians and nine non-Christians meet together, all twelve people can learn from one another in community by engaging in meaningful conversations about God and the Bible, even though they may not all believe the same thing. Because Jesus is at the center of the three initiators' relationship, the nine are not only experiencing a trusting relationship with the three, but they are also seeing Jesus in them!

Launching the Jesus 3:12 strategy works best when church leaders follow the same principles themselves—forming a leadership triad to pray, grow, and serve, and then inviting nine Christians who are capable of developing these groups into a community where they can learn and discover together from each other, catching the vision of how this works.

Prayer Is Essential

When I (Mary) started a Q Place in the Northwest several years ago, I began by asking God who would be the two who could facilitate the group with me. I had several people in mind who I thought could do it, but I really wanted them to be God's pick. Over a couple of months, two names consistently began to rise to the top: Krissy and Colin. Krissy was a good friend of mine who had a naturally compassionate heart for people. Colin was an associate pastor in my church. Both were familiar with Q Place. Once I was pretty sure that they were God's choice for my triad, I asked whether they would be interested in starting a group with me for the spiritually curious. They both prayed about it and sensed that the Lord was leading them to try it.

The three of us began praying for people whom God had laid on our own hearts who might be open to coming. Soon, we were praying for about twenty people compiled from our three separate lists. Our hearts were knit together as we prayed for each other's friends and for what God might be doing in their lives.

We also prayed that God would show us new friends who had questions about God. We encountered dozens of people every day who were not Christians. Had we taken the time to know their names or their stories? Which of them would benefit from ongoing spiritual discussions about God and the Bible? We knew the people most likely to accept an invitation were those who already knew and trusted us.

Without much extra effort, we started to get to know people who had come to our minds as we prayed together. For example, when I stopped for coffee in town, I made a point of meeting the couple who owned the café, and I started to learn some of their story. Tim had been in the army and stationed in Germany when he met his wife, Manuela. They had two kids and now lived in our town. He knew a lot about coffee before he launched the cafe, since he had worked for a local coffee roaster.

I was mindful of following Jesus as I encountered people in my everyday path. Before he called Peter and Andrew to follow him, Jesus related to them as fishermen, taking an interest in their work and even helping them catch a record number of fish (Luke 5:2-11). The miracle he performed in the great catch of fish was followed by an invitation given in terms that they would understand: "Follow Me, and I will make you become fishers of men"

(Mark 1:17, NASB). I wanted any invitations I offered to come out of genuine relationships I'd developed with people.

In Luke 6:12 we read that Jesus went to a mountainside to pray all night, asking God to show him which of the men he knew would be his twelve disciples. No doubt he prayed for each individual one by one, and he may even have identified the closer relationship that he would have with Peter, James, and John. Not many of us would think to pray all night for our three and additional nine, but Jesus' actions show us that identifying people to invite merits concentrated time in prayer to discern God's will.

Getting Started

If you want to have ongoing discussions about God with people who are spiritually open and curious, you and your other triad members are the *initiators* of the process. To turn your initiative into action, *set a date*. Setting the start date adds a common focus for your triad, increases your passion for prayer and dependence on God, and provides accountability for following through with your plan.

You'll have to resist the temptation to judge who will be interested when you are assembling a list of people to invite. As mentioned earlier, let God help you select the potential attendees through prayer and quiet listening to him. You might be surprised at who ends up attending that first gathering. God is going before you and softening people's hearts to accept the invitation.

Make it clear to people that they are coming *one time* to hear about the *possibility* of a discussion group on spiritual topics about God and the Bible. In presenting the idea, emphasize some or all of these points taken from our book *How to Start a Q Place*:

1. This group will discuss questions about God. People are respected as thinking adults and are not judged. No previous knowledge about God or the Bible is necessary.

2. The group is not for experts. It's for new discoveries. People who think they are experts are especially encouraged to listen and ask questions so that all group members can discover answers for themselves. Everyone is a learner.

3. The format is informal discussion, not lecture. Questions on life, God, and the Bible can provide material for the discussion.

4. People are encouraged to share their ideas honestly and openly.

5. People learn as they express their discoveries. One person's insights sharpen another's understanding as the group discusses a topic together. Participation in the discussion increases. Interest grows. The focus is not on the leader but on the questions (and possibly the Bible passage) being discussed.

6. It is helpful for the group to consist of people from different backgrounds who are willing to share their perspectives as the group learns together from each person.

7. Most groups meet weekly for about an hour and a half. Some groups meet for a shorter period if there is a time limitation, such as a lunch hour at work or child-care constraints.[6]

After the initial meeting, a group typically is open to getting together for six to eight weeks. The group members decide on the topic they are most interested in discussing, which often stems from the questions people raised about God in the first meeting. When the group has completed a six- to eight-week session, they can decide whether to continue beyond that period. If people are benefiting from the discussions and a caring community has started to develop, they will want to keep meeting. Most people recognize the rarity of this kind of gathering.

Typically, the people you invite will have some fears about attending a group like this. Understanding potential concerns ahead of time will help you be empathetic as you extend an invitation. People are afraid to expose their ignorance and be judged. They don't know what to expect, and they worry they'll be stuck in a long-term commitment. If you have built trusting relationships with those you are inviting, some of these fears will be minimized or can be discussed openly as you invite them. It helps to ask open-ended questions to find out more about any concerns they express. Listen well to what they share and address their fears with short but clear answers.

Colin, Krissy, and I set a date, but we faced some challenges when we began inviting people to our newly forming group. I was relatively new to the area and didn't have a lot of non-Christian friends. I didn't know if the people I was thinking of asking would trust me enough to seriously consider my invitation. Colin worried that inviting his non-Christian friends would ruin or change the relationships he had with them. Krissy planned to invite a few friends from her workplace, and she was not only afraid to ask but also was concerned that asking would cause trouble with her job.

We prayed that God would make it easy for Krissy to extend invitations. One day she went to work knowing that the time had arrived for her to invite her friend Laurie. But as soon as Krissy arrived, Laurie came right up to her and asked if Krissy knew of a Bible study that she could join! *Are you kidding?* Krissy thought. *Did God ever make it easy!*

Laurie became one of our group's most faithful participants. She had many questions and was eager to learn. The group meant so much to her, giving her a good understanding of what it meant to be a Christian and why it was important to study the Bible. With a growing foundation of what she believed about God, she attended her Catholic church with a new sense of purpose. I loved Laurie's seeking heart. The prophet Jeremiah speaks on God's behalf when he writes, "When you call on me, when you come and pray to me, I'll listen. When you come looking for me, you'll find me" (Jeremiah 29.12-13, MSG). Our invitation gave Laurie the chance to look for God. He was already at work in her life before Krissy invited her to join us.

Paul was another regular participant in our group, and he had not been on anyone's list! Here's what happened: Colin asked his friend Ed to join our group, and in turn, Ed invited Colin to a different event about a spiritual topic where Colin met Paul. Paul was interested in biblical prophecy and the Bible, but he wasn't sure whether that meant he wanted a personal relationship with Jesus. After being part of our group, Paul is a now a strong believer who loves Jesus. He'd say he grew to love everyone in our group too. He also met his girlfriend, Anna, there—a huge added bonus!

Establishing Guidelines

When you begin to talk about spiritual matters with a diverse group of people, they are likely to be uneasy. People relax when there are clear ground rules that will guide the discussions, maintain a safe environment, and respect each person's opinions and time.

Q Place guidelines have been developed and time-tested by thousands of small groups. They are printed in the back of every Q Place discussion guide and are also available on a separate guidelines card so that each participant in a Q Place can have them in hand for every discussion.[7] When initiators go through the guidelines together at the first meeting, they set the stage for everyone to understand the nature of the group and the tips for a healthy discussion. The guidelines help everyone feel from the beginning that the group will be a safe place for exploring the real questions they have about life, God, and the Bible.

Whenever a new person joins the group, it's good to read the guidelines again with everyone. Over time, initiators can have the group self-evaluate, discuss areas for improvement, and encourage everyone to keep each other—including the initiators themselves—on track.

One of the basic guidelines is to begin and end on time. Another reminds everyone not to judge others. Each participant then knows that he or she can share a belief that won't be criticized or immediately "fixed" by a well-meaning facilitator or participant. When there is acceptance and respect regardless of opinions shared, people can feel safe to express themselves honestly in the group discussions.

More Prayer

Did I mention that prayer is essential? I'll say it again. Prayer is the foundational building block of any Q Place. From the beginning, prayer is needed to *start* an ongoing spiritual discussion group, and it will continue to be a necessary component as you meet because this is God's work. He certainly invites you to participate with him, but as Jesus says in John 6:44-45, "No one can come to me unless the Father who sent me draws them, and I will raise them up at the last day. It is written in the Prophets: 'They will all be taught by God.' Everyone who has heard the Father and learned from him comes to me."

In the beginning of a group, prayer will not be visible to participants. It's something that happens behind the scenes. It's good to pray before the participants arrive, after they leave, and during the days between your meetings. At some point in time, when you sense it is appropriate, let the participants know that you and your co-initiators are willing to pray for them as they are willing to share prayer requests. You could keep a prayer journal in which someone from the group writes down requests. Toward the end of the meeting, before you conclude, you could ask the group if there are things about which they'd like prayer. Assure them that what they share is confidential. After prayer requests are shared, one of the initiators could briefly close in prayer, covering those requests, if your triad believes the group is ready for praying out loud.

Choosing Curriculum

We talked a lot in chapter 9 about the importance of being learner centered as we facilitate. But if the facilitators are not teaching during these ongoing discussions, then how will people learn and grow in their understanding of God? It may start with very simple, icebreaker-type questions that encourage people to share honest thoughts about life and to discover that the group really will be a nonthreatening place to explore what they believe.

When the group communicates specific needs or questions about God, you may suggest a topic that you could discuss together. Having a good discussion resource helps to support topical discussions. While you will find thousands of possibilities out there, not all of them use the inductive or asking approach, focused on the learner. Many Bible study resources are designed to show you the conclusions of the author of the study rather than to help you make discoveries and reach conclusions for yourself. Also, while there are many great books and great DVDs out there about God and the Bible, often the authors or teachers become the main text rather than the Bible itself.

Here are two helpful criteria for choosing discussion resources for your group:

1. Is the curriculum inductive, promoting self-discovery by asking open-ended, discussion-producing questions?
2. Does the curriculum point participants to the Bible and to Jesus?

Getting people into the Bible is the best vehicle for reaching the ultimate destination of knowing God completely through Jesus Christ. People are often ambivalent or even resistant to the Bible, but it's the best source we have to understand God's plan, purpose, and love for us. The greatest story of all time, the living Word of God can expose our need for him better than any Christian trying to "convert" someone. The author of Hebrews declares, "The word of God is alive and active. Sharper than any double-edged sword, it penetrates even to dividing soul and spirit, joints and marrow; it judges the thoughts and attitudes of the heart" (Hebrews 4:12).

Prayer is essential in your triad as you seek discernment about your group's readiness to read Scripture together. Many people are not willing to look at Scripture when they first join a group; they are not sure it has something to say to them personally, and they are not convinced that it is true. In the trial meeting, where participants get a taste of what it would be like to discuss important questions of life, God, and the Bible, it usually works well to read a short section of Scripture and ask questions that help the group discuss it.

The trial meeting usually reveals the interest of the participants. Often groups just want to discuss their questions about God, and initially there isn't a lot of reference to Scripture. It's good to be careful. Rushing into something that participants are not ready to discuss is likely to reduce trust, causing them to feel that you have an agenda. As initiators are sensitive to the readiness of group participants, they can take Spirit-led risks to introduce Scripture into the group in a way that honors their level of openness.

It may start with reading a short section of Scripture printed on a sheet of paper, having copies for everyone to read and discuss, or pulling up a verse through an app like YouVersion. You could ask five simple questions of each passage:

1. What does this reveal about God?
2. What does this reveal about people?
3. What else did you learn?
4. If you believed this was true, how would you apply it in your life?
5. If you put it into practice, what could be the challenges? What could be the benefits?

Later, if your group is ready to look at what the Bible says in more depth, together either choose a book of the Bible that is likely to answer the main questions the group is asking, or see what the Bible has to say about a topic the group has picked. If participants are curious about Jesus, study the Gospel of Mark, which is the shortest and simplest account of his life and teachings.

Scripture is a powerful tool for transforming the human heart. In 2011, Lifeway Research did a study to discover the common traits of disciples who were maturing in their faith. They surveyed one thousand pastors and four thousand Protestants in the US and Canada. The survey identified eight attributes of discipleship: (1) Bible engagement, (2) obeying God and denying self, (3) serving God and others, (4) sharing Christ, (5) exercising faith, (6) seeking God, (7) building relationships, and (8) being unashamed and transparent. They found that Bible engagement was the top attribute that affects one's spiritual maturity—more than the rest of the seven discipleship attributes combined! Not only that, but growth in Bible engagement is correlated with growth in all seven of the other attributes.[8]

One thing is clear: As God leads, he will also use his Word in the lives of everyone in the group. In Isaiah 55:10-11 God declares:

As the rain and the snow
    come down from heaven,
and do not return to it

> without watering the earth
> and making it bud and flourish,
> so that it yields seed for the sower and bread for the eater,
> so is my word that goes out from my mouth:
> It will not return to me empty,
> but will accomplish what I desire
> and achieve the purpose for which I sent it.

Doubting and Drop-Off Is Normal

People living far from God may not be predictable when it comes to regular attendance and preparation for a group. That's another reason prayer is so important; it protects participants from some of the normal distractions that could keep them from coming, and it protects initiators from discouragement.

In one of the final scenes the Bible shows us of Jesus with his disciples, we see them gathered on a mountain just before he ascends to heaven. Over the previous three years, Jesus had spent the majority of his time with these men. One of the Twelve had betrayed him. The remaining eleven had seen him die and then experienced the miracle of his resurrection. Yet in Matthew 28:17, we read astonishing words about these remaining eleven: "When they saw him, they worshiped him; but some doubted."

I am blown away that these guys who saw Jesus perform countless miracles, speak with more authority than anyone, and conquer death still had doubts that made them hesitant to worship Jesus. What's more, although Jesus knew their doubts, he proceeded to commission them, with "all authority in heaven and on earth" backing him, to "go and make disciples of all nations, baptizing them in the name of the Father, Son, and Holy Spirit" (28:18-19). The good news about this passage is it reminds us that doubting doesn't faze Jesus. It's normal. Believers have doubts at times, and people who are on a journey of seeking God will have plenty of them too. Our job is to guide them toward unchanging truth as they seek to resolve those doubts in the context of caring community, where healing, love, and spiritual growth can flourish.

Power of Community and These Nine Arts

When Don Ross, the senior pastor at Creekside Church in the Seattle area, was introduced to The 9 Arts of Spiritual Conversations, they immediately resonated with him. He decided to try to incorporate the nine practices into his own life. In the middle of writing a book called *The Turnaround Pastor*, he decided to write at a local McDonald's; it had free wi-fi and decent coffee at a reasonable price. And although he hadn't been aware of this before or seen it as a need, McDonald's was a place where he could meet people.

After sitting in the same spot almost every day for a few weeks, Don *noticed* a man who sat at the next table nearly every day he was there. At first all they did was nod a brief hello. Eventually Don learned the man's name was Carl, and he started to regularly *pray* for Carl without knowing much about him. Before long the men had a brief conversation every time they saw each other, with Don *asking* Carl some questions and *listening* to what he shared. Carl had been married three times and had eleven women in his past. He'd been to jail and had battled alcoholism. Don had a common challenge with recovery from an addiction. Carl must have sensed that Don was relating well with him because at one point, Carl said, "I don't know why I feel like I can tell you all this stuff!"

One day, Carl came into McDonald's very upset as Don was on his way out. Carl said that his four-year-old grandson, Truin, was having open-heart surgery that day to repair two holes in his heart. He asked Don if he would mind praying for Truin, since Carl didn't think he "had the right kind of pipeline to God." So right there, near the trash cans outside of McDonald's, Don said a short prayer for Carl's little grandson. The next time Carl saw Don at their usual spot, he could hardly contain himself! He said that his grandson was fine now. Somehow the bottom hole in his heart had healed itself, and the top hole had been an easy fix for the surgeon. Carl said, "This prayer stuff really works!"

Pretty soon there was a community of guys—some of whom were homeless—gathering around Don at McDonald's. Don gave them a booklet to read called "What on Earth Am I Here For?" by Rick Warren. He told them to underline everything they were curious about, and then they'd talk about it. During one of their conversations about the book, Don asked Carl if he was ready to start walking with Jesus. Carl said yes, and the two prayed together once again. After that, the two prayed together regularly.

A few of Carl's friends who also had lived hard lives began to get sick and were dying. Carl wanted Don to visit them, but Don encouraged Carl to go instead and to share what he was learning about Jesus. One of these friends ended up praying to have a relationship with Jesus just before he died. Carl said he "could feel the Spirit of God moving through him" as he made these visits. Don describes Carl's impact on his friends as a spiritual chain reaction.

When Don asked Carl how his life is different since they met, Carl said, "I used to feel so alone. But now I feel like I have a regular friend in Jesus who's always with me. And I feel like I have a purpose in life with those around me."

Don is now the Pacific Northwest regional director of the largest denomination in the Pacific Northwest, the Assemblies of God. Because of his experiences with Carl and his other McDonald's friends, he has encouraged his network of nearly three hundred churches to practice The 9 Arts of Spiritual Conversations and start Q Places.

What challenges you about putting all of the 9 Arts of Spiritual Conversations into practice? Can you begin praying about whom

God would have you partner with to start a Q Place? We see that on average, about half of the people who join a Q Place end up placing their faith in Jesus as a result of their exploration of God and the Bible. If eight spiritually curious people joined a Q Place to discuss faith matters, that means that about four people could make a decision to follow Jesus through your initiative, enabling you to faithfully live out the Great Commission and make new disciples. What an impact for God's Kingdom!

Discover

1. Have you ever had the privilege of walking alongside someone on their faith journey? What impact did it have on your own faith?

2. Review your list of people God is calling you to engage with in spiritual conversations. Who would benefit from a small group where they could figure out what they believe about God? Pray about developing a group and inviting those people.

Practice

1. Talk to someone you know who is not a Christian but may be spiritually curious, and ask them what they think of this small-group concept. Would they ever consider becoming a participant? Why or why not?

2. Host a movie night or a book discussion that would prompt some good spiritual discussion with a few good open-ended questions. What went well? What did you find challenging? How might this experience prepare you for starting a Q Place?

CHAPTER 13

From Cups of Cold Water to Rivers of Living Water

*Jesus stood and said in a loud voice, "Let anyone who is thirsty
come to me and drink. Whoever believes in me, as Scripture has
said, rivers of living water will flow from within them."*

JOHN 7:37-38

*I believe this moment is unlike any other time in history. Its
uniqueness demands an original response. If we fail to offer a different
way forward, we risk losing entire generations to apathy and cynicism.*

GABE LYONS

IN MAY 1943, Army Air Forces bombardier Louis Zamperini's plane
crashed, shot down in an air battle over the Pacific Ocean. He and
two other airmen found themselves floating aimlessly in tandem
rafts in the middle of the Pacific, desperately hoping to be rescued
by their fellow countrymen. To their utter disappointment, the
three men discovered that their rafts were stocked with only a few
bars of chocolate, several half-pint tins of water, and a few other
supplies. In the remarkable true story about Zamperini's life, titled
Unbroken, author Laura Hillenbrand writes, "Most worrisome was
the water situation. A few half-pints wouldn't last them long. The
men were surrounded by water, but they couldn't drink it."[1]

After their supplies were gone, Zamperini and his friends went
three days without water before a storm produced a most welcome
drink, which the three men consumed voraciously by throwing
back their heads and opening their mouths to catch the raindrops.

Hillenbrand describes it as a "sensory explosion" to these three desperate men. Over the course of the storm, they figured out how to capture the rain with canvas and funnel it to refill the tins with fresh drinking water to keep them alive.

Very few of us reading this in the Western world with almost unlimited access to good drinking water can grasp how difficult it is to survive each day without water. But people living in the first century and those in developing countries today know all too well the value of a tin of fresh drinking water.

Arid Palestine in AD 30 had too few wells and fresh bodies of water for the basic needs of its people and animals. Obtaining water would have been close to the front of everyone's minds. When Jesus used the example of giving a cool cup of water as a way to show mercy and love (see Matthew 10:42), his hearers would have understood it on a visceral level. Giving people something as simple as a cup of cold water was probably a sensory explosion then, too!

What's the spiritual equivalent of a cup of cold water today in the Western world? We think it is genuine mercy and love, shown through the nine simple practices we have described in this book. When people get a taste of it, they have a sensory explosion, like Louis Zamperini and his friends on the raft, who desperately needed fresh water to survive. People are so thirsty for someone to pay attention to them and show that they have value in this world. When they experience the attention of people who notice, pray for, listen to, ask questions of, love, welcome, and serve with them, they are drawn to that attention. It is good news to them, and they want more.

West Point graduate and former Army Ranger Greg Plitt was an imposing physical specimen. He was a fitness model and actor who seemed to have everything: health, fame, and fortune. Yet he was searching for truth, wondering whether it could give him the contentment and peace that had eluded him. For eighteen months he met regularly with Dave, his former high school wrestling coach, and talked about God and what he believed. The two of them would sit in an LA restaurant for a couple of hours once a quarter and talk about Jesus. Greg trusted Dave, as he didn't feel judged or coerced to believe as Dave did. The conversations were lively and full of questions from both men.

On January 17, 2015, Dave received a distraught call from Greg's brother-in-law. There had been a tragic accident; Greg had been killed by a commuter train in Burbank as he was filming a video on the train tracks that promoted his new protein drink. This tragic accident cut short Greg's search for God. Dave was asked to conduct two memorial services for Greg and to somehow make sense of it all. Here's what Dave said:

> Greg wanted to know Jesus. But his lifestyle and never-ending pursuit of excellence kept him from creating space for God. He once said to me, "I'm thirty-five years old but I feel like I'm eighty." Our times together were the few times he could take a break and talk about his emptiness and how God may be the answer to his lifelong pursuit of fulfillment, meaning, and worth.

Then there's Laura (not her real name), a thirty-year-old divorced hairdresser in the western suburbs of Chicago who thought she had found the man of her dreams. She had dated Doug, an electrician, for about six months when they decided to get married. Within a year they had a baby. Looking back, Laura would say the marriage showed signs of trouble even before their son, Charlie, was born. Doug liked spending time with his buddies watching sports at the local pub more than being with his wife. When his son was born, it seemed as if he spent even more time away from his young family. Laura confronted Doug about this several times, but he became increasingly distant. Eventually the couple divorced, and Laura is now raising eight-year-old Charlie on her own, fighting Doug for every dollar of child support and trying to make ends meet with her income at the beauty salon.

Laura was not raised with any faith background. She is more open to spiritual matters now than ever because life is difficult. After going to three different churches in the area to check out "whether they might have something to offer" her, she said she gave up because "they didn't seem like a fit" for her. In the meantime, she goes on every day the best she can, raising her son and making ends meet, wondering why life is so hard. For a while I (Mary) was getting my hair cut by Laura. We've had several conversations about God. I've prayed for her and have asked her several questions about what she believes, listening attentively to her answers and, when asked, sharing with her what I believe. I sense that she is thirsty for this meaningful dialogue. She has expressed interest in going to a group where she could interact with others who are similarly searching for God.

Laura is high on my list to invite to a Q Place, but she doesn't live close by. I wonder whether there are Christians in her apartment building or at the playground she visits with her son. What if they began to notice, pray for, and listen to her? And what about Doug, her ex-husband? Has he begun to recognize the dismal consequences of his choices? Could he be open to talking about God? Is there a fellow electrician at work who is a Christ follower, who could ask questions and listen?

And there are Darla and Steve (names changed), whose son Richard was a consultant at a large aerospace company in the Pacific Northwest. They got a call in the middle of the night from the police saying that their son had jumped out of a fifth-floor hotel window. Darla and Steve don't have any connection with a church. Do they have Christian neighbors and friends? Do these friends know how to engage in meaningful conversations about God with people who are suffering deep grief and loss? Did Richard have

Christian friends at work who could have given him an opportunity to explore the offer that Jesus gives and see it for himself?

I am sure you could list many people in your life who are untouched by a local church yet have a story of brokenness and a need for God's redemptive power.

The Church in Crisis

As I (Mary) was writing this final chapter, I happened to talk with two Christians who shared what was going on in their own churches. Barbara, along with her husband, has belonged to an Episcopalian church in a small resort town for most of her life. She said that their church is dwindling and that she and her husband, in their sixties, are the youngest people there. "In the summer, we'll have tourists and snowbirds there and it seems a little more vibrant. But on Sundays the rest of the year," she says, "I have a pew to myself."

Another friend belongs to a Bible-based nondenominational church not too far from Barbara's. He said that his church had a congregation of about 120 people less than five years ago. "We now have thirty people who would call it their church home. People moved or left because they didn't agree with some things we were doing. I still love it, and those who have stayed are growing mature in their relationship with Christ," he said.

While some of the "big box" churches are seeing vibrant activity primarily from transfer growth of Christians leaving their smaller churches, the overall picture of shrinking churches is becoming increasingly clear. I am sure everyone reading this could give more examples that point to a less-than-hopeful path for the institutional church in the US. And yet there are people like Greg, Laura, Doug, Steve, Darla, and Richard all around us in our daily lives!

These anecdotal stories are pretty discouraging, and so is the data. David T. Olson, author of *The American Church in Crisis*, claims that by 2020 only 14.7 percent of the American population will be attending a Christian church on any given weekend. He doesn't think the conditions that could produce growth are present, and he believes that the downward trajectory will continue.[2] That tells us we can't rely on pastors to be the only ones doing the work of making disciples through a one-hour teaching on Sunday, especially if fewer people are coming to hear it.

According to John Dickerson, author of *The Great Evangelical Recession*, "Christianity as we know it is receding." Speaking primarily about the Western world, he writes about the 10-percent drop in evangelicals over the last several decades. He defines "evangelical" as "churches and individuals who believe a salvation-by-faith-alone 'gospel.' We're talking about American Christians who believe the Bible is God's Word, that it is without error, and that Jesus is the only way to salvation and to God."

Dickerson believes that evangelical Christians in 2014 made up between 7 and 9 percent of the US population, or 22 million people. He expects this figure to decline to about 4 percent in the next thirty years.[3] However, he believes that "the evangelical recession offers us a window of opportunity, during which we can re-center Christ's church on *His* mission."[4]

Pollster and author George Barna writes:

> The church landscape will continue to evolve into something that would have been unrecognizable a quarter century ago. . . . The mainline churches and even some of the evangelical and fundamentalist groups that were solid at the end of the last millennium and the beginning of this one will lose altitude unless they substantially reinvent themselves.[5]

If making disciples is the mandate of the Great Commission, and if church growth and attendance are lead indicators that we are accomplishing this important mission, we have got to understand that something is seriously wrong and needs to be addressed.

Perhaps we've somehow made fulfilling the Great Commission too hard? Too complicated? Too institutional? Perhaps we don't see our individual responsibility as followers of Jesus to make disciples? Perhaps we are not noticing all of the people like Greg and Laura around us who are searching for God but have not found him in the church building on Sunday? Perhaps we've relied too much on a telling approach that appears transactional and prescriptive to many around us?

Jesus reminds us in John 17:18, "As you [the Father] *sent* me into the world, I have *sent* them [believers] into the world" (emphasis added). We have been sent. Are we willing to go? I love *The Message*'s paraphrase of this same verse: "In the same way that you gave me a mission in the world, I give them a mission in the world." It's not just the paid professionals. We all have a mission to make new disciples. It's like in Isaiah 6:8, where Isaiah describes hearing God ask the question: "Whom shall I send? And who will go for us?" Isaiah said in response, "Here am I. Send me." Are you willing to be sent?

Bystanders?

A phenomenon called the "bystander effect" may help explain why an individual Christian is unlikely to view making disciples as his or her own personal responsibility. The bystander effect refers to people's tendency not to help someone in need when other people are present. In fact, the more bystanders who are present, the less likely they are to do anything.

There are many heart-wrenching examples of the bystander affect. Hugo Alfredo Tale-Yax was stabbed to death in 2010 after trying to help a woman who was being attacked by a robber in Queens, New York. Over the course of an hour, almost twenty-five people walked by while he lay dying on the sidewalk. No one helped him. One person even took a picture.[6] Medical professionals have learned that when there is an emergency, it is critical to point to one person, ask his or her name, and then tell that person to call an ambulance or take some necessary action. Being asked directly and personally increases the likelihood that someone will see it as his or her job to help.

Parents can identify with this phenomenon. When they simply ask, "Can someone clear the dishes from the table?" all of the children will slowly slink away, with none of them thinking that it is their responsibility. Everyone assumes that someone else will do it.

Jesus sent *you* on a mission in the world. His commission to make new disciples has *your* name all over it. And he has shown you how to walk the way, modeling how simple it is. As simple as giving someone a cold cup of water.

Let's look again at *The Message*'s version of Matthew 10:42, which we referenced in chapter 2. Jesus sent his disciples out into ministry with these words:

> This is a large work I've called you into, but don't be
> overwhelmed by it. It's best to start small. Give a cool
> cup of water to someone who is thirsty, for instance.
> The smallest act of giving or receiving makes you a true
> apprentice. You won't lose out on a thing.

We all have a chance to bring the Kingdom of God to this sinful world. It is a Kingdom of love, and we're part of it through our relationship with Christ and through his life in us. We'll be able to share it a little bit at a time by noticing, praying, listening, asking questions, loving, and welcoming. But we have to start doing something. As Matthew West's song "Do Something" reminds us, "If not us, then who? . . . If not now, then when?"[7]

We can do something! Within the covers of this book, you have seen nine simple practices that get Christians off the bleachers and into the action. At the same time, followers of Jesus have an ongoing "ringside seat" for what God is doing all around them in people's lives. This fuels their own faith journeys and points other people directly to the love of Jesus. Giving people continual, steady sips of grace and truth builds a solid foundation of faith in the lives of those unreached by the institutional church. With The 9 Arts of Spiritual Conversations, churches have the opportunity to equip almost everyone in their congregations for vibrant, vital outreach.

Gabe Lyons, a young evangelical leader and the author of *The Next Christians,* says:

> I believe this moment is unlike any other time in history. Its uniqueness demands an original response. If we fail to offer a different way forward, we risk losing entire generations to apathy and cynicism. Our friends will continue to drift away, meeting their need for spiritual transcendence through other forms of worship and communities of faith that may be less true but more authentic and appealing.[8]

Streams of Living Water

The apostle John records an event that happened at the Temple courts in Jerusalem while Jesus and his disciples were there for the Jewish Festival of Tabernacles:

> Jesus stood and said in a loud voice, "Let anyone who is thirsty come to me and drink. Whoever believes in me, as Scripture has said, rivers of living water will flow from within them." By this he meant the Spirit, whom those who believed in him were later to receive. Up to that time

the Spirit had not been given, since Jesus had not yet been glorified.

JOHN 7:37-39

It seems from these verses that anyone seeking God is invited to come to Jesus for a satisfying drink. And those who believe in Jesus will be astonished by the rivers of water that will flow out from within them, naturally pointing those who are seeking God to Jesus. I can't help but picture millions of followers of Jesus with living water flowing from their lives—rushing, transformative water that started as a simple drink.

In Ezekiel 47:1-12, the prophet Ezekiel recounts a vision of water bubbling up from the altar in the yet-to-be-built Temple. The stream of water heads eastward through the inner court, then through the outer court, and out the Temple complex along the southern side of the outer eastern gate.

A man with a tape measure takes Ezekiel eastward, measuring off the equivalent of seventeen hundred feet, and then leads him through water that is ankle-deep. The depth increases at each interval: from his ankle, to his knee, to his waist, and finally to such depth that it cannot be crossed. This river continues to run southeasterly toward the Jordan Valley and then flows into the Dead Sea.

The Dead Sea got that name because nothing can live in it. You certainly would never want to drink its water. From Hebrew, the name is often translated as "the Sea of Death." With 34.8 percent salinity, the Dead Sea is 9.6 times as salty as the ocean. It is 47 miles long, 11 miles wide at its widest point, and 1,300 feet deep—the deepest salt lake in the world. The water is so salty that it cannot sustain any life.

In Ezekiel's vision, the expanding, abundant freshwater stream causes the Dead Sea—this well-known body of lifelessness—to become alive with sea life! The man takes Ezekiel back to the riverbank, where he sees a great number of trees on each side. The man, who seems to be an angel, tells Ezekiel that wherever the river flows there will be fish of many kinds and fishermen spreading their nets. The fruit trees will bear fruit every month, and the leaves not only will never fall off the trees but also will be used for healing. Wherever it flows, this divine river brings life.

The water here comes from God's residence, the Temple, beginning as a trickle at the altar. This river seems similar to the one that John sees in his vision of heaven, a river that flows down the city's street from the throne of God (see Revelation 22). Both rivers are similar in purpose and indicate that fruitfulness and healing come from God and his throne.

I find it intriguing that water is sometimes a barrier in Scripture (such as in Exodus, when the Jewish people are trying to leave Egypt and the Red Sea is in their way) or a source of destruction (such as during the plagues when God turned the Nile River to blood, killing the fish and removing the Egyptians' source of drinking water). But at other times Scripture mentions that God is the source of water, and it is life giving and healing:

This is what the LORD says—
    he who made a way through the sea,
    a path through the mighty waters,
who drew out the chariots and horses,
    the army and reinforcements together,
and they lay there, never to rise again,
    extinguished, snuffed out like a wick:
"Forget the former things;
    do not dwell on the past.
See, I am doing a new thing!
    Now it springs up; do you not perceive it?
I am making a way in the wilderness
    and streams in the wasteland."
ISAIAH 43:16-19

What if God is doing a new thing right now, mobilizing and equipping all of us who are followers of Jesus to be rivers of living water in the wastelands of our neighborhoods, communities, and workplaces? What if we knew how to bring Jesus to a hurting world right where we are, without all of the answers but with a willingness to engage the questions people are asking? Our purpose is to bring life to the dead sea of humanity living each day without Christ.

Hugh Halter reminds us of "four incarnational nuances of speaking of Jesus" that are worth sharing as we encourage you to have ongoing spiritual conversations with the people God has placed around you. He says, "Keep a running conversation. Talk when they ask you to. Talk about the kingdom. Talk about the King."[9]

Many people are harassed and helpless, living in quiet desperation, thirsty for a taste of a better life. Within us, we have a never-ending supply of living water to share. But making disciples is not easy. It requires staying close to the source of the water, living in complete dependence on Jesus.

In his book on the great evangelical recession, John Dickerson concludes:

> We stand at the hinge of a great moving in Christ's church. God, in His plan, placed us at this time of historic opportunity. His most valuable possession—His bride—is ours to guide gently and boldly through the 21st century. She will either draw closer to His heart and plan, or drift further from it. Her spiritual decay or restoration depends, in your sphere, on you and your leadership.[10]

It will take all of us walking the way of Jesus to change the trajectory of the church. By noticing, praying, listening, asking questions, loving, welcoming, facilitating, serving together, and sharing the Good News, we give people tangible expressions of the fruit of the Holy Spirit in our lives, expressed as nine compelling qualities in Galatians 5:22-23: "love, joy, peace, patience, kindness, goodness, faithfulness, gentleness, [and] self-control" (NASB).

The 9 Arts of Spiritual Conversations are cups of cool water that will open the floodgates of curiosity and draw people—your own friends, family, neighbors, and coworkers—to become engaged in ongoing conversations about God. Walking the way of Jesus means that we create small group communities where it is safe to explore what we believe, just as Jesus provided for his twelve disciples when he was on earth. When we actively walk the way of Jesus, we will grow spiritually and in fellowship with other believers. Churches will spring to new life. Inviting people we know to come to church will be more natural, and the result will be more satisfying.

As people taste the cups of cool water for themselves, discover Jesus' offer to them, and believe in him, they will experience for themselves the transformation, life, and healing of those abundant rivers of living water.

Discover

1. Which people in your life might be "thirsty" for God?

2. What would be a good next step or "cup of cold water" that you could give to each of them?

Practice

1. Ask God to show you what he wants you to do as a result of reading this book to get you on a new path of making disciples as Jesus did?

2. Aim to begin incorporating The 9 Arts of Spiritual Conversations into your life every day. Pick one a week and focus on improvement.

3. Keep praying for the list of people you developed in an earlier chapter—the people you believe God may be calling you to engage in spiritual conversations. Consider putting copies of the list where you'll see it each day, such as in your car, on your bathroom mirror, or at your desk. As new relationships form or existing relationships deepen, keep praying about next steps with each of them.

Acknowledgments

Mary Schaller:

When I was introduced to "the art of noticing" back in 2010 at a Q Place event, I was intrigued but concerned it was too elementary. How wrong I was! In our busy, self-focused culture, we are hungry for simple practices that enable us to live more like Jesus in our conversations and relationships with others. Jesus was the ultimate noticer, prayer, listener, question asker, welcomer, and lover of people.

Slowly, over time, we identified nine common behaviors that Jesus regularly exhibited when engaging people in meaningful conversations about God and the Scriptures. Hence, the foundational principles for *The 9 Arts of Spiritual Conversations* were born. Colleagues Judson Polling, Doug Pollock, and Jeff Klein were tremendous partners in creating the thirty-six inductive learning modules that eventually made up the Q Place 9 Arts curriculum in the subsequent three years.

I am deeply grateful to John Crilly for his outstanding contribution to this content, and to the rest of the team for your creativity, insights, and hard work on this important project. Special thanks to Karen Schleicher, our Q Place publishing leader, who worked diligently behind the scenes in all aspects of its creation and refinement; and to Kristin Thompson, my beloved daughter and the mother of three of my precious grandchildren, who stayed up long after her bedtime to read and edit my writing.

We are truly grateful to Tyndale House for publishing our discussion guides back in the 1970s and '80s, and now for publishing this important book. We have thoroughly enjoyed working with your entire talented team once again.

This book's evolution goes back to 2001, when my dear friends Judy Squier and Kristin Day unwittingly accepted my invitation to start a spiritual conversation group for women with diverse beliefs about God in a small San Francisco Bay–area town called Portola Valley. I would have neither story to tell nor wisdom to share if not for that group. They changed my perspective on how ordinary Christians can talk about God with people who believe differently. Though I can't list each of the dozens of people who came into my living room over those years, you know who you are. I hope you know how grateful I am for what you taught me about God, this fascinating relational process, and myself. We had a lot of fun, too.

I'm grateful for my dear friends Caron Heimbuck, Barby Farmer, Eloise Pollock, Ethel Newell, LJ Anderson, and others who helped me grow in my relationship with Jesus. Many thanks to pastors Ben Pierce, Tim Sandquist, and Eric Rust, who walked alongside me as encouragers during those formative years, helping me to understand the theological meaning of these group encounters and their relevance to the church. It was during those years that Lee Strobel, Mark Mittelberg, and Garry Poole were helpful to me as mentors while my vocational call came into focus. I'm thankful that I met Fran Goodrich, who introduced me to Neighborhood Bible Studies (now known as Q Place) and the board that ended up hiring me as president of this remarkable ministry.

Thank you, Colin Moody and Krissy Rosedale, for helping

me better understand triads and how they provide such a solid foundation for Q Place facilitation and launching groups. Our own Q Place in Sandpoint, Idaho, taught me so much and kept my internal fire red-hot for this form of relational, conversational discipleship while I led the ministry during those years.

Thank you, Rich Berg, for your unconditional support of my leadership and the ministry of Q Place over the past several years. You are a tremendous reminder to me of God's provision and faithfulness! How can I ever thank you enough?

I am so grateful to my dad for loving and believing in me always, providing a perfect illustration of our heavenly Father's love for me. I wish you were still alive today, Dad, to see this book come out and read how it talks about our spiritual conversations and how much impact they had on both of us. Terry and Tom, my two wonderful siblings, thanks for all of our conversations about God and how you've been so supportive of my own spiritual journey.

The most gracious gift God has given me in this lifetime (next to Jesus, of course) is my amazing husband, Paul. You have always been my biggest cheerleader and life partner. Your family of origin's nickname for you, Gibraltar, still fits you well today, as you have been a foundational rock in our family, enabling us to grow and flourish. I love you with all of my heart. Thank you! And thank you to my three adult children—Kristin, Mike, and David—and your wonderful families, who give our lives such meaning and joy.

Jesus, thank you for your amazing grace that has saved a wretch like me. It's that saving grace, which changed my life, that I want to share with everyone I meet. Your love and forgiveness give true hope to this broken world. This verse in Acts 20:24 is increasingly true for me: "I consider my life worth nothing to me; my only aim is to finish the race and complete the task the Lord Jesus has given me—the task of testifying to the good news of God's grace." Let it be so.

John Crilly:

There are so many books—so many good books. So why write another one? We felt compelled to write this book as our contribution to the conversation—as an encouragement to ordinary Christians, inviting them into the adventure of having conversations about God with people who believe differently, and giving them a natural on-ramp to greater love and understanding using Jesus' behavioral practices. Our crazy dream is that more Christians would rise up in love and engage their cultures with the alluring, dynamic truth and beauty of the gospel of Jesus Christ.

But a book can never be born in the absence of ideas. So I want to thank the many people who influenced the creation and content of this book. First, I want to thank my cousin Andy, who chose to engage with me when I was very far from God. Andy was a safe place for me to begin my spiritual journey toward Jesus. Thank you, God-of-the-Second-Chance, for pursuing me, transforming my life, making me into a "new creation," and leading me to an amazing church home. I want to thank my pastors at Willow Creek Community Church throughout the years, whose incredible teaching, leadership, insight, and wisdom informed my worldview and taught me about God's immense heart for people. Thanks especially to Bill Hybels, John Ortberg, and Lee Strobel. You have mentored me from a distance.

I am grateful to Randy Siever and Jim Henderson for introducing us to the simple but profound concept of noticing ("the cultural equivalent of a cold cup of water") and for continuing to be supportive friends. Thanks to great friends and core volunteers Jack Armbruster and Dave Demas, who wrestled with these ideas in their early stages, including countless discussions on everything from sabermetrics to the four stages of learning. Your sacrificial investment of time and thought helped form and advance these ideas. And, of course, I am thankful to my coauthor, Mary Schaller, for her significant contribution to this material, for collaborating with me on the content, and for striving for excellence, simplicity, and clarity throughout the entire process.

I am thankful for the great people I have known through the years who have provided me with real-life opportunities to test and live out these behavioral "arts" as I have tried to walk the way of Jesus—in the day-to-day moments with my colleagues over twenty-three years, in the marketplace crucible of dissatisfied customers, difficult coworkers, deadlines, mistakes, and stress; in the week-to-week moments around my neighborhood; and in the year-by-year friendships that have the history and hidden knowledge of seeing me fail, succeed, and grow in Christ over time and with many apologies. In all these times, I was able to see Jesus show up in their lives and mine.

Once the ideas were hatched, they needed to be developed. I am thankful to the team that helped support us in developing the content for the training curriculum that eventually formed the basis of this book, including Karen Schleicher, Jeff Klein, Doug Pollock, and especially Judson Poling. Judson, your contributions were incredibly valuable. Also, a big thank-you to Doug Knox and his team at Tyndale House Publishers for seeing the value in these concepts and believing in the project.

Any good writing demands a good editor, and we had the best—both of them! Internally, our deepest gratitude goes to Karen Schleicher, who handled the editing with poise, passion, class, and exacting excellence. She was a true partner in the ultimate creation of the core content. Then, Tyndale House provided us with a gift by assigning Karin Buursma as our editor. Karin provided exceedingly helpful feedback, wise insights, and a balanced perspective, all with an encouraging and diplomatic touch. I felt God's care from both editors throughout the writing process.

In addition, I am grateful to my family—especially my parents, who sacrificed greatly to lay the foundations of faith and learning in me. Thanks so much to my friends (you know who you are!)

who encouraged me throughout this project—especially my friend and mentor David Mains, who often acted as a sounding board during my writing.

A good chunk of my writing was done at the best café on the planet, LaBriola Café. Thanks to the hospitable team and ownership there that welcomed me, served me wonderful food, and allowed me to drink gallons of my favorite iced tea!

Finally, I want to thank my wife, Danielle. I won the lottery when I married this woman—full of elegance, discernment, creativity, beauty, and compassion. A wife of noble character who brings me good, not harm. I am the grand-prize winner.

To all of these folks mentioned, and the many others unnamed, you have been difference makers in my life. I hold each of you in high regard.

Notes

CHAPTER 1: THE HEART AND HABITS OF JESUS

1. Alan Hirsch, *Disciplism: Reimagining Evangelism through the Lens of Discipleship* (Exponential Resources, 2014), 27.
2. Francis Chan, *Crazy Love: Overwhelmed by a Relentless God* (Colorado Springs: David C. Cook, 2008), 93.
3. Greg Ogden, *Discipleship Essentials* (Downers Grove, IL: InterVarsity, 2007), 21. Italics added.
4. Hugh Halter, *Flesh* (Colorado Springs: David C. Cook, 2014), 182.

CHAPTER 2: REDISCOVERING NINE RELATIONAL PRACTICES OF JESUS

1. David Kinnaman, *You Lost Me: Why Young Christians Are Leaving Church . . . and Rethinking Faith* (Grand Rapids: Baker, 2011), 202.
2. Peter Scazzero, *Emotionally Healthy Spirituality* (Franklin, TN: Integrity, 2006), 178.
3. Brené Brown, *Daring Greatly: How the Courage to Be Vulnerable Transforms the Way We Live, Love, Parent, and Lead* (New York: Gotham, 2012), 150.
4. Brian Orme, "A Candid Talk with Francis Chan on Evangelism and Mission," *Outreach* magazine, October 25, 2012.
5. Fritz Erpel, *Van Gogh: The Self-Portraits* (New York: New York Graphic Society, 1969), 17.
6. H. H., "Love and Praise the Lord." Used by permission.

CHAPTER 3: THE ART OF NOTICING

1. Doug Pollock, *God Space* (Loveland, CO: Group, 2009), 38.
2. John Ortberg, *Grace: An Invitation to a Way of Life* (Grand Rapids: Zondervan, 2000), 16.

3. John Paul Lederach, *Reconcile: Conflict Transformation for Ordinary Christians* (Harrisonburg, VA: Herald, 2014), 45–48.
4. Chaim Potok, *My Name Is Asher Lev* (New York: Fawcett Columbine, 1972), 108.
5. Jerry Root and Stan Guthrie, *The Sacrament of Evangelism* (Chicago: Moody, 2011), 17.
6. Melody Allred, *The Next Door: That They May Believe* (2010), 16.
7. Kallistos Ware, "Cycle Two: The Law of Bearing," in *Ordinary Graces: Christian Teachings on the Interior Life*, ed. Lorraine Kisly (New York: Harmony/Bell Tower, 2000), 28–29.
8. Ken Sande, "Charitable Judgments: An Antidote to Judging Others," Peacemaker Ministries, http://peacemaker.net/project/charitable-judgments-an-antidote-to-judging-others. Accessed September 20, 2015.
9. Simone Weil, *Waiting for God* (New York: Harper Perennial, 2009).

CHAPTER 4: THE ART OF PRAYING

1. C. S. Lewis, "Christianity and Culture," in *Christian Reflections* (Grand Rapids: Eerdmans, 2014), 41.
2. Lon Allison, Q Place Vital Conference presentation, October 1, 2011.
3. Rick Richardson, Q Place Vital Conference presentation, September 25, 2010.
4. Ibid.
5. Henry T. Blackaby and Claude V. King, *Experiencing God* (Nashville: Broadman & Holman, 1994), 55, 70.
6. Ibid., 56, 69.
7. Richardson, Q Place Vital Conference presentation.
8. Basil Miller, *George Müller: Man of Faith and Miracles* (Minneapolis: Bethany House, 1972), 146.
9. Mark Batterson, *The Circle Maker* (Grand Rapids: Zondervan, 2011), 11–13.
10. Quoted in Dick Eastman, *The Hour that Changes the World* (Grand Rapids: Baker, 1986), 80.
11. Richard Foster, *Prayer: Finding the Heart's True Home* (New York: HarperCollins, 1992), 191.

CHAPTER 5: THE ART OF LISTENING

1. "Every Breaking Wave," *Songs of Innocence*, U2, 2014.
2. Garth Stein, *The Art of Racing in the Rain* (New York: HarperCollins, 2008), 101–102.
3. For research on the importance of listening well, see "Listening Facts," the International Listening Association, http://d1025403.site.myhosting.com/files.listen.org/Facts.htm. Accessed September 20, 2015.

4. Anikó Ouweneel-Tóth, "Love = Time + Attention," Artway.com, www
   .artway.eu/content.php?id=1826&lang=en&action=show. Accessed
   September 20, 2015.
5. John Paul Lederach, *Reconcile: Conflict Transformation for Ordinary Christians*
   (Harrisonburg, VA: Herald, 2014), 119.
6. David Whyte, *The House of Belonging* (Langley, WA: Many Rivers, 1996).
   Used by permission.
7. Dietrich Bonhoeffer, *Life Together: The Classic Exploration of Faith in
   Community* (New York: HarperCollins, 1954), 98.
8. Todd Hunter, quoted in Doug Pollock, *God Space* (Loveland, CO: Group,
   2009), 54.
9. Alice Fryling, *The Art of Spiritual Listening: Responding to God's Voice amid the
   Noise of Life* (Colorado Springs: WaterBrook, 2003) 20.
10. Doug Pollock, *God Space* (Loveland, CO: Group, 2009), 118.
11. Seth S. Horowitz, "The Science and Art of Listening," *New York Times*,
    November 11, 2012, page SR10.
12. Karen Kimsey-House, "Disrupt Your Life in a Good Way, Pt. 6: Learn to
    Listen Well . . . Newsflash: It's Not about the Words," The Blog, Huff/Post50,
    July 23, 2012, www.huffingtonpost.com/karen-kimseyhouse
    /listening_b_1681469.html.
13. Ram Charan, *Harvard Business Review*, HBR Blog Network, "The Discipline
    of Listening," June 21, 2012.
14. Pollock, *God Space*, 60–61.

CHAPTER 6: THE ART OF ASKING QUESTIONS

1. William Miller, "Old Man's Advice to Youth: 'Never Lose a Holy Curiosity,'"
   LIFE, May 2, 1955, 64.
2. Jedd Medefind and Erik Lokkesmoe, *The Revolutionary Communicator* (Lake
   Mary, FL: Relevant Media Group, 2004), 53, 61.
3. Edgar H. Schein, *Humble Inquiry* (San Francisco: Berrett-Koehler, 2013), 2.
4. David Maxfield, "How to Change People Who Don't Want to Change,"
   CrucialSkills.com, www.crucialskills.com/2015/01/how-to-change-people
   -who-dont-want-to-change. Accessed September 25, 2015. Quoted text was
   transcribed from the embedded video.
5. StoryCorps, "About Us" page, http://storycorps.org/about. Accessed
   September 10, 2013.

CHAPTER 7: THE ART OF LOVING

1. Frederick M. Lehman (1917), public domain. Lyrics are based
   on "Haddamut," by Meir Ben Isaac Nehorai, 1050.
2. Aaron Niequist, "Changed," copyright © 2003 by AARONieq Music. Used
   by permission.

3. Brent Curtis and John Eldredge, *The Sacred Romance: Drawing Closer to the Heart of God* (Nashville: Thomas Nelson, 1997) 73, 98.

4. Max Lucado, *No Wonder They Call Him the Savior* (Nashville: Thomas Nelson, 2004), 131.

5. Fredrick Buechner, *The Magnificent Defeat* (New York: HarperCollins, 1985), 105.

6. Francis Chan, *Crazy Love* (Colorado Springs: David C. Cook, 2013), 128.

7. Gabe Lyons, *The Next Christians* (New York: Doubleday Religion, 2010), 170.

8. Peter Kreeft, *Making Sense out of Suffering* (Ann Arbor, MI: Servant, 1986), 133.

9. The authors gratefully acknowledge that content for this section comes from Robert Bugh, *When the Bottom Drops Out* (Carol Stream, IL: Tyndale, 2011). Used by permission.

10. Don Ever, *Jesus with Dirty Feet: A Down-to-Earth Look at Christianity for the Curious and Skeptical* (Downers Grove, IL: InterVarsity, 1999).

11. Bugh, *When the Bottom Drops Out*, 144.

12. D. R. Lehman, J. H. Ellard, and C. B. Wortman, "Social Support for the Bereaved: Recipients' and Providers' Perspectives on What Is Helpful," Journal of Consulting and Clinical Psychology, volume 54(4) (August 1986), 438–446.

13. Dr. Camille Wortman, Ph.D., "This Emotional Life: Offering Support to the Bereaved: What Not to Say," www.pbs.org/thisemotionallife /blogs/offering-support-bereaved-what-not-say.

14. Bugh, *When the Bottom Drops Out*, 162.

CHAPTER 8: THE ART OF WELCOMING

1. American Time Use Survey, US Department of Labor, Bureau of Labor Statistics, last modified July 10, 2013, www.bls.gov/tus/charts.

2. Henri J. M. Nouwen, *Reaching Out: The Three Movements of the Spiritual Life* (New York: Doubleday, 1986), 65, 71.

CHAPTER 9: THE ART OF FACILITATING

1. Greg Green, "My View: Flipped Classrooms Give Every Student a Chance to Succeed," *Schools of Thought* (blog), CNN, January 18, 2012, http:// schoolsofthought.blogs.cnn.com/2012/01/18/my-view-flipped-classrooms -give-every-student-a-chance-to-succeed.

2. Karen E. Yates, "Flipping the 40-Minute Sermon," *Christianity Today*, May 24, 2013, www.christianitytoday.com/women/2013/may/flipping-40 -minute-sermon.html?paging=off. Accessed September 20, 2015.

3. William Barclay, *Daily Celebration: Devotional Readings for Every Day of the Year*, Denis Duncan, ed. (Waco, TX: Word, 1971).

4. Peter Block, *Community: The Structure of Belonging* (San Francisco: Berrett-Koehler, 2008), 95.

5. Maryellen Weimer, *Learner-Centered Teaching: Five Key Changes to Practice* (San Francisco: John Wiley and Sons, 2013), 15.

6. Bill Mowry, *The Ways of the Alongsider* (Colorado Springs: NavPress, 2012), 14.

7. Tim Keller, *Encounters with Jesus: Unexpected Answers to Life's Biggest Questions* (New York: Dutton, 2013), ix. Italics in the original.

8. Bill Donahue, *Leading Life-Changing Small Groups* (Grand Rapids: Zondervan, 1996), 36.

CHAPTER 10: THE ART OF SERVING TOGETHER

1. "The Constitution of the Soviet Union, 1918," www.abc.net.au/concon/ constitutions/sov1918.htm. Accessed October 1, 2013.

2. Rick Rusaw and Eric Swanson, *The Externally Focused Church* (Loveland, CO: Group, 2004), 118.

3. Brené Brown, *Daring Greatly* (New York: Avery, 2012), 176–177.

4. Gabe Lyons, *The Next Christians* (Colorado Springs: Multnomah, 2012), 216.

5. Ibid., 159.

6. Ibid., 158.

7. Ray Vander Laan, *Faith Lessons on the Promised Land* (Grand Rapids: Zondervan, 1999), 14.

CHAPTER 11: THE ART OF SHARING

1. Quoted in Larry Ondrejack, "What Is Relational Evangelism?" Grace & Truth, October 2000.

2. *The Big Kahuna*, directed by John Swanbeck (Lions Gate Films, 2000).

3. Jonathan Gottschall, "Why Storytelling Is the Ultimate Weapon," May 2, 2012, www.fastcocreate.com/1680581/why-storytelling-is-the-ultimate-weapon.

4. Bill Hybels, *Just Walk across the Room* (Grand Rapids: Zondervan, 1994).

5. David Heim, "The Gospel in Seven Words," *Christian Century*, 128, no. 18 (2012).

6. *Courageous*, directed by Alex Kendrick (Sherwood Pictures, 2011).

7. See "The Bridge to Life," The Navigators, January 31, 2006, www.navigators .org/Tools/Evangelism%20Resources/Tools/The%20Bridge%20to%20Life.

8. For a video example of "Do versus Done," see www.youtube.com/watch? feature=player_embedded&v=54jPcucSOvE#.

CHAPTER 12: STARTING A Q PLACE

1. Greg Ogden, *Transforming Discipleship: Making Disciples a Few at a Time* (Downers Grove, IL: InterVarsity, 2003), 135.

2. Ibid., 141.

3. Ibid., 182.

4. Ibid., 153–174.

5. Neil Cole, *Cultivating a Life for God* (Long Beach, CA: CMA Resources, 1999), 54.
6. Mary Schaller, *How to Start a Q Place* (Carol Stream, IL: Q Place, 2010), 38.
7. A copy of the Q Place guidelines and some discussion tips can be viewed online at www.qplace.com/howqplaceworks/guidelines.
8. Eric Geiger, Michael Kelly, and Philip Nation, *Transformational Discipleship: How People Really Grow* (Nashville: B&N Books, 2012). For more information, see http://tda.lifeway.com.

CHAPTER 13: FROM CUPS OF COLD WATER TO RIVERS OF LIVING WATER

1. Laura Hillenbrand, *Unbroken* (New York: Random House, 2010), 128.
2. David T. Olson, *The American Church in Crisis* (Grand Rapids: Zondervan, 2008), figure 11.7.
3. John S. Dickerson, *The Great Evangelical Recession* (Grand Rapids: Baker, 2013), 33.
4. Ibid., 17.
5. George Barna, *Futurecast: What Today's Trends Mean for Tomorrow's World* (Carol Stream, IL: Tyndale, 2012), 198.
6. Ikimulisa Livingston, "Stabbed Hero Dies as More Than 20 People Stroll Past Him," *New York Post,* April 24, 2010, http://nypost.com/2010/04/24/stabbed-hero-dies-as-more-than-20-people-stroll-past-him. Accessed September 20, 2015.
7. Matthew West, "Do Something," copyright © 2012.
8. Gabe Lyons, *The Next Christians* (Colorado Springs: Multnomah, 2012), 11.
9. Hugh Halter, *Flesh* (Colorado Springs: David C. Cook, 2014), 185.
10. Dickerson, *The Great Evangelical Recession*, 218.

About the Authors

Mary Schaller is president of Q Place, a ministry that empowers Christians to engage in meaningful conversations about God with people who believe differently. After twenty-two years as an entrepreneurial marketer and a founder of three technology-related business ventures in Silicon Valley and the Boston high-tech corridor, Mary turned her attention to ministry in 1999 as a minister of small groups at Menlo Park Presbyterian Church in the San Francisco Bay Area. In 2006, she graduated from Fuller Theological Seminary with a master of divinity. She is the author of *How to Start a Q Place* and a coauthor of *The 9 Arts of Spiritual Conversations* inductive curriculum series for Q Place small groups. Mary and her husband, Paul, have three adult children and four grandchildren. They divide their time between Chicagoland and Sandpoint, Idaho.

John Crilly is the son of a construction worker and is married to a farmer's daughter. Before serving Q Place as national field director, he spent nearly twenty-three years in leadership and management positions in the engineering and construction fields. John is a writer, poet, and certified professional life coach. He coauthored the Q Place *9 Arts of Spiritual Conversations* training curriculum. John has been married to Danielle since 1990. They live in the Chicago area, where John mentors international refugees.

How effective are you in the 9 Arts
of spiritual conversations?

Check out our free online assessment tool:

www.QPlace.com/resources/assessment